Rum Punch and Revolution

D1153725

EARLY AMERICAN STUDIES

Richard S. Dunn, Director, The McNeil Center for Early American
Studies, Series Editor

A complete list of books in the series is available from the publisher.

Rum Punch & Revolution

Taverngoing & Public Life in Eighteenth-Century Philadelphia

Peter Thompson

UNIVERSITY OF PENNSYLVANIA PRESS • Philadelphia

Copyright © 1999 University of Pennsylvania Press
All rights reserved
Printed in the United States of America on acid-free paper

10 9 8 7 6 5 4 3 2 1

Published by
University of Pennsylvania Press
Philadelphia, Pennsylvania 19104-4011

Library of Congress Cataloguing-in-Publication Data
Thompson, Peter, 1960–
    Rum punch and revolution : taverngoing and public life in
eighteenth century Philadelphia / Peter Thompson.
        p. cm. — (Early American studies)
    Includes bibliographical references and index.
    ISBN 0-8122-3459-6 (acid-free paper).
    ISBN 0-8122-1664-4 (pbk. acid-free paper)
    1. Philadelphia (Pa.)—History—Colonial period, ca. 1600–1775.
2. Philadelphia (Pa.)—History—Revolution, 1775–1783—Social
aspects. 3. Philadelphia (Pa.)—Social life and customs.
4. Taverns (Inns)—Pennsylvania—Philadelphia—History—18th
century. 5. Political culture—Pennsylvania—Philadelphia—
History—18th century. I. Title. II. Series.
F158.4.T47   1998
974.8'1102—dc21   98-27389
                                                      CIP

For Alex

Contents

Illustrations

Introduction

Colonial Philadelphians, like other Americans of the time, regarded habitual drinking as sinful but the moderate consumption of beer, cider, rum, and wine as healthful and unremarkable.[1] Of course, definitions of "moderate" consumption varied. Ministers, magistrates, and moralists regarded some forms of drinking, and some varieties of drink, as pernicious. Nevertheless, among the population at large, alcohol was held in great affection and attitudes toward drunkenness were indulgent. "Top'd," "tann'd," and "tipium grove," "buskey," "bowz'd," and "burdock'd": these are a sample of some one hundred fifty synonyms for inebriation employed in colonial Philadelphia.[2] As a song had it:

> There's but one good reason I can think
> Why people ever cease to drink
> Sobriety the cause is Not,
> Nor fear of being deem'd a Sot,
> But if liquor can't be got.[3]

Both William Penn and Benjamin Franklin, colonial Philadelphia's most celebrated residents, shared their neighbors' affection for alcohol. Penn made considerable efforts to ensure that his household was well supplied with drink. He engaged, for example, in a lengthy and ultimately fruitless effort to establish vineyards on his Pennsbury estate.[4] Franklin, despite his penchant for drinking water while at work, enjoyed wine when in company. In fact he wrote a drinking song, circa 1745, in which he averred:

> Virtue and Safety in Wine-bibbing's found
> While all that drink Water deserve to be drown'd . . .
> . . . .
> So for Safety and Honesty put the Glass round.[5]

Convinced that there could be no "good living where there is not good drinking," Franklin, like Penn, hoped that Pennsylvania's soil and climate

would support the production of fine wines.⁶ And although he was concerned that dram drinking among the poor might bring to Philadelphia
scenes comparable to those depicted by Hogarth in the print *Gin Lane*,
Franklin composed an affectionate tribute to the virtues of rum punch:

> Boy, bring a bowl of China here
> Fill it with water cool and clear:
> Decanter with Jamaica right,
> And spoon of silver, clean and bright,
> Sugar twice-fin'd in pieces cut,
> Kni[f]e, sieve and glass in order put,
> Bring forth the fragrant fruit and then
> We're happy till the clock strikes ten.⁷

The emergence of a tavern trade in colonial Philadelphia would, at first
glance, seem to pose no great explanatory problem. Taverns were a familiar
and cherished feature of the landscape of northwestern Europe, and Philadelphians, emigrants to an unfamiliar land, had a fondness for alcoholic refreshment. But many eighteenth-century paeans to drink and "noble living"
made no mention of taverns and indeed suggested the countervailing attraction of sociability in private or domestic settings. There were, throughout the
colonial period, sites other than taverns in which Philadelphians might
conjoin "soft wit with pleasure."⁸ Philadelphians drank and socialized at
home, at work, along the city's riverbanks, and in its streets and squares.
Many of the other functions served by taverns, and often cited by historians
seeking to explain the public house's appeal, could be found elsewhere. Philadelphians used taverns to exchange gossip and information, but they had
alternative sources of news and opinion. Thanks not least to Franklin, colonial Philadelphia had competing weekly newspapers and an efficient postal
service from a relatively early date. Residents and strangers did not have to
value—still less rely upon—tavern talk, and yet such talk fascinated them.
    The sheer size of the city's tavern trade testifies to the peculiar attrac-
tion taverns held for colonial Philadelphians, who founded new taverns at a
rate that far outstripped the increase in the city's population. The Quaker
city had more public houses per capita than corrupt old world metropolises
such as Rotterdam and Paris.⁹ Within a year of the first Quaker settlers'
arrival in the Delaware Valley, two Philadelphians were keeping tavern in
caves dug into the Delaware riverbank. By 1686 there were at least 6 taverns
in operation in the city, and by 1756 there were 101 licensed premises in

operation.[10] Although Philadelphians occasionally and inconsistently applied British distinctions between different types of public house—inn, tavern, and alehouse—to their tavern trade, the city's stock of public houses tended to uniformity in size, tone, and service. Even when conducted above ground, colonial Philadelphia's public houses were cramped venues. Until the middle of the eighteenth century, all taverns were run in buildings designed as private residences. The amenities colonial Philadelphia's taverns offered to the public were basic; most taverns had a single bar room, where customers sat around a common table, usually drinking from inexpensive pewter canns and tankards but sometimes sharing a communal bowl. Although food could be obtained, it was not until the mid-eighteenth century that a handful of Philadelphia's tavernkeepers began to attempt to provide a regularly scheduled "ordinary," or table d'hôte. Travelers lucky enough to find lodgings in a tavern could expect to share a bed, sometimes with a stranger and always in rooms close to both the bar area and the licensee's family. Some publicans performed small favors for their customers in return for a consideration. They kept packages, delivered messages, loaned small sums of money, or rented horses. Many licensees did little for their clients, however. Although licensed taverns were required to display a sign, it was not easy (even for a local) to tell a good house from a bad one. In colonial Philadelphia, a city with an ethnically and culturally diverse population and a relatively fluid social hierarchy, taverns drew together customers from a wide variety of backgrounds in conditions of enforced intimacy.

Colonial Philadelphians, like other Americans, believed that taverns housed a distinctive kind of sociability—one that, for better or worse, exerted an influence beyond its immediate setting. They struggled to understand the attraction of this sociability, often locating its appeal in the intrinsic merit, or sinfulness, of the activities—especially heavy drinking—with which it was associated. The inhabitants of the Moravian settlement of Nazareth, Pennsylvania, captured something of the peculiar allure of taverngoing when they asked church elders to build a tavern before they set about building a church on the grounds that a community without a public house was like *Hamlet* "without the Ghost."[11] Philadelphians also recognized that the influence and appeal of taverngoing (by which I mean the use of those licensed and unlicensed premises selling liquor variously, and inconsistently, designated alehouse, beershop, coffeehouse, dramshop, inn and tavern), were greater than the sum of the often bare-bones service that publicans offered. They identified taverngoing as a powerful form of sociability, within whose ambit lay changing attitudes, assumptions, and be-

Silver Punch Bowl. Simon Coley. New York. C. 1755–1760. Philadelphia Museum of Art: Gift of Susanne Strassburger Anderson, Valerie Anderson Readman, and Veronica Anderson Macdonald from the estate of Mae Bourne and Ralph Beaver Strassburger. (*Facing page*) Silver Cann, Inscribed "The Barley Sheath." Joseph Richardson, Philadelphia, date unknown. Philadelphia Museum of Art: Gift of Mr. and Mrs. Wister H. MacLaren. Eighteenth-century Philadelphians developed a huge body of drinking lore, which was expressed in both oral and material cultures. The silversmiths who crafted these vessels would have interrupted their working day for drink and conversation in Philadelphia's taverns. The wealthy Philadelphians who bought and used these status symbols attempted to demonstrate that their enjoyment of drinking and convivial conversation was of a more refined nature than the laborer's. The silver cann celebrates healthful beer drinking, linking the brewing trade with a rural economy.

haviors that constituted the very marrow of the culture of the eighteenth-century city. This book investigates and explains Philadelphians' passionate attachment to the tavern—their yearning to make the privately owned "public house" a site where they could express and, if necessary, defend their complicated and contested notions of community and society in a new world environment.

I have chosen to situate this study in the city wards of Philadelphia, home to a tightly packed and culturally diverse population. Most colonial Americans lived within rural communities whose spiritual or secular patriarchs were more assertive than Philadelphia's inwardly directed founding

The Bell Tavern. 1858. Photograph. The Free Library of Philadelphia. This tavern on the west side of Eighth Street and the north side of Sansom was built in the late eighteenth century. Its dimensions typify the cramped scale of most taverns in colonial Philadelphia. A visitor to a colonial tavern could expect little in the way of privacy.

fathers. The uncommon heterogeneity of Philadelphia's population also promoted competition between cultural and religious values of an intensity largely unknown in the towns and settlements of colonial New England. In the early stages of its growth Philadelphia provided opportunities for economic security and advancement that were the envy of laboring men elsewhere. In contrast, toward the close of the eighteenth century, the city's economy was evolving in ways which brought hardship and even destitution to many workingmen. These factors conspired to militate against the replication of those contested yet often deferential relationships that characterized the social life of communities in the Chesapeake and Carolinas. The interaction of these distinctive features of Philadelphia's economic and social development with the peculiarities of Pennsylvania's politics in the waning years of proprietary rule helps explain why residents of the Quaker city gave voice to an uncommonly broad spectrum of political opinion, including some of the most radical propositions uttered in the American Revolution.

Precisely because colonial Philadelphia was a burgeoning and prosperous city, numbering among its population representatives of various sects, ethnicities, and stations in life, it possessed a multiplicity of meeting places, information networks, exchanges, clubs, and civic buildings. Yet taverngoing was as popular with colonial Philadelphians as it was with the residents of New England towns or Chesapeake communities, even though Philadelphians were confronted with a greater range of alternatives to the tavern than most other Americans. Since the authors of those eighteenth-century documents describing taverngoing in Philadelphia were aware that alternatives to tavern sociability existed, it is possible to glean from surviving letters and diaries some sense of the peculiar appeal the tavern held for residents of the Quaker city. Because Americans in communities all along the Atlantic seaboard visited taverns as much out of choice as out of necessity, the reasons Philadelphians chose to frequent taverns are of more than local interest.

The peculiarities of Philadelphia's history make it a particularly promising site in which to examine the appeal taverns held for colonial Americans. But if we are to understand the popularity of taverngoing and the role it played in the political history of early Pennsylvania, we have to investigate the forces that shaped Philadelphia's profoundly undeferential culture. Philadelphia was, from its founding, the scene of a particularly pure form of the interplay between communal and social impulses that is arguably the dominant theme of early American history.[12] William Penn sought to attract to his "holy experiment" settlers who would act with "an eye to Providence of

God" and maintain "natural affection . . . and . . . friendly and profitable correspondence" with their new neighbors in the city of brotherly love.[13] Yet in the promotional tract *A Further Account of Pennsylvania*, published soon after the colony's founding, Penn accepted that for current and prospective settlers, "the improvement of this place is best measured by the advance in value on every man's lot."[14] Penn himself brought a mixture of motives to the task of founding a holy experiment. "Though I desire to extend religious freedom" he declared, "yet I want some recompense for my trouble."[15] The proprietor of what has been described as a vast "semi-feudal barony," Penn proposed "that which is extraordinary . . . to leave myself and successors no power of doing mischief, that the will of one man may not hinder the good of the whole country."[16] Unfortunately, as Penn saw it, Pennsylvania's political leaders took advantage of his self-sacrifice to engage in a mischievous "governmentishness" that added to his troubles while denying him recompense. In 1688 Penn (who had once averred "let men be good and government cannot be bad") appointed a stern Puritan, John Blackwell, to discipline his disputatious Quaker colonists.[17]

Lurking behind this contradiction between self-interest and community development was a fundamental tension between the values and imperatives of private life and those of an idealized but imperfectly realized public world. My study of Philadelphia's tavern sociability is set in the hundred years or so between the city's founding and the end of the American Revolution, when what Roger Chartier has dubbed a "fascination with publicness" gripped peoples in Europe and America who had spent generations inventing, and investing meaning in, the private self.[18] Fascination with the public world, exemplified in the widespread popularity of taverngoing, can be seen at its most paradoxical in Philadelphia. The Quaker city counted among its population some of the most private, inwardly directed sectarians in the Atlantic world. Penn's plans for the development of Philadelphia appealed to their sense of privacy and sought to build upon their fascination with the inner self. The city's wholesome grid of streets and squares—a source of comment among scores of subsequent visitors—spoke of a desire to harness the public thoroughfares of the holy experiment to the task of inculcating in a heterogeneous citizenry a sustained examination of their consciences. Penn changed the street that he might change the man.[19] Yet even intensely private settlers felt the need to demonstrate something of the quality of their beliefs to a wider world through distinctive patterns of speech, clothing, and behavior. Quakers, for example, drank and conversed in taverns, even though in these cramped houses they found little respect for their sense of privacy and, on occasion, outright contempt for "broadbrimmery."

Although founded by one of colonial America's greatest idealists, William Penn, Philadelphia nurtured the era's preeminent pragmatist, Benjamin Franklin. Franklin's interests included the inward and the personal, but as a self-consciously self-made man, Franklin deployed the greater part of his energies in the public world. He laid his own grid—composed of civic associations, municipal initiatives, and the orderly and rational exchange of news and information—over the fabric of Philadelphia. Where Penn had sought to reform the world indirectly through the workings of conscience, Franklin sought its direct reformation by the mid-eighteenth century through the workings of voluntary associations. Where Penn had spoken the language of community, emphasizing family and congregation, Franklin spoke the language of society, emphasizing above all the public actor. On issues such as the defense of the city and the relief of its poor, Penn and many of his co-religionists upheld the primacy of the private conscience, while Franklin and many of his associates argued the case for its subordination before an abstract public welfare. In practice the work of voluntary associations demanded orderly and detailed discussion among men committed to shared goals. Paradoxically, lest their motives be misunderstood as secretive or subversive, voluntary associations held many of their meetings in the distracting confines of public houses. Here the business of working through an agenda was liable to be disrupted both by other tavern customers and by the bowls of punch that generally graced the tables around which civic associations met.

Both Penn and Franklin influenced the development of the city's tavern trade in ways that demonstrate the interplay of community and society in eighteenth-century thought. Conscious of the failings of previous colonial ventures, Penn sought the speedy settlement of Philadelphia. He believed that in order to create godly and peaceable communities, his province needed a thriving, populous seaport. He believed a handful of taverns in the city would speed the work of development, not only by serving the needs of travelers and workmen but also by convincing potential emigrants that Philadelphia was habitable. At the same time, to safeguard his broader aim of moral reformation, Penn in 1683 drew up the city's first tavern regulations and thereafter continued to urge magistrates, assemblymen, and councillors to work together to regulate the trade.[20] Far from seeing their attempt to separate the needs of the community from the imperatives of society as futile, Penn and subsequent Quaker magistrates put the best face on their efforts, arguing that taverns could be brought, via the licensing law, to serve a wide variety of policing functions.

But how many taverns ought a community to possess? Could a healthy community tolerate as many licensed public houses as there were individuals willing to run them? Franklin thought not. In the preamble to a grand jury presentment in 1744 that called for a drastic suppression of public houses, Franklin argued that as the number of public houses in operation in Philadelphia rose, distinct clusters of taverns began to emerge in particular locations. As a result, even licensees who came into the trade with a modicum of financial independence and moral integrity were forced to compete for customers with less scrupulous neighbors by ignoring those restrictive aspects of the licensing law designed to suppress drunkenness, disorder, and vice. Thus the more taverns there were, the more likely it was that their influence would be pernicious. Unless and until the number of public houses in operation was anchored well below the level of demand, the evils associated with taverns would overwhelm and outweigh their positive influence on community life.[21] Franklin's grand jury report was the clearest, and most forcefully argued, example of a quasi-mercantilist approach to licensing policy that became dominant in mid-eighteenth-century Philadelphia.

Although both Franklin and Penn toyed with the notion that some, or all, tavernkeepers encouraged Philadelphians to drink to excess, patronize prostitutes and gaming attractions, and nurture impious, improvident, and impudent attitudes and behavior, neither man believed that a city without licensed public houses would be free from drunkenness, vice, or sedition. Perhaps more worrying was the recognition that, for better or worse, the influence of tavern sociability transcended its origins. Even men and women who made a point of rarely visiting taverns, even Philadelphians who saw little purpose and less wisdom in the uses their deluded neighbors made of the city's public houses, realized that tavern sociability had the power to threaten, or overturn, those values that they themselves held dear. As a result, even those Philadelphians who could conceive of the existence of more "rational" or wholesome forums of discussion occasionally acknowledged the power of tavern debate by entering into discussion and argument within it. Tavern talk was often compared unfavorably with the discourse of the printed text. Yet licensed public houses were wellsprings of indigenous textual production in Philadelphia, and many pamphlets and newspaper features mirrored tavern speech precisely in order to sway a readership that continued to hold oral discourse in high regard.[22] Contemporaries recognized the difficulty of sustaining the proposition that taverns did no more than create vice and disorder. Even critics who maintained that some portion of the taverngoing population was motivated by varying measures of frivolity, immorality, or criminal intent recognized that countless of their neighbors found taverngoing to be unremarkably natural, enjoyable, and valuable.

It would have been extraordinary indeed if the tavern's unique position, serving as home to assumptions and practices which lay somewhere between the private world of the householder, pietist and reader, and the public world of commerce, government, and citizenship, had permitted a neat resolution of the conflicts created by the variety of backgrounds, behaviors, and beliefs Philadelphians brought with them to the tavern. Yet much of the literature on public drinking in colonial America makes what was messy unduly tidy. The first writers to attempt scholarly histories of American taverns tended to gloss over elements of contest within tavern sociability and to underestimate the hostility toward taverns that existed in the colonial communities that supported them. Benjamin and Mary Boggs, Alice Morse Earle, and Edward Field saw taverns as quaint, if doomed, "traditional" institutions whose effect was to pull fledgling communities together.[23] More recent treatments of the social history of public drinking in America have begun to stress the conflicts taverngoing created and sustained in their communities. Roy Rosenzweig, writing of nineteenth-century Worcester, Massachusetts, argues that although drinking was not restricted to the working class, saloongoing was. He concludes that Worcester's saloongoers fashioned a working-class leisure institution that rejected, but did not actively challenge, the moral order of the town's bourgeoisie.[24] David Weir Conroy, in the first study of colonial taverngoing to employ modern social history techniques, has detailed "the course, significance, and outcome" of "temperance-tavern conflict" in colonial Massachusetts.[25]

Conroy presents a convincing case for the importance of taverngoing while avoiding an overly simplistic reading of the nature of tavern sociability and opposition to it. He explains demand for taverns by reference to the persistence in Massachusetts of old world "drinking habits." In a new world environment, these habits "came to be considered dysfunctional."[26] This promoted a friction between old and new value systems that he summarizes as "temperance-tavern conflict" and illuminates through an exhaustive survey of attempts made by ministers and legislators to regulate tavern culture and suppress the tavern trade. In Conroy's words:

Public houses provide a window into much more than the drinking habits of colonists. . . . From the first years of settlement, public houses were controversial gathering places. Rulers perceived them to be a threat to order and suppressed their number and use as much as possible. Nevertheless, taverns became a public stage upon which colonists resisted, initiated, and addressed changes in their society. Indeed, in these houses men gradually redefined their relationships with figures of authority.[27]

By demonstrating just how deep-seated the conflicts associated with taverngoing were, and by pointing to their political as well as their cultural significance, Conroy succeeds in establishing taverngoing as a subject of central importance to the social history of southeastern Massachusetts and, by implication, colonial America.

However, Conroy's work demonstrates the ways in which taverns functioned as a "stage" upon which New Englanders addressed and resisted the hegemony of the culture that comes to us via the writings of ministers, legislators, and journalists with greater success than it elucidates the ways in which taverngoers initiated change in society. Despite his efforts to discuss the taverngoer's cultural agency, Conroy tends to present tavern culture as essentially oppositional: a source of popular alternatives to the social and political values and beliefs of a limited number of authoritative provincial leaders whose views, formed and shaped by university education, church conclaves, and government service, continued to constitute New England's dominant culture. Here Conroy displays the main intellectual influence on his analysis: studies of popular culture and social change in England in the seventeenth and eighteenth centuries.[28] Yet there are good reasons to doubt that a model that stresses the "oppositional" quality and "traditional" roots of popular culture provides the best means of approaching the extraordinary popularity and cultural influence of the early American tavern.

Of course much of the subject matter of tavern conversation in the eighteenth-century Atlantic world—for example, religious controversy or political dispute—was generated well away from the confines of the public house in particular cultures not easily accessible to the vast majority of the population. However, the culture of the cleric or assemblyman and the culture of the parishioner or constituent were situated in far greater proximity in eighteenth-century America, and especially eighteenth-century Philadelphia, than they were either in eighteenth-century Europe or in our age of ivory tower universities and televised evangelism. Colonial America's ministers, assemblymen, and men of learning were themselves taverngoers; they lived and worked in communities, like Philadelphia, which they shared with their subjects.[29] Partly as a result, the frontier between "popular" culture and official or "high" culture was far from distinct in colonial America. Of course many individuals and various groups sought to establish a clear boundary between the cultures of the many and the culture of the few in eighteenth-century America.[30] But for most of the eighteenth century, in New England as Conroy himself notes, and especially in Philadelphia as I demonstrate, the "ordinary" men and women who kept taverns in business did not see themselves as living and thinking outside a cultural mainstream, and they did not view their activities as presenting a "popular" alternative to some other body of assumptions and values only within which might their world be made truly coherent.

Moreover, in the case of Philadelphia, the political influence of tavern sociability was not—to adapt Conroy's metaphor of the stage—restricted to the role of the chorus in a Greek tragedy, commenting on events that they could do little to influence. The American Revolution followed very different courses in Massachusetts and Pennsylvania. Massachusetts's first state constitution actually disenfranchised poor white adult males who had been eligible to vote under British rule. In contrast, Pennsylvania's first state constitution was arguably the most radical and democratic statement of political values that the American Revolution produced.[31] The egalitarian values of tavern sociability in colonial Philadelphia were reflected in Pennsylvania's first state constitution; thereafter the continuing influence of tavern discussion on political affairs helped inspire a conservative backlash against an overly "democratic" frame of government. Tavern talk and behavior were much more intimately bound up with both the prosecution and the main themes of the Revolution in Philadelphia than in southeastern Massachusetts.

My thinking about both the extraordinary popularity and the social and political significance of taverngoing in eighteenth-century Philadelphia has been influenced heavily by Thomas Brennan's study of public drinking in eighteenth-century Paris, which strives to understand the appeal of the public house from the customer's perspective. Brennan juxtaposes evidence from elite sources with "attempts to discover the positive uses of public drinking through evidence that has come more directly from the people in taverns."[32] His main source of such evidence is a body of police records that contain detailed transcriptions of Parisian taverngoers' speech and behavior. Brennan describes laboring Parisians engaging in the "public reproduction of their social relations" in taverns. He concludes that "public drinking in taverns reenacted a fundamental communion among men, a symbolic consumption and sharing [through] which they created their solidarities and reaffirmed their values."[33] Brennan's account of the developing mores of taverngoing in an old world city stresses the interplay of change *and* tradition in the cultural rules which Parisians imposed on the organization of public drinking. During the eighteenth century, well-to-do Parisians chose in increasing numbers to abandon the tavern terrain, with the effect that the public reproduction of social relations in the tavern milieu encouraged the development of a working-class culture that appropriated elite values (especially in respect to honor and reputation) and at the same time promoted an assertive and undeferential understanding of the relationship between patrician and plebeian. Brennan demonstrates a genuine dialectic between elite and popular culture whose force stems not from the survival of tradition but from the changing patterns of tavern usage. His account stresses the depth, ambition, and coherence of the culture Parisian workers constructed through taverngoing and the ways that culture appropriated elite values, rather than its isolation from a putative mainstream or its disruption by attempts at regulation from above.

David Shields's *Civil Tongues and Polite Letters in British America*, published while this book was in the final stages of preparation, has described brilliantly how the reception of literary productions was manifested in taverngoing and other forms of sociability, and refracted by the desires, tensions, and cultural insights associated with, and inherent in, a range of sociable forms. I welcome his emphasis on the ways in which those who share cultures make sense of them. However, my own interest lies in the ways the passions bound up with taverngoing were played out in social behavior. I seek to ask questions of a specific location—eighteenth-century Philadelphia—that are similar to, but ultimately different from, those posed by Shields. What did Philadelphians do in taverns and with whom did they do it? Why, if taverns were sites of both conflict and contest, was taverngoing so popular? What was the relationship between tavern sociability and the broader social and political culture? Like Shields and Brennan, I try to treat taverngoing as eighteenth-century drinkers might have approached it—a popular activity through which a range of desires were expressed—rather than follow Conroy's approach by presenting taverngoing as the manifestation of deep-seated trends in a popular culture whose origins lay outside the tavern and perhaps outside America itself.

Taverngoers left relatively few accounts of their drinking habits or of the positive attraction of taverns. The nature of the evidence available is such that a number of issues concerning the uses to which Philadelphians put their taverns must remain obscure. It is not possible to gauge with accuracy how the unemployed or idle worker saw the culture of the tavern, whereas it is all too easy to be swayed by the opinions of wealthy and respectable citizens who left more in the way of written records. I can say far less about women as taverngoers than I wish. Although some women used taverns, most of the surviving evidence on taverngoing in colonial Philadelphia is written from a male perspective. For this reason, although I cite instances of gender conflict in taverns, I have not attempted to investigate in depth the relationship between the public house and the private home. But for all its infuriating silence on some of the issues which most interest historians today, the variety and quality of the extant documentary evidence makes it possible to investigate with some rigor both the structure of Philadelphia's tavern trade and the changing cultural assumptions that informed the practice of taverngoing over time.

A first step toward writing a history of the passionate attachments and desires bound up with taverngoing is to develop an understanding of the peculiarities of the space enclosed within public houses. Although taverns were privately owned, licensees, magistrates, and customers competed for control over them. Despite their quasi-public function, taverns could not be written into Philadelphia's plan in the same way as public squares or broad streets. Taverns existed in Philadelphia because their keepers thought they would profit from running them. Yet the logic of the licensing legislation was to treat taverns as wards of government. In order to protect the public, the price of drinks and services sold in taverns was strictly regulated. This legislation enjoyed widespread support among drinkers. Yet some taverngoers sought to exploit relationships with particular publicans in order that "their own" neighborhood tavern might ignore aspects of licensing law that restricted access to prostitution, attempted to control drunkenness, or limited a tavern's opening hours. No magistrate, publican, or customer ever "won" the battle for control of the tavern conclusively, yet each party viewed the contest with the utmost seriousness. Magistrates closed taverns they deemed disorderly, licensees banned particularly "obnoxious" customers, and customers coerced publicans and defied magistrates. The depth of this struggle and the intimacy of the terrain over which it ranged are what made the public house such a distinctive cultural site.

The first two chapters of this book introduce the public house by discussing the changing influence of licensing policy and the economics of the tavern trade on the creation of this distinctive site. Chapter 1 describes the workings of Philadelphia's licensing system, detailing its effects on both the size of the licensed trade and the social characteristics of the city's cadre of publicans. Chapter 2 examines the trade from the publican's perspective, describing the services publicans offered and the potential economic reward to be gained from keeping a tavern. By setting and enforcing what were, from the customer's perspective, relatively affordable maximum retail prices for drinks and services sold in taverns, Philadelphia's magistrates encouraged licensees to offer services of generalized rather than specialized appeal. Publicans could profit from the trade, but to do so they needed to exercise tact and diplomacy in dealings with clienteles typically drawn from across the city's spectrum of wealth and background. Legal and economic factors helped create the colonial tavern's distinctive status as a site that brought together men, and sometimes women, from diverse backgrounds who sought to use a shared space for varied, and sometimes incompatible, purposes.

These chapters form a necessary prologue to the discussion of the actions and mores of taverngoers and the political significance of taverngoing presented in Chapters 3, 4, and 5, which links both the popularity and the political significance of taverngoing to the public house's legal and cultural status as "public space." Taverns were, I believe, the most enduring, most easily identifiable, and most contested body of public space in eighteenth-century America. Public spaces were those, like taverns, in which colonial Americans believed that neither the laws and usages of private property, private meetings, and private societies nor those of public property, public gatherings, and public associations fully applied.[34] In topographical terms, public space would encompass not only taverns but also colonial Philadelphia's unapportioned lands, including the banks and waters of its rivers, the town's squares, public landing stages such as those at Dock Creek and Pegg's Run, and the city's roads, bridges, and streets. In social and cultural terms, Philadelphia's public space, above all the tavern, brought together rich, poor, and middling, Quaker, Presbyterian, and Anglican. Almost all human communities have some body of public space. In some communities, whether as a result of apathy, obedience, or unanimity, public space emerges and flourishes without ever becoming the subject of cultural contest arising from rival claims to its definition and ownership. In contrast, in colonial Philadelphia a densely packed and heterogeneous population engaged in countless competing and often incompatible acts that sparked insoluble cultural contests, reinforcing Philadelphians' awareness of the tavern as a distinctive setting that was neither private nor fully public.

Taverngoers' behavior and the interpretive framework they applied to speech and action encountered in taverns were shaped by an awareness of the tavern as public space.[35] Taverngoing was a form of social action, the product of conscious decision rather than of habit. When Philadelphians chose to drink in a public house, in preference to the home, workplace, or the city's streets, they did so in order to make particular statements and to enact and assess values that seemed distinctive to them. Always conscious that there might be dissemblers and designing men in their midst, and that comments offered innocently might be misconstrued, Philadelphia's tavern-goers cast themselves nevertheless as performers and judges of public speech and behavior. Alive to every nuance of the presentation of self in public, they panned for nuggets of character insight even in the dross of humdrum tavern sociability. The tavern maintained its popularity for as long as Phila-delphians hoped or believed that the peculiar space enclosed within a public house offered unparalleled possibilities to address and perhaps even resolve cultural concerns that to them seemed pressing. Only when, in the last third of the eighteenth century, Philadelphians reassessed the possibilities of tav-ern space, and began to toy with the notion that speech and behavior in this singular setting might not offer any distinctive or compelling illumination of cultural concerns, did the tavern trade begin to change in ways (described in Chapters 4 and 5) that reflected the declining appeal of the type of public house most commonly encountered in the colonial city.

Since I argue that taverngoers' consciousness of the tavern as public space is the most important factor explaining both the popularity and the cultural significance of taverngoing, I ought here to compare and contrast my use of the term "public space" with the concept of the "public sphere" as formulated by Jürgen Habermas and applied by him to some types of public house in the eighteenth century, especially coffeehouses.[36] As Keith Mi-chael Baker has noted, Habermas's work "presents the appearance of a bourgeois public sphere simultaneously in two registers: as the emergence of a normative ideal of rational public discussion from within the distinctive social formation of bourgeois civil society and as the realization, or rather the fleeting, partial realization, of this ideal within that society."[37] The concept of the "public sphere" invites the reader to consider the emergence and the function within civil society in eighteenth-century Europe of a set of relatively inflexible rational-critical discursive assumptions and practices. In contrast, I intend the term "public space" to indicate the essentially ethnographic origins and emphasis of my examination of a range of chang-ing forms of tavern behavior and interaction.

Public space was shared space. Philadelphians from various back-grounds sought to use the tavern for purposes that were often in conflict and sometimes incompatible. In contrast, Habermas's concept of the public sphere is built around the examination of gatherings drawn from a particular category of civil society—the bourgeoisie—brought together by a shared commitment to the normative ideal of rational-critical debate. The relationship between Habermas's public sphere and the concept of public space is best described as dialectical. A Habermasian public sphere could have emerged in any or all of Philadelphia's taverns only when and if resolution of most of the contests over "ownership" that characterized the public house as a public space had been achieved. But these contests never were resolved in eighteenth-century Philadelphia. Some of the well-to-do men who gathered at exclusive venues like Bradford's Old London Coffeehouse or the City Tavern resolutely refused to discuss politics or even business. When well-to-do clienteles *did* discuss politics they disagreed just as readily, and with as much violence, as laborers gatherings for similar discussions. Searching for a means of expressing consensus, Philadelphia's elite staged lavish entertainments more often productive of drunken excess than rational debate in the final quarter of the eighteenth century. In the context of spiraling inflation and the initial popularity within Philadelphia of the radical state constitution of 1776, the cautious and generally conservative patrons of the City Tavern were forced to deny that they sought to exercise the functions of a quasi-public body constituted as an alternative to the power of the state. In short, even within the category of Philadelphia society that could most plausibly be described as "bourgeois" there was, in the late eighteenth century, at best a limited acceptance of Habermas's normative ideal of rational public discussion. Moreover, the fact that some of the men who drank at the City Tavern steered clear of political discussion, while others, for example, fought duels arising from personal slights, real or imaginary, encountered in that setting, suggests that even in this exceptional establishment, the ideal of rational discussion among men self-consciously assembled as "public" figures was, at best, imperfectly realized.

The specialization of service and clientele that made "saloon" and "hotel" meaningful distinctions to nineteenth-century Philadelphians began to enter into the tavern trade in the second half of the eighteenth century and became ever sharper with the collapse of retail price controls in the aftermath of the Revolution. Moreover, the final quarter of the eighteenth century witnessed the emergence in Philadelphia of new forms of public space—including hotels and pleasure gardens—whose use is described in the Epilogue.

The main focus of my inquiry rests on the description and analysis of tavern culture in colonial Philadelphia. I believe that taverngoing initiated political as well as social change in the city. In Chapter 4, I explain the influence taverngoing had on the creation of the singularly "accessible" political culture that Alan Tully has recently argued dominated the political history of colonial Pennsylvania.[38] Chapter 5 assesses the political consequences of an observable and increasing reluctance displayed by taverngoers in the revolutionary era to drink and talk politics in the "mixed" company that had typified tavern gatherings in the first half of the eighteenth century. In the years after the French and Indian wars, especially in the early years of Pennyslvania's existence as an independent state, Philadelphians from all walks of life began to express through their choice of where and with whom they would drink an increasing preference for sociability among men of "their own kind." This further promoted the impression that there existed in the city at least two distinctive modes of political and social discourse, each of which became associated with particular political values. In this way, the changing *context* of public political discussion, most clearly visible in changing practices of taverngoing, began to inform some part of the *content* of politics in revolutionary America's largest city.

Despite my disinclination to hunt out the existence or origins of a public sphere in eighteenth-century Philadelphia, there is no doubt that the increasing preference expressed by the city's taverngoers for sociability among men of similar background or belief—symbolized by the founding of establishments such as the City Tavern—altered the context of public political discussion in ways that suggest Habermasian themes. Tavern assemblies in which men from different ranks and ethnicities discussed politics in an atmosphere remarkably free from deference had helped create in Philadelphia in the first two-thirds of the eighteenth century a political culture uncommonly open to the influence of laboring men. Few of Philadelphia's artisans became officeholders and their votes may have counted for little in a political system weighted toward rural and mercantile interests but, as members of tavern companies that drew in men from all walks of life and all shades of opinion, laborers could participate in the creation of the public opinion that many believed should complement voting in determining and informing provincial policy. Philadelphians continued to discuss news and politics in taverns during the Revolution, and taverngoers continued to claim that their views ought to inform in some way the policies of state and national government. However, changes in the structure of government and a widening of the franchise altered the relationship between the formal act of voting and informal discussion of officeholders and policies in the tavern setting. Moreover, political discussion in public houses occurred increasingly within gatherings in which only a portion of the city's spectrum of opinion or hierarchy of rank were represented. In this changed context, the very fact that public political discussion continued to exist became an issue in the American Revolution and the link between rum punch and revolution was forged.

I

"For Strangers and Workmen"

The Origins and Development of Philadelphia's Tavern Trade

As he considered the place of taverns in the development of his colony, William Penn was ever mindful of the biblical injunction "righteousness exalts a nation but sin is the shame of any people."[1] In an early draft of Pennsylvania's "Fundamental Constitutions," Penn reasoned that "virtue and industry" could be nurtured only if the "letts to both are . . . removed" and went on to assert that no taverns or alehouses would be "endured" in Pennsylvania. Yet Penn hoped that the holy experiment to be conducted on the banks of the Delaware would encourage men to remake themselves. He avoided measures designed to coerce outward appearances of piety from his colony's diverse citizenry. Accordingly, he reversed an initial decision to ban taverns and alehouses from Pennsylvania. Instead, while still in England, he drafted tavern regulations through which he believed he could turn an institution synonymous with the creation and perpetuation of sinful behavior in the old world to the task of fostering righteousness in the new.[2] Philadelphia's taverns were to serve liquor of standard quality, in standard measures, and at set prices. They would provide necessary amenities. They would not be permitted to harbor sedition, gambling, or drunkenness. Only licensed houses would be permitted to trade, and these would trade openly, in full view of magistrates, constables, and neighbors. Only men and women of sober character, who could be relied upon to uphold the letter and spirit of the law, would be granted licenses. Thus in Pennsylvania citizens would be supplied with taverns that would do them—and their communities—more good than harm.

Yet in narrow, specific, and irritating ways even the retention of those public houses established before his arrival stood at odds with Penn's larger plans for Philadelphia. For example, in order for Thomas Holme, Penn's surveyor, to complete the superimposition on the city's land of the grid of

A South East Prospect of the City of Philadelphia. Peter Cooper. 1708. Library
Company of Philadelphia. William Penn's astute management helped ensure that
Philadelphia grew with extraordinary rapidity in the first generation of settlement.
Cooper's view captures the city's flourishing trade and a skyline impressive in a city
founded so recently. To the left of center, John Whitpain's "great house"—once the

streets and squares necessary to conjure into existence a wholesome "green
country town," the Blue Anchor tavern had to be demolished. Had it remained standing, it would have blocked Front Street and required an un-
seemly deviation in the orderly progression of the city's streets.[3] Griffiths
Jones, the owner of the Blue Anchor, was a justice of the peace who enjoyed
Penn's friendship. Yet Jones demanded substantial compensation for the
demolition of the tavern—despite the fact that he had been charged with
keeping it without a license.[4] Equally troubling were the caves dug into the
bank which ran up from the edge of the Delaware River westward to Front
Street, which were soon a site for public houses. The behavior of the patrons
of such primitive riverbank taverns, indeed the property rights of the city's
cavedwellers, soon became matters of judicial and governmental concern.[5]

There are other equally revealing testimonies to the first Philadelphians' willingness to put private profit before public morality by involving
themselves in the liquor trade. Thomas Wynne, who as its speaker was the
man charged with representing the Pennsylvania assembly in negotiations
with Penn over a provincial charter, was presented by a grand jury soon after
his arrival in the city for keeping a public house without a license.[6] John
Test, sheriff of Philadelphia County, and Thomas Hooton, chairman of the

site of tavern and brewery—is shown. William Frampton's brewery and the Scales tavern feature in the center of the view. Samuel and Joshua Carpenter built taverns on the complex of wharves shown nearby. The Pennypot tavern is depicted to the extreme right.

Philadelphia grand jury, men with responsibilities for prosecuting unlicensed houses, each built a tavern on their city lots.[7] When Penn tried to interest William Frampton, a wealthy Quaker merchant, in building a brickworks in Philadelphia, Frampton built a brewery and tavern instead.[8] In 1684, when an excise on liquor was mooted, a group of nine merchants, five of whom owned public houses, petitioned the provincial council claiming that the tax would ruin their trade. The group argued that if the government needed money, they would voluntarily subscribe to give it £500. The provincial council accepted this proposal, although it received no money in return.[9]

Soon after Philadelphia was founded, an anonymous "planter" reminded Penn that although the first settlers had come to a "wilderness," it was "not meet" that "they should continue it so."[10] One enduring contemporary definition of a wilderness—encapsulated in Franklin's quip that there could be no good living where there was not good drinking—was a place without taverns or breweries.[11] Penn himself sympathized with this view. In *A Further Account of Pennsylvania* he went so far as to boast that there were in Philadelphia alone "seven ordinaries for the entertainment of strangers and workmen . . . [with] a good meal to be had for sixpence."[12] But while he

and the city's founding fathers may have been prepared to equate the building of public houses with the successful development of their city, they were
also quick to lay the blame for visible immorality among Philadelphians at
the tavern door. As early as 1684, Nicholas More was pointing to illicit
tavernkeeping and public drunkenness as evidence that "vice" was creeping
into the colony "like the old serpent."[13] When, in 1698, Penn wrote to the
provincial council demanding an explanation for the reports of Philadelphia
received in Britain that claimed "there is no place more overrun with wickedness, [with] sins so scandalous, openly committed in defiance of law and
virtue," the provincial council admitted that "as this place has grown more
populous and the people increased, looseness and vice [have] also crept
in . . . although endeavors have been used to suppress it by care and industry
of the magistrates from time to time." The council attributed the increase in
vice to the growth in the number of taverns, arguing, "as for ordinaries, we
are of the opinion that there are too many in this government, especially in
Philadelphia, which is one great cause of the growth of vice and makes the
same more difficult to be suppressed and kept under."[14] Having decided to
permit taverns in the province, Penn now urged that their numbers be kept
down. Taverns, Penn had discovered, could not be treated as civic amenities,
to be woven into the city's planned development as seamlessly as broad
streets or healthy, leafy squares. The men and women who founded the city's
first taverns were motivated by considerations of profit rather than public
service.

The speed with which Philadephians opened taverns illustrates a tension between ideals and material interests that can be identified, in various
forms, in the history of every settlement in colonial America. How well
could planned communities fulfill their supporters' aims, whether spiritual
or commercial? Philadelphia's earliest taverns, sites potentially both profitable and productive of vice, raised issues that were not unique. However,
although it was never controlled as effectively as magistrates and moralists
might have wished, Philadelphia's tavern trade was, from first settlement to
the end of the colonial period, subject to effective legal authority. Philadelphia's licensing authorities took a distinctive approach to regulating their
city's burgeoning tavern trade. In the first generation of settlement, Philadelphia's magistrates licensed men and women who in another city, such as
Boston, probably would have had to trade illegally. In contrast, at the close
of the colonial period, when magistrates elsewhere were abandoning efforts
to suppress the licensed trade, Philadelphia's licensing authorities presided
over a relative contraction in the number of licensed houses.

Demand for tavern licenses always outstripped supply; many Philadelphians who wished to try their luck in the tavern trade were barred from
its practice. Moreover, especially after the first generation of settlement, the
steadiest source of demand for licenses came from impoverished men and
women who, so magistrates and moralists reasoned, might be least able to
uphold those aspects of the law designed to restrict vice and protect the
community's health. But legislators and magistrates made numerous concessions to the realities of demand. The most influential of these was the
introduction in 1704 of a partial license, permitting the holder to sell small
measures of rum or beer alone, whose cost lay within the reach of impoverished householders. The effect of this decision on the size of the trade
was inflationary. Licensing policy was an important secondary cause of the
rapid growth in the number of licensed public houses of all kinds in the first
third of the eighteenth century that prompted efforts to restrict the growth
of the tavern trade—especially dramshops—in the final twenty-five years of
proprietary government. Critics of the tavern trade argued that the fact that
the growth in the number of licensed houses first outstripped, and then
matched, the increase in their city's population indicated that Philadelphia's
licensing policy had failed. In fact, Philadelphia's licensing authorities pursued with a good deal of consistency a policy that sought to bind publicans
to the task of moral reformation both by restricting possession of tavern
licenses to men and women of suitable character and by prosecuting, and
removing from the trade, men and women who broke licensing legislation.
Their decisions—and their occasional squabbles—contributed to a rapid
increase in the number of taverns in operation, but they stuck to a policy that
mixed pragmatism with idealism and thereby continued to influence the
development of the trade.

Ordinary citizens' propensity to evade or ignore the law by keeping
unlicensed houses even at the height of Quaker influence on the development and governance of the city raises questions regarding the efficacy of the
design and actual operation of licensing policy in Philadelphia that bear not
only on temperance-tavern conflict but also on the mores of tavern sociability. I argue, in Chapters 2, 3, and 4, that in colonial Philadelphia rich
and poor frequently drank in one another's company in licensed public
houses partly because the city's magistrates set maximum prices on liquor
sold in taverns at levels affordable for the poor as well as the rich. But if the
law was flouted in the matter of licenses, then it is open to doubt whether it
was obeyed with regard to retail prices. Similarly, if at any one time most of
the city's taverns were operating illegally, then one might doubt that "re-

spectable" citizens would have visited them and could question the representativeness of those licensed taverns where interaction between rich and poor can be shown to have occurred. In short, it is extremely important to understand exactly how much influence licensing law and policy had on the city's tavern trade. A detailed examination of licensing issues forms a necessary prologue to the discussions of the services taverns offered, their profitability, and the mores of taverngoing that follow later in this book.

*   *   *

A simple enumeration of the changing number of public houses in operation in the city suggests that, from first settlement to the close of the colonial period, Philadelphians were generously supplied—perhaps over-supplied—with licensed taverns. Table 1 sets the growth in the number of taverns in Philadelphia against the growth of the city's population. As early as 1686, six Philadelphians posted bonds as security for good behavior on their licensed premises, and court records show that there were already unlicensed publicans trading in the city.[15] There were about a dozen more or less above board public houses in operation in 1693, the year the city's first tax assessment was conducted. Court records from that period suggest we should probably increase that figure by two-thirds to arrive at an estimate of the total number of drinking houses, legal and illegal, then in operation.[16]

In the first two decades of the eighteenth century, the number of public houses in operation increased dramatically. During this period the province's governing bodies squabbled over licensing procedure. They also enacted a fundamental change in the licensing law. In 1704 a full license entitling its possessor to serve wine, beer, and spirits was made more expensive, at £5, than a partial license, costing £2 10s., permitting its possessor to sell beer or spirits alone.[17] In 1721 the city's constables drew up a list of all public houses, legal and illegal, in operation in their wards. These constables' returns are only partially extant and do not distinguish between licensed and unlicensed establishments. But if we assume that the distribution of the city's taverns by ward was the same in 1721 as in 1756 and extrapolate from the partial returns, there were ninety-four public houses, licensed and unlicensed, in operation in the city that year.[18] Compared to the city's population, this figure suggests an extraordinary level of provision: one public house for every sixty-five men, women, or children residing in the city. But the fact that in 1720 the city's licensed publicans, in a rare collective expression, had petitioned the assembly for relief from competition from unlicensed houses suggests that the

TABLE I   Ratio of Taverns to Philadelphia's Population, 1693–1769

	Taverns		Population	Ratio
1693	(Est. legal)	12	2,100	1:175
	(Est. total)	20	2,100	1:105
1721	(Est. total)	94	6,096	1:65
1756	(Est. legal)	101	16,182	1:160
1767	(Est. legal)	153	26,460	1:173
	(Est. total)	176	26,460	1:150
1769	(Est. legal)	155	28,042	1:181
	(Est. total)	178	28,042	1:158

Population totals as given by P.M.G. Harris in Susan E. Klepp, "Demography in Early Philadelphia, 1690–1860," *Proceedings of the American Philosophical Society* 133 (1989), 274.

startling ratio of taverns to citizens indicated by the fragmentary constables' returns is plausible.[19]

The 1744 grand jury Franklin chaired put the total number of houses in operation at one hundred.[20] In 1756 magistrates issued 111 licenses for the city wards. The coincidental survival of a tax list and a list of licensees (which does not, unfortunately, distinguish full from partial license holders) allows us to put a precise figure—101—on the number of licensed houses in operation in the city in 1756.[21] We can compare the 1767 and 1769 tax lists against similar lists of licensees to arrive at an informed estimate of the number of licensed houses in operation in these years as well. In 1767 Philadelphia's mayor's court issued 170 recommendations for licenses; in 1769, 172 recommendations. In each year, approximately 90 percent of those recommended lived in the city wards and actually took up their license.[22] Meanwhile, the frequency with which the mayor's court prosecuted unlicensed or disorderly houses, or specifically withdrew previous recommendations, suggests that in 1767 and 1769 the unlicensed trade was at least 15 percent of the total size of the licensed trade.[23]

The steady growth in the number of taverns in operation in colonial Philadelphia can be explained by the determination of Philadelphians from all walks of life, especially those who were disadvantaged, to enter the trade to secure a livelihood. But in the first generation of settlement, the tavern trade expanded with particular rapidity because it also attracted Philadelphians of varying degrees of wealth who sought a speculative return on investment.

Among this latter group were Samuel and Joshua Carpenter, Philadelphia's first plutocrats. Samuel Carpenter came to Philadelphia in 1684 at the behest of William Penn, and his brother Joshua joined him within two years. Samuel was a Quaker merchant who had made a fortune in trade in Barbados. As a reward for purchasing five thousand acres in Pennsylvania, Penn rewarded him with a prime waterfront lot in the city of Philadelphia, a portion of which Samuel sold to Joshua. The relationship between Penn and Samuel Carpenter was cordial, but it soon became apparent that the Carpenters were bent on developing their holdings in accordance with self-interest rather than the needs of the holy experiment. Samuel planned a wharf to stretch across the Delaware "so far as I might see fit." Joshua built a brewery.[24] Samuel refused to collect taxes for Penn; Joshua, who converted to the Church of England soon after he arrived in Philadelphia, led a tax revolt in the early 1700s.[25]

Both brothers established, but did not personally operate, public houses. In 1686 Joshua Carpenter built the Tun on the cartway that led to what had become known as Carpenter's Wharf. This cartway, in turn, became known as Tun Alley and was the site of Joshua Carpenter's brewery.[26] Samuel Carpenter built two taverns on the east side of Front Street: the Globe and an establishment that became known as Carpenter's Coffee-house. Like the Tun, these taverns were conducted by tenants.[27] For the Carpenters, and men in their position, building a house that could be rented as a dwelling or, perhaps more profitably, as a tavern was attractive because it promised the creation of commercial synergies; Samuel Carpenter's wharf attracted ships, which in turn attracted merchants, traders, sailors, and stevedores. These men could meet and discuss business at the Carpenter brothers' taverns, where they would drink Joshua Carpenter's beer.

This developmental logic was replicated by men and women possessed of rather fewer resources than the Carpenters. James West, a shipbuilder by trade, came to Philadelphia in 1684. He founded his own shipyard and in 1689 purchased the Pennypot tavern at Pegg's Run, just north of Vine Street.[28] West's account book makes clear that he continued to practice as a shipbuilder even after he bought the Pennypot. We do not know why he bought a tavern, but his investment allowed West to profit from the thirst of his workforce. A fragmentary record relating to the Pennypot show that one of West's shipbuilders, John King, regularly drank three quarts of beer a day and occasionally consumed, or at least purchased, seven or more quarts.[29] West paid his laborers, at least in part, by writing off the debts they contracted at the Pennypot, thus reducing the amount of hard cash he had to spend on wages. Such arrangements challenged the spirit of legislation

The Pennypot Tavern and Griscom's Academy. (After Edward Munford?) *Annals of Philadelphia*, ed. John Fanning Watson. Philadelphia: E. L. Carey, 1830. Library Company of Philadelphia. An artist's impression of the Pennypot as it might have looked in the early eighteenth century. (The same artist drew an accurate depiction of William Bradford's Old London Coffeehouse, reproduced below, suggesting that this view of the Pennypot is reliable.) The Pennypot, identified by its sign, was larger than most taverns built in the first generation of settlement, perhaps because its first owner, James West, could draw on labor and materials from his adjacent shipyard.

designed to prevent publicans from inveigling customers into debt, but given the shortage of specie in Pennsylvania, they may have been not only attractive but necessary.[30] Many of the transactions recorded in West's ledger involved barter. Dennis Rathford, for example, paid for repairs to his boat with cider and rum as well as molasses, corn, and turnips.[31] West could use his tavern to "launder" Rathford's cider and rum, and perhaps even the turnips. Moreover, ownership of the Pennypot allowed West to entertain the owners and purchasers of the vessels in his yard.

It is difficult to determine precisely how profitable an investment in the tavern trade was for men with a portfolio of assets. George Emlen came to Philadelphia from Shepton Mallet in Somerset in the 1680s. He established a public house at the sign of the Three Tuns on his Chestnut Street lot. The 1693 Philadelphia tax list valued Emlen's taxable estate at £150. The Three Tuns was clearly a busy house; an inventory conducted on Emlen's death in 1710 showed that the tavern's cellar contained ninety gallons of wine, three barrels of strong beer, and numerous casks and tierces of cider—in all, stock valued at £18. The tavern's kitchen was equipped with nearly one hundred sets of pewter utensils. Emlen's ownership of the Three Tuns must partly explain why, on his death, he left cash in silver worth £69 and gold worth £11. However, at his death, Emlen was no longer simply a tavernkeeper. The probate inventory shows that he had erected another house, a stable, a brewhouse, a bakery, and sundry outhouses in addition to the tavern on his Chestnut Street lot. The Three Tuns and its brewhouse valued at £325 were but a sizable fraction of an estate valued at £1,091.[32] Emlen's hoard of coins was probably built up as much from the turnover of the brewery and bakehouse as from the tavern. Thus, in all likelihood, simply owning one or even two taverns, for those who had the luxury of considering such a course for potential return on investment, was commercially appealing but hardly irresistible. As the city grew, the value of a tavern may have fallen. Samuel Carpenter complained that when he was forced to sell one of his taverns, probably the coffeehouse, he did not recoup his outlay on construction costs.[33]

Even in the first generation of settlement, and thereafter more generally throughout the colonial period, the majority of those who sought to enter the trade were less concerned with its commercial potential than with matters of daily survival. In an early example of a type of petition with which licensing authorities became all too familiar, Enoch Hobart brought to the magistrates' attention his inability to support his wife and six children by a regular trade. Since his neighbors were sometimes desirous of having a cup of meat dressed, and since they liked to drink beer with their meal, he "humbly appealed" for a license to sell liquor. Another applicant, Susannah Read, had been left a "destitute stepmother of four." She had made a "hard shift to earn a poor subsistence," and "pinching necessities" now "constrained" her to apply for a license to retail liquor.[34] Men and especially women who had fallen on hard times presumed themselves to have a customary right to alleviate their distress by keeping a tavern. Since the Middle Ages Britons who would otherwise have had no means of supporting a household had sought to enter the tavern trade, often with the tacit encouragement of licensing bodies.[35] In Philadelphia, as in England, desperate and impoverished citizens felt they had a right to try to scrape together a living by selling liquor. Indeed, from their point of view, restrictive licensing legislation was unnatural. If Enoch Hobart's neighbors wanted someone to sell them food and drink from time to time, why should he not oblige them?

Men and women who came to the trade in Hobart's circumstances were not necessarily unsuccessful tavernkeepers. Especially in the first generation of settlement, some Philadelphians who took up the trade out of necessity became prosperous and well-regarded publicans. On Benjamin Franklin's first visit to Philadelphia, a Quaker recommended the Crooked Billet as a reputable tavern. This house, founded by Alice Guest, began its trading life in a riverside cave. Alice Guest came to Philadelphia in 1683 when her husband, George, obtained a warrant from Penn to found a brickworks on the Delaware. George Guest died soon after the couple arrived in Philadelphia, leaving Alice neither brickworks nor a conventional house. She began keeping a tavern in her waterfront cave. In 1686 she put up a bond of £20 as security against good behavior on her premises. The property rights of Guest and the other dwellers in the bank became a matter of some dispute. However, in 1687 Guest received a confirmed patent to her land. Her cave was deemed to be worth more than £30 and she was thus exempted from the order that evicted most riverbank dwellers. Within five years of receiving the patent, Guest had built a conventional structure on her lot that housed a tavern she named the Crooked Billet. In 1693 Alice Guest's estate was assessed at £250. By the time of her death in 1705, she had wharfed out her riverfront holding, equipped it with warehouses, an additional dwelling, and access via Crooked Billet Alley. She had also acquired a house on the west side of Front Street. Perhaps because she was a devout Quaker, Guest appears to have kept house in full compliance with the law.[36]

Most of Philadelphia's first generation of publicans, keeping tavern in rented premises, would have regarded simply staying in business as an achievement. Grimstone Boude served for nearly twenty years as the tenant of Samuel Carpenter's Globe tavern. He went to court to testify against unlicensed competitors and, in turn, was himself presented by the grand jury and fined, for refusing to serve on the nightly watch and for failing to renew his license. At the time of his death he was still keeping the Globe. His will describes an estate that, when viewed as the product of twenty years' daily labor, can only be described as modest. Boude bequeathed to his four children a gold ring, three silver drinking vessels, four silver spoons, three feather beds, and small sums of cash. Boude may have been wealthier than these specific bequests suggest. His wife, Mary, received the unenumerated remainder of his estate, which might have included a slave woman named Joan. However, both Boude's court appearances and the value of his estate at his death suggest that tavernkeeping provided him with only tenuous economic security.[37]

Many Philadelphians attempted to profit from their neighbors' thirst without establishing a legitimate, licensed public house. Scores of Philadelphians serviced their neighbors with occasional clandestine or "back-door" sales of liquor. Many, perhaps most, of the householders who engaged in this activity as a means of securing a competency would not have regarded themselves as criminals. As late as 1746, Rebecca Warder alluded to the imprecise boundary between the economy of a private household and full-fledged involvement in the tavern trade when she contested a fine for keeping public house without a license with the argument that she had been "unwarily drawn" into selling liquor by small measures.[38] But although magistrates showed some sympathy in cases where desperate persons, and especially impoverished women, sold drink without a license as a short-term expedient—by accepting promises to desist, even allowing defendants to dispose of their existing stocks—the letter and spirit of the licensing law sought to detach the sale of liquor from individual household economies on one hand and from the market-based retail trades in consumer essentials such as bread on the other.[39] Philadelphians could buy liquor wholesale from merchants or alewives, but they were not permitted to purchase and drink small measures of liquor in stores or other unlicensed houses. Persons who attempted to incorporate unlicensed sales of small measures of beer, wine, or spirits into their business—for example, storekeepers who allowed customers to "taste test" liquor in their shops—were vigorously prosecuted.[40] Such prosecutions enjoyed the support of the city's licensees as well as at least some portion of the wider community from which taverns drew their customers. The circumstances surrounding the sixty-one known cases involving alleged breaches of licensing law brought to trial between 1685 and 1703 suggest friction between publicans trading openly in conformity with the law and illicit retailers attempting to make quick profits while evading restrictive legislation.[41] In 1686, for example, a grand jury presented Richard Russell, identified as a ship's carpenter, for keeping tavern without a license. A number of Russell's neighbors testified against him. One of them, a legitimate tavernkeeper, Thomas Holleman, told the court that he had heard "unhandsome" noises coming from Russell's house at "unseasonable" hours and had it on good authority that money was changing hands for drink there.[42] In a similar case, Grimstone Boude testified against one Hendrik Faullonberg for keeping an unlicensed and disorderly house.[43] In other cases, licensed publicans were accused by their neighbors of serving Indians or servants, or of keeping unseasonable hours.[44]

Legislators attempted to force Philadelphians to drink on private property under the supervision of a householder or employer or in licensed public houses under the supervision of a licensee answerable to the state. Nevertheless, in the first generation of settlement, at the height of Quaker influence, Philadelphia's drinkers were faced with an array of houses selling liquor openly or covertly, legally or illicitly. Shady drinking dens found customers, even if the prosecution of unlicensed or scofflaw retailers attracted a measure of community support. Although many drinking establishments had brief trading lives, the overall number of taverns in operation in the city at any given moment rose steadily in the first generation of settlement because men and women of many degrees of wealth and honesty were prepared to take their chance, illegally if necessary, in the business of attempting to cater to their neighbors' apparently insatiable thirst.

In response to the realities of demand, Pennsylvania's licensing bodies developed a policy that differed in subtle yet significant ways from those pursued in other English colonies or in England itself. The province was founded and developed during a period in which English magistrates permitted a dramatic expansion in the number of licensed houses, not only, notoriously, in London, but also in those provincial towns with which many Philadelphians were familiar and against which they might compare the well-being of their adopted city. In Shrewsbury, for example, 23 innkeepers practiced their trade in 1668. In 1709 the town had 60 innkeepers; by 1731, 52 innkeepers and a score of lesser alesellers. In 1702 Preston had 5 publicans; in 1722, 28.[45] To English critics, such sharp increases in the number of licensed taverns signaled not just the corrupt abandonment of any commitment to reform popular morality but also a positive encouragement to vice.

In light of English experience, magistrates and lawmakers in Britain's American colonies adopted a far more rigorous approach to the regulation of the tavern trade. Under the duke of York's laws, which governed the west bank of the Delaware and the Jersies before Penn's arrival, no settlement was permitted more than three licensed houses. In 1677 Virginia's House of Burgesses stipulated that no county might license more than two taverns.[46] In 1681 Massachusetts set upper limits on the number of taverns to be permitted in each of its towns and began a policy that aimed to reduce drastically the number of taverns and liquor sellers in the city of Boston by restricting the number of licenses granted.[47] The chief targets of such pre-

scriptions were small houses, trading in the twilight of legality, which offered few amenities of use to travelers or others deemed to have legitimate
need of a tavernkeeper's services. Such houses were difficult to suppress
because, in the colonies as in England itself, they were kept by poor and
disadvantaged citizens struggling to keep a household afloat. If they could
not trade legally, they would trade illegally. In Boston a policy of suppression pursued doggedly for more than twenty years failed, not least because
many Bostonians refused to cooperate in the prosecution of unlicensed
publicans by evading terms of service in the office of tithingman that would
have required them to inform magistrates of illegal houses.[48] In contrast, by
introducing graduated license fees, Pennsylvania's legislators gave impoverished Philadelphians who wished to sell drams or pints alone an opportunity to do so legally. Moreover, unlike other colonial legislatures, Pennsylvania's did not attempt to stipulate in law the precise number of public
houses that might constitute a healthy provision for any given community.

Penn and the city's founding fathers were as concerned as their counterparts in Boston about the potential vices of the tavern trade. Yet Pennsylvania's authorities did not attempt a sustained draconian "suppression" of
public houses such as that pursued in Boston. On the other hand, Philadelphia's licensing bodies never adopted the lax attitudes to regulation of the
trade common in England. Instead, they attempted to check what they did
not doubt were the pernicious effects of a surfeit of taverns by restricting
practice of the trade to licensees of suitable character. All the available
evidence suggests that Philadelphia's licensing bodies held a tavern license
in high regard, as a prize to be won rather than the mere legislative acknowl-
edgment of a customary entitlement. From the city's founding until roughly
the middle of the eighteenth century, Philadelphia's licensing authorities,
despite criticism, paid as much attention to the character of the men and
women they licensed as they did to the overall number of taverns in operation. In the third quarter of the eighteenth century, at a time when Boston's
magistrates had largely abandoned any effort to control the size of the trade,
Philadelphia's licensing bodies may have presided over a slight contraction
in the licensed trade. Yet even in this period the number of tavern licenses
granted in Philadelphia more or less matched the increase in the city's
population. Philadelphia's licensing bodies continued to pay close attention
to the character of the men and women they were licensing; the extant
records suggest that throughout the colonial period Philadelphia's licensing
authorities made character judgments, listened to neighborhood sentiment,
and considered the good of the community in an effort to regulate the trade.

They pursued a flexible and even handed licensing policy with a fair measure of success.

Nevertheless, in the first generation of settlement, squabbles between competing branches of government over which of them was best qualified to judge suitable licensees, how many persons should be recommended, and how the revenue from fees should be collected and spent threatened to stymie the development of a coherent approach to licensing. Critics of the tavern trade assumed that its pernicious influences could be traced to the fact that it was being conducted by the wrong sort of person. In 1695, for example, the provincial assembly received a petition from forty-four Philadelphians who demanded that only "sober, honest and conscientious persons" be licensed to keep tavern in their city.[49] In 1697 Penn informed the provincial council that henceforth licenses were to be issued only on the recommendation of the county courts of quarter sessions. This stipulation was incorporated within the Charter of Privileges agreed in 1701.[50] However, the provincial council continued to interfere in licensing decisions made by magistrates, while arguing that it should have the power to recommend licensees.[51] Meanwhile, the magistrates of Philadelphia's mayor's court, claiming jurisdiction over the city wards, wrangled with their colleagues on the Philadelphia county court of quarter sessions over the licensing of houses on the margins of the city in Southwark and Northern Liberties.[52] Lieutenant governor John Evans entered into these disputes, ostensibly in order to protect the proprietary interest in the matter of revenue but in reality as part of his campaign to cut Quaker justices and assemblymen down to size. In February 1707, in a speech designed to woo voters, he argued that more taverns were needed in the province.[53] In the spring of 1707, despite Evans's last-ditch attempt to attach to the governor's office the power both to recommend and to issue tavern licenses, local magistrates consolidated their power over the appointment and removal of licensed publicans. In the system that developed, the license itself carried the seal of the provincial secretary and was issued on behalf of the proprietary interest. But the licensee took possession of the license from the clerk of the local court of quarter sessions, following a recommendation from the justices. This procedure allowed the courts to confirm the identities of those men and women they licensed, or removed from the trade, within their jurisdiction.[54] Magistrates now began to enact a policy that sought to restrict possession of a tavern license to those of sober character.

In *Some Account of the Province of Pennsylvania*, William Penn assured those "universal spirits that have an eye to the good of posterity, and that both understand and delight to promote good discipline and just government among a plain and well intending people," of an especially warm welcome in the province.[55] Presumably it was these "spirits" Penn hoped would apply for tavern licenses. The law required licensees to act against their own economic interests by, for example, not allowing locals to "tarry" on their premises, not serving servants, Indians, or slaves, and not allowing even legitimate customers to drink to excess. Publicans had to observe limits, designed to protect customers from "gouging," on the prices they could charge for the drinks and services they provided. They also had to court unpopularity by suppressing gambling, swearing, and revelry during the hours when they might open their houses to the thirsty public. In short, the law presumed a suitable licensee would possess a degree of detachment from paying customers that would enable him or her to act as a guardian of public morality.

Apart from the requirement that a licensee possess wealth enough to pay a license fee, licensing law made no stipulation linking an applicant's eligibility for a license to his or her station in life or gender. In this respect the law was out of keeping with community sentiment. On one hand, many wealthy Philadelphians, mindful perhaps of Sir William Blackstone's precept that some persons lived in "so mean a situation as to be esteemed to have no will of their own," doubted whether poor and impoverished citizens could act as guardians of public morality.[56] On the other hand, as we have seen, Philadelphians who actually lived in mean situations, and impoverished women in particular, regarded themselves as having almost a right to alleviate their distress by retailing liquor. This sense of customary entitlement enjoyed substantial support among the population at large. Philadelphia's licensing bodies therefore faced a dilemma with which their counterparts elsewhere were familiar. If they issued licenses in quantities close to the level of demand, they risked bringing into the trade men and women unwilling or unable to enforce those aspects of the licensing law designed to safeguard the health of the community. But if they held the number of licenses issued well below the level of demand, they risked creating an illegal trade and, consequently, a freer market in drink than moralists, taverngoers, and existing publicans would tolerate.

An examination of decisions reached on petitions for tavern licenses by the city's licensing authorities suggests that Philadelphia's magistrates retained an extraordinary faith in the efficacy of the licensing system as a means of combating vice. Their decisions assumed that suitable, licensed publicans were more likely than unlicensed, and therefore unsuitable, vendors to uphold laws governing permissible tavern behavior and retail practice. Magistrates paid attention to neighborhood assessments of an individual publican's character. They scrutinized all petitions, not just those that sought the award of a full license (which is as impressive in hindsight as it must have been irksome for unsuccessful petitioners at the time). If a person broke the licensing law by keeping a disorderly house, he or she could expect to be barred from the trade, but unless or until a publican broke the law, he had a reasonable chance of keeping house for as long as he desired. Whereas in other communities licensing policy veered wildly from draconian suppression to world-weary toleration, in colonial Philadelphia licensing authorities clung tenaciously to a policy that attempted to control the trade by examining its practitioners on a case-by-case basis. The chief beneficiaries of this policy were men and—especially—women of modest means.

More than one hundred petitions submitted between 1704 and 1760 by individuals seeking tavern licenses survive in the archives of the Historical Society of Pennsylvania.[57] Many of these are formulaic, stating simply that an existing license was about to expire. Even detailed petitions do not generally specify whether a full or partial license was being sought and it is not always possible to determine the verdict reached by magistrates. Nevertheless, some of these petitions offer fascinating descriptions of the applicant's background and motivation. Moreover, the very existence of a body of petitions, as well as the information supplied in them, suggests that a licensing policy which sought to restrict the possession of licenses to men and women of "suitable" character exerted an effective influence on the development of the tavern trade.

Tales of misfortune were commonly cited as a reason for seeking to take up a tavern license. Petitioners mentioned their age, their inability to find other means of support, or the weight of their family commitments. Moses Durel, for example, appealed for a license on the grounds that he was "very infirm" in body, frequently sick "to the degree that he [had] to spend eight to ten days in bed," and hard-pressed to support his several small children. The magistrates, Durel continued, should express their compassion for his "poor low condition" by favoring him with their "bountiful recommendation."[58] William Watkin was a mariner who had formerly sailed out of Philadelphia. Unfortunately, he had begun to labor "under several violent and severe disorders" and was troubled by "pleurisy, rheumatism and gravel" to such a degree that he was "incapable of doing any hard manual labour." Nevertheless he had taken over an "accustomed house" on the corner of Mulberry and Fifth Streets and several friends and neighbors supported his petition for a license to keep tavern.[59]

In all likelihood, such petitions offered a more or less accurate description of the petitioners' circumstances. There was little incentive for a petitioner to fabricate a heart-rending picture of poverty, since magistrates were
perfectly prepared to reject petitions grounded in dire distress. Elizabeth
Spoom petitioned for a license on the grounds that she had an "old diseased
mother" and was already receiving assistance from the overseers of the poor.
She was rejected. John Stacey's wife petitioned for a license on the grounds
that her husband had but one eye and that was "ill." He was unable to work
and the family was living in extreme poverty. A laconic summary on the
reverse of the petition noted that the magistrates had rejected this appeal
and that John Stacey was now blind.[60] It is of course possible that such
decisions were capricious or even corrupt. More likely, magistrates kept
faith with the unstated assumptions of the law—namely that the vices of the
trade could be controlled by the right sort of practitioner—by looking beyond a petitioner's material circumstances in an attempt to form a judgment
based on an individual's character and motivation.

Prosperous petitioners were subjected to a scrutiny as rigorous as that
applied to the disadvantaged. In 1704 Gabriel Wilkinson, a freeman of the
city with property worth £225, argued rather haughtily that "since it is nearly
fishing time," there would be a "necessity" of a public house of entertainment on the banks of the Delaware. He informed the magistrates that
"because the fishermen always come ashore at my house and most of the
shipwright's yards are thereby and none lives near that sells drink," to "deny
a license would be very prejudicial, and inconvenient to many."[61] Despite
Wilkinson's wealth and his announced willingness to serve the community,
his petition was rejected. That this decision was founded on an assessment
of Wilkinson's character is suggested by a second petition in which Wilkinson protested that despite reports received by the magistrates from unknown
sources, he had kept neither "bad orders nor ill company."[62]

In most cases a court appearance on a charge related to an offense
against public order or licensing law was enough to disqualify a person from
the trade. John Spering, for example, persuaded a number of well-off neighbors to testify their "willingness that he be recommended" for a tavern
license. Spering's friends told the court that he had for "some time kept a
public house of entertainment" in their neighborhood. The tavern itself was
"ancient" and "very commodious for that imploy." Last, they attested that
they looked upon Spering as not only "fully qualified" but also as a man who
would keep "no disorderly house."[63] Unfortunately he had previously been
presented for selling strong drink without a license. No witnesses were

called, since he was "known to the jurors" and had entered a guilty plea.[64] Spering's subsequent petition for a license was in vain.

Magistrates clearly paid attention to neighborhood views on the suitability of a potential keeper, often to the applicant's detriment. Although many petitioners gathered signatures, or alluded to support from neighbors prepared to vouch for their character when they applied for a license, hostile neighborhood sentiment could drive established licensees from the trade. Sometime before 1740, Thomas Carrol was granted a license after he submitted a petition that made frequent references to an "ancient mother," nine children, and the difficulty he faced supporting himself by trade. In 1740 Carrol was writing again, saying that "by the information of some person to your Worships of some misbehavior of which your petitioner is altogether ignorant . . . and [of which] he has not had a chance to prove his innocence, your petitioner was refused a license at the last court." Carrol now brought to the court's attention the fact that he was "stricken in pain" and unable to support his large family even though he had already parted with most of his worldly goods. His petition was rejected, as was another submitted a year later, which repeated that he was "stricken" and added that he had had to sell the remainder of his household goods at vendue.[65]

Licensing authorities generally rejected petitions submitted by men who sought a short-term stint in the trade to secure a temporary means of support. George Antwerp broke his arm and applied for a license to support himself while his arm mended. He was unsuccessful. A blacksmith, William Perkins, "mashed and broke" his leg and thigh and, wanting to keep his family together while it healed, sought a publican's license with the "encouragement" of his neighbors. He was not granted one. Thomas Hamper spoke of his many misfortunes in the distilling business. He felt he could no longer carry on that trade but believed that his "sobriety and honesty" qualified him as "a proper person for retailing liquor." He wanted a license to sell drams in order to "amend the bad situation of his affairs" and procure a "livelihood" for himself and his family. The magistrates refused his request.[66] They may have assumed that a publican seeking to profit from a short stint in the trade would have less incentive to uphold the letter and spirit of the law than a man or woman committed to the trade as their sole means of support. Such decisions show that magistrates attempted to maintain a distinction between tavern licenses and articles of outdoor charitable support.

Nevertheless, while poverty, even distress, did not in themselves qualify a person for a license, the surviving records suggest that magistrates may have made some concessions to considerations of charity. When magistrates

were convinced that a petitioner had no other means of supporting or keeping together a family except by selling liquor, they usually granted a license.
Some men benefited from this bias, but the chief beneficiaries were women
who found themselves in circumstances similar to Isabella Neal's. Neal had
been abandoned by her husband, and her efforts to support a family had
been hampered by the seizure of all her household goods. Although one
wonders how Neal would have been able to equip a tavern, her request for a
license was granted.[67] We can be sure of the outcome of thirty-two petitions
grounded in personal and family misfortunes and submitted by men and
women between 1704 and 1760. Nine women in this category were granted a
license; only three were rejected. In contrast, among men, nine such petitions were approved but eleven were rejected.[68] Although many wives,
daughters, women servants, and slaves helped men run taverns, women
were licensed only when—as a result of bereavement or abandonment—they
found themselves heading a household. Even women who had previous
experience in the trade stressed their desperation not their expertise when
petitioning for a license of their own. I know of only one case in which a
woman successfully petitioned for a first tavern license on the grounds that
she had effectively run a tavern licensed in her former husband's name.[69]
The vast majority of women who specified their reasons for seeking a license
alluded to the need to maintain a family, spoke often of their poverty and
distress, and made no mention of any previous involvement in the trade. Of
course many men made exactly the same pitch, but it seems to have been
more successful when made by women.

Most of the surviving data on licensing decisions forces us to consider
whether women seeking to enter the tavern trade were encouraged or discriminated against in isolation from the distinction between a full and partial license. At no point in the colonial period is it possible to determine
whether, for example, magistrates applied "charitable" considerations
toward women who sought become alehousekeepers but discriminated
against women who sought to take out a full license. But if we look at overall
rates of approval and rejection in licensing decisions it seems that magistrates treated men and women equally. Between 1759 and 1761, for example,
Philadelphia's mayor's court considered 206 petitions for tavern licenses.
They approved 32 and rejected 16 submitted by women. In the same period
they approved 102 petitions filed by men and rejected 56.[70] In other words,
although at the close of the colonial period fewer women than men sought
to take out a license, those women who did petition the courts received

treatment comparable to that afforded men. Once licensed, women were relicensed with the same frequency as men.[71]

Throughout the colonial period, but especially in the first two generations of settlement, some women, like Alice Guest at the Crooked Billet, kept prominent houses that enjoyed a good reputation. Nevertheless, although their ranks always included some comparatively wealthy widows, women licensees were generally poorer than their male counterparts and may, as a result, have chosen to apply for licenses to run dramshops or alehouses more frequently than they applied for full licenses.[72] The available licensing data does not permit even this speculation to be investigated exhaustively. However, court records from the first generation of settlement, impressionistic evidence derived from newspaper advertisements and other sources describing the trade in the second quarter of the eighteenth century, and licensing records from the 1760s suggest that throughout the colonial period women publicans maintained a visible presence in Philadelphia's tavern trade. Two of Philadelphia's first six licensees were women. Seventy-two women were among the 243 persons recommended for tavern licenses between 1767 and 1771. At any given stage in the city's development, women licensees could be found managing approximately a quarter of the city's public houses. Shopkeeping was the only trade in the city similarly open to female participation.[73]

However impressive its mix of idealism and pragmatism appears in hindsight, Philadelphia's licensing policy attracted criticism. Efforts made by magistrates to respond to, and even anticipate, fears concerning the growth and size of the licensed trade, the advisability of licensing dramshops, and the continuing presence of substantial numbers of women among the city's cadre of licensed publicans helped shape further the development of Philadelphia's tavern trade. As we have seen, in 1704 legislators established a distinction between a "full" tavern license permitting, and implicitly requiring, its holder to offer a wide range of goods and services and a partial license permitting its holder to sell drams or pints alone. Although lawmakers subsequently tinkered with the price differential, the basic distinction between full and partial licenses remained in effect for the rest of the colonial period. This decision recognized the realities of the demand for licenses and sought to encourage respect for the law. But, regardless of its intent, its effects on the size of the trade were inflationary. As Philadelphia's tavern trade grew, critics demanded that the city's licensing authorities adopt a more restrictive policy.

Critics of licensing policy proceeded from the assumption that the existence of affordable partial licenses encouraged poor and desperate Philadelphians to take up the trade. The inevitable result would be that unsuitable keepers, that is, the poor, would establish vice-ridden groggeries, bringing to Philadelphia the scenes of debauchery made infamous by William Hogarth in *Gin Lane*. A mercantilist view of the trade held that as the number of licensed premises of all sorts increased, so competition among licensees increased. It was assumed that dramshopkeepers, being poorer than full licensees, would feel competition most keenly and would therefore be tempted to ignore laws designed to regulate the trade. This in turn would lead tavernkeepers to compete with dramshops for customers until, in a manner similar to Gresham's law, "bad" publicans would drive out "good."

In 1744 these critical perspectives were drawn together in an astringent grand jury presentment. Chaired by Benjamin Franklin, the grand jury reported "with great concern" on the "vast number of tippling houses within this city." These were unlicensed houses, generally specializing in the sale of spirits. A shopkeeper who allowed customers to drink rum in a secluded back room was keeping a tippling house. Tippling houses also served those persons barred from licensed premises, including slaves, apprentices, and Indians. The grand jury presentment claimed that Philadelphia's tippling houses were "nurseries [of] vice and debauchery," the homes of "profane language, horrid oaths and imprecations," and a cause of poverty to themselves and their neighbors. The jurors also noted the increased number of licensed public houses and the clustering of those houses in particular neighborhoods. They argued that at least some tavernkeepers, "for want of better customers, may through necessity, be under greater temptation to entertain apprentices, servants and even negroes." This, they maintained, was already the case in a section of the city known as "Helltown." Since it was unlikely that tavernkeepers could be provided with "better customers," to prevent the creation of future Helltowns some method of "limiting or diminishing the number of public houses" should be found. This would lessen competition and encourage tavernkeepers to better enforce existing laws.[74]

Magistrates were profoundly angered by this report, not least because they seem to have anticipated some of the concerns it expressed.[75] For example, there are indications that as the total number of licensed premises in operation rose, licensing authorities paid closer attention to the location of the houses they were licensing. Philadelphia's drinkers regarded a tavern on their doorstep as a right. This was one reason why unlicensed houses found customers and indigent petitioners found supporters. Some petitions alluding to this presumptive right—for example, John Johnston's, which argued there was no public house at his end of Walnut Street, Alice Devonshire's, which pointed out her house was a long way from any other tavern, and William Hawkins's, which argued that a house was "needed" at his end of the city—were approved.[76] On the other hand, in 1759 James Mullan informed magistrates that he had lost one of his eyes to smallpox and was "compelled to follow some other trade for a livelihood." He had taken over the "accustomed" tavern known as the Sloop. This house, Mullan argued, was "commodiously situated for the entertainment of shallopmen and others attending the drawbridge." His petition was denied on the grounds that there was already a tavern at the head of the dock.[77] Throughout the colonial period, magistrates operated in accordance with their own estimation of community needs. Thus they invariably allowed ferry operators a tavern license—in order that passengers might be provided with a terminus in which to wait for, or recover from, a river crossing—but drew the line at licensing Richard West, a "small trader chiefly dealing with those that go to and fro by water."[78] The magistrates seem to have concluded that West did not offer a regular ferry service to the public and that he sought a license solely to entertain his trading partners. Similarly Bartholomew Baker—a shopkeeper who had "at great labour and expence" erected "a large stable," furnished a house for the accommodation of strangers, and gathered more than a hundred signatures attesting to his "suitability" to keep a public house—was denied a license on the grounds that his house would only "entertain country market people." Ann Donner's argument that her house was the "daily resort" of several "friends and acquaintances from the country" who came to her to buy rum cut no ice with the licensing magistrates.[79] Contrary to the 1744 grand jury presentment, licensing decisions reached in the half century prior to independence show that magistrates gave consideration to the potential location of a tavern and its likely clientele, as well as the character and circumstances of the petitioner.

Franklin's grand jury report formed the preamble to a specific presentment against nine publicans, six of whom were women, for keeping disorderly houses. The gendered language of the report—for example its reference to "nurseries" of vice—highlights critics' continuing concerns over a licensing policy that was relatively friendly to women. By granting licenses to women tavernkeepers, magistrates implied that women were as capable as men of running a respectable independent business. Franklin doubted whether women ought to conduct any independent business enterprise, let alone tavernkeeping.[80] In the community at large, while women householders might have been regarded as deserving objects of charity, there seems to have been some reluctance to affirm that they were as capable as men of running a respectable tavern. A number of extant petitions for a tavern license include the signatures of the petitioner's neighbors. In only one such case was the petitioner a woman.[81]

Those features of the trade that made it attractive to women seeking to support a household triggered concerns regarding gender roles that could act to the detriment of women tavernkeepers. The attraction of tavernkeeping for independent women householders may have been that it brought workplace and household together, affording women seeking to juggle a variety of demands upon their time some degree of flexibility. Viewed from a different perspective, tavernkeeping brought drunkenness, bad language, and vice into buildings that doubled as private homes. Magistrates seeking to uphold the sanctity of the private home must have been tempted to judge cases involving disorder in taverns run by women differently from similar cases involving male licensees. On the night of August 10, 1695, for example, constable Thomas Morris, acting on complaints from neighbors about "unseasonable drinking," called in at the Blue Anchor, a tavern kept by the widow Cox. There he was abused by assembled drinkers as a "cur," "rascal," and "impudent dog." Cox was charged with keeping a disorderly house. In her defense, she maintained that she could not, for reasons unspecified, force her customers to stop drinking at the appointed hour. She was stripped of her license.[82] Magistrates, familiar with gender stereotypes that characterized some women as scolds, shrews, or harridans, may have doubted that a woman in Cox's position would not have been able to staunch the torrent of abuse offered to constable Morris. Some women publicans enjoyed strong-willed personalities and kept good order on their premises by turfing out drunks. Moreover, many women tavernkeepers could have relied on help from male relatives or servants to control their customers. (The presence of male dependents in a house run by a woman could be a mixed blessing. Hannah Gooding, for example, was convicted of keeping a disorderly house because the court believed that her son was using her riverside cave to sell liquor to servants and to trade in stolen goods.)[83] Even so, it must have been difficult for a woman, especially a woman desperate to support a household via income from liquor sales, to control troublemakers in her tavern.

However, the language Franklin chose to castigate tippling houses—"nurseries of vice"—implied that women tavernkeepers might actually be responsible for encouraging vice. This assumption also haunted charges brought against women accused of keeping disorderly or bawdy houses. It raises a question that is impossible to answer from the data available: namely, did the likes of Margaret Cook, charged in 1741 with receiving and entertaining, "whores, vagabonds," and idle men of "bad conversation" in her house set out to keep a tavern brothel, or did economic necessity and social pressure force her, against her will, to serve "whores and vagabonds" on her premises?[84] It seems that, except in one important area, Philadelphia's magistrates gave women publicans the benefit of the doubt. Where Franklin toyed with the notion that some women tavernkeepers were encouraging vice, magistrates adopted the more charitable assumption that, like men, women were in certain circumstances unable to control their customers. The surviving court records yield details of seventy-one cases involving the charge of keeping an unlicensed or tippling house brought between 1701 and 1771. Seventeen individuals in this sample were women. Roughly a quarter of those prosecutions brought against keepers of disorderly houses in the same period involved women defendants.[85] In other words, magistrates prosecuted women for keeping unlicensed or disorderly houses roughly as often as one might expect given the fact that women ran around a quarter of the licensed houses in operation in the city at one moment in time. On the other hand, both men and women who were convicted of keeping a disorderly house were removed from the trade with little or no right of appeal.

A possible exception to the general rule that magistrates did not employ pejorative gender characterizations in their licensing decisions concerns the role of prostitution in taverns. Between 1701 and 1771 eighteen women and twenty-five men were specifically accused of keeping bawdy houses.[86] Women ran approximately a quarter of the city's taverns, but nearly half the total number of prosecutions for keeping a bawdy house were brought against women. The disparity is striking but perhaps not surprising. If it was difficult for a woman publican to stop a male customer from drinking or fighting, it must have been even harder for her to stop a man from gratifying his sexual appetites or a woman from plying a trade even older than tavernkeeping. The low frequency with which charges of keeping a bawdy house occur in the extant court records lends little substance to Franklin's claim that Philadelphia possessed rookeries of vice notorious as "Helltowns." Moreover it is possible that whether run by men or women, the city's bawdy houses were not conducted in licensed premises.[87] By operating a relatively accessible licensing policy, Philadelphia's magistrates gave even poor publicans running modest dramshops an incentive to keep prostitution out of public houses.

Dramshops were an enduring source of concern among critics of the tavern trade, especially since there is some evidence that they tended to be run disproportionately by women. In 1721, for example, constables found that there were no taverns in the city's South Ward, but four women dramshopkeepers. There may have been as many as fifty dramshops, most of them unlicensed, in operation in 1721.[88] Between 1767 and 1771, 243 individuals were recommended at least once for a license to keep public house. Of this group, only 31 were recommended for a license to sell only spirits or beer. (This figure suggests that magistrates had responded to concerns that they were licensing too many dramshops.) However, 14 of those recommended for a partial license between 1767 and 1771 were women. There were, at this time, proportionately more women among the ranks of the city's dramshopkeepers than there were among the ranks of its "full" tavernkeepers.[89] Only 8 of the men and 2 of the women recommended for a license to sell spirits alone from 1767 to 1771 appeared on either the 1767 or 1769 tax list and the mean value of their estates was £5. In contrast, the mean value of the estates possessed by the far greater number of publicans recorded on the tax lists of 1767 and 1769 under the designations tavernkeeper or innkeeper was slightly above £20. This disparity in mean values is slightly misleading. The median wealth of the city's pool of licensees full and partial in 1767 and 1769 (£10 and £9 respectively) suggests that poorer Philadelphians took out full as well as partial tavern licenses.[90] Nevertheless, by the close of the century, the city's poorest publicans, especially its poorest women publicans, were likely to be found behind the bar of a rented dramshop. It is important not to rush to the conclusion that all establishments licensed to sell drams or beer alone were marginal. In Chapter 2, I present evidence, drawn from brewers' account books, that shows some beerhousekeepers purchasing and presumably selling beer in quantities dwarfing those of fully licensed neighbors. Poor dramshopkeepers could conduct a high-volume and profitable trade. Nonetheless, most dramshops and alehouses traded at the margins of profitability, enjoyed brief trading lives, and provoked fears that their keepers were under special pressure to evade laws designed to control vice.

The 1744 grand jury's charge that magistrates were not sufficiently rigorous in rooting out illegal or disreputable publicans was a hardy perennial. But in both the first generation of settlement and again toward the close of the colonial period, we can find evidence of magistrates making strenuous efforts to root "undesirable" publicans out from the trade. On December 26, 1701, John Simes's tavern was the site of an event that a subsequent grand jury thought "disturbing of peaceable minds" and liable "to propagate the throne of wickedness amongst us." Simes allowed—and in the grand jury's eyes encouraged—John Smith and Edward James to "dance and revel" dressed in women's clothes while Sarah Stivee and Dorothy Canterill were present masked in men's clothes. Simes contested his presentment for keeping a disorderly house and found a tailor, John Williams, to stand bond for his appearance in court. Simes kept his license. But in 1703 one John Saltell was brought to court accused of passing counterfeit coins in Simes's tavern. In 1704 Simes's wife, Anne, was accused of using the tavern to forestall the market, and following this charge the tavern and its keeper disappear from the records.[91] It is possible that as the number of licensed public houses, especially those selling only rum or beer, rose, magistrates and grand juries were less able to supervise the trade. However, even if magistrates and grand juries had been lax in the first half of the eighteenth century, by the third quarter of the century they were conducting a vigorous prosecution of licensing offenses. Indeed, during this period, only felonies and assaults took up more of the court's time.[92]

Even as the volume of business conducted by the courts rose, magistrates actively pursued recidivist and scofflaw liquor sellers like Bryan and Susannah Connolly. In May 1760 Bryan Connolly was convicted and fined for keeping a disorderly house. At the same sessions, his wife, Susannah, was convicted of stealing goods belonging to Andrew Braykill. Later that year the Connollys were jointly accused of stealing property belonging to Anne Rakeshaw and John Lawer. Bryan Connolly was found guilty and fined £10. However, Connolly was able to find a neighbor prepared to post a £200 bond for his future good behavior and this bond was not called in when, in 1761, Connolly was haled before the court accused of breaking one of John Hood's windows. In January 1764 Bryan Connolly was once again found guilty of keeping a disorderly tippling house, and of assault and battery upon Mary Campbell and Daniel Jerman. Susannah Connolly was found guilty of assault and battery on Jerman. The court demanded a bond of £800 for their future good behavior. When they could not come up with this bond, the Connollys petitioned for relief. They were freed on the condition that they be shipped to "some country to the southward of Georgia."[93]

Such persistence in enforcing the terms of licensing law almost matched the regularity with which it was flouted by some Philadelphians. Yet contemporaries remained convinced that vice was going unpunished. As late as 1761, the Pennsylvania assembly discussed a petition from the Philadelphia Monthly Meeting "earnestly recommending to ye care of the legislature the increase of vice occasioned by the enormous increase of taverns and tippling-houses."[94] The same year, Philadelphia's mayor, Benjamin Shoemaker, undertook nocturnal tours of the city to check on the behavior of the city's licensees and taverngoers. In 1768 the *Pennsylvania Chronicle* inveighed against what it took to the harboring of slaves and apprentices by the city's publicans.[95] Given this climate of concern, it is perhaps no coincidence that the most detailed extant lists of licensees date from the third quarter of the eighteenth century.[96]

The size and, more important, the effect the existence of unlicensed houses might have had on the licensed trade in colonial Philadelphia present formidable problems of evidence and interpretation. Even at the close of the colonial period a Philadelphian could plausibly claim to recognize by sight every one of the city's inhabitants.[97] The judicial formulation "known to the jurors" employed in many grand jury presentments captures the intimacy of the city. It was feasible for magistrates, grand juries, and constables to exercise watch and ward over their community. Philadelphians would have had suspicions as to which taverns in their midst were operating illegally. (As we have seen, unsuccessful petitioners for tavern licenses complained bitterly about both the intensity of neighborhood scrutiny and the credence given to it by magistrates.) Extant court dockets show magistrates acting vigorously against bawdy or disorderly public houses. It is entirely possible then that very nearly all unlicensed houses were detected and their keepers brought to court. One could, therefore, extrapolate a plausible estimate of the size of the unlicensed trade from the number of prosecutions for licensing offenses contained in extant court dockets. The number of licensing prosecutions in any given year was generally between 15 and 20 percent of the total number of licenses issued.

However, any estimate of the size of the unlicensed trade derived from judicial activity against unlicensed keepers is accurate only if magistrates were aware of each and every unlicensed house operating in their community and proceeded against them immediately. The surviving court records, which show periodic crackdowns against unlicensed houses, suggest that magistrates did not always pursue the keepers of illicit houses as soon as they were identified. Using judicial activity against individuals charged with keeping house without a license might therefore seem liable to produce a serious underestimate of the size of the unlicensed trade. On the other hand, it is surely significant that, with one exception, licensed publicans made no complaint about competition from unlicensed keepers.

The exceptional petition presented to the Pennsylvania assembly by Philadelphia's licensees in 1720 bears closer examination since it speaks to both the size and possible effects of the unlicensed trade.[98] The licensees' petition was prompted by what they felt was unfair competition from unlicensed "tippling houses." The licensees' complaint—that although they were bound to keep good order when they sold drink, the unlicensed keeper was not—assumed, self-interestedly, that tippling houses were especially subversive of order. Licensees warned that competition from unlicensed houses might force them to turn a blind eye to those features of licensing law designed to control the behavior of their clients. Unfortunately, presentments brought against the keepers of tippling houses offer no information on the identities or behavior of the men and women who used them. We simply cannot substantiate the licensees' allegation that a combination of rum, race, and youth made tippling houses peculiarly volatile establishments. But neither can the licensees' petition be dismissed as special pleading.

A portion of an enumeration of Philadelphia's drinking places undertaken in 1721 by the city's ward constables survives in the miscellaneous papers of the Philadelphia county court of quarter sessions.[99] Despite the fact that this census of drinking houses was probably taken in response to the licensees' petition of 1720, the constables who conducted it did not distinguish licensed from unlicensed houses in their returns. Nevertheless, the fragments that survive permit some speculation as to the size and composition of the unlicensed trade in 1721. The constables who surveyed South Ward—one of Philadelphia's less densely populated wards—reported that their neighborhood had no taverns but four women who were "retailers of liquor." Middle Ward, on the south side of High Street, had sixteen public houses in operation, of which seven were dramshops. Assuming that the distribution of public houses by ward was the same in 1721 as in 1756 (a year for which surviving data provides an accurate picture of the distribution of licensees), and extrapolating from the returns from South and Middle Wards, Philadelphia had slightly more than forty taverns and fifty dramshops and retailers of liquor in 1721. The majority of those named as retailers of liquor or dramshopkeepers in Middle and South Wards make no appearance in any other surviving document and were, therefore, likely representatives of the rootless, illicit, or unlicensed sector of the trade that threatened licensees and troubled moralists. In contrast, the names of most of the tavernkeepers identified in the returns recur in other records. If South and Middle Wards were representative of the city as a whole, then in 1721 the greater part of Philadelphia's forty taverns were properly licensed whereas nearly all of its dramshops were unlicensed. In other words, there was in all likelihood, in the 1720s at least, a substantial unlicensed trade in spirits, especially rum. Whatever success magistrates may have had in restricting the trade to licensed practitioners in earlier and later periods needs to be seen against the background of the existence of this trade.

It is not entirely surprising that if the unlicensed trade was more than double the size of the licensed trade, legitimate publicans felt sufficiently threatened to petition the authorities for redress. But did the existence of an unlicensed trade, whether of the apparently substantial size visible in the 1721 constables' returns or of the more modest proportions suggested by extant court records, have the negative effects on the quality of licensed trade that licensees feared and critics of licensing policy, such as the 1744 grand jury, claimed to have identified? Three factors suggest that the un-licensed trade, even if it assumed the proportions that can be estimated in 1721, did not drag the licensed trade "downmarket." First, at all times colo-nial Philadelphians were offered a wide choice of licensed houses. A drinker might buy an illicit dram at a vendue or horse race but he did not have to rely on unlicensed vendors. Magistrates took advantage of Pennsylvania's rela-tively enlightened legislation to license dramshops and alehouses, even if they did not license as many as Philadelphia's drinkers could have sup-ported. Second, Philadelphia's licensing authorities were prepared to license impoverished men and women who might otherwise have been especially tempted to sell drams illicitly. It is possible that the illicit trade grew to its apparent size in 1721 precisely because magistrates at that time were restrict-ing access to partial licenses, thereby encouraging impoverished house-holders to sell spirits illegally.[100] If so, the magistrates learned their lesson, since by the 1760s licenses, especially "partial" licenses, were granted to men and women possessed of extremely modest taxable estates. Finally, as Chap-ter 2 demonstrates in greater detail, where it is possible to compare tax and licensing data with records that speak to the value of individual publicans' trade, we can see that some poor licensees ran houses with an impressive turnover. Licensed dramshopkeepers and alehousekeepers were not locked in the desperate competition for customers with unlicensed houses that Franklin believed he had observed. The licensed trade was competitive, but an energetic alehousekeeper could draw in daily custom that many a "full" licensee would have envied. If a licensee's business acumen and motivation was the crucial determinant of his profit, it seems unlikely that the mercantilist calculations of the 1744 grand jury presentment against unlicensed houses exercised great influence on the colonial trade.

At any time in the colonial period, taverngoers could choose from a wide range of licensed public houses, each upholding legal requirements in matters of minimum standards and maximum prices. These taverns were run by men and women drawn from a broad spectrum of wealth and experience. From time to time licensing authorities, publicans, and critics of the tavern trade expressed concern that modest alehouses and dramshops posed a particular threat to public order. Yet Pennsylvania law placed a partial license within the reach of impoverished Philadelphians and to some extent legitimated the presumptive right of the poor to support themselves by selling beer or rum. Philadelphia's magistrates, attempting to restrict the trade to licensees of suitable character, placed relatively little weight on a petitioner's wealth when making their licensing decisions. They brought into the licensed trade precisely those impoverished men and women whom critics believed were the most likely to keep pernicious houses.

Licensing policy tended to assume that regardless of the wealth or experience a man or woman possessed on entry into the tavern trade, a suitably honest publican could trade both legally and profitably. If we turn from licensing data to extant business records, we can see that this assumption was more or less correct. Legislation setting maximum prices for the goods and services publicans could offer to customers limited the profitability of keeping a tavern and added to the burdens of poorer licensees, who kept house in small, rented properties. But, by the same token, they militated against the provision of expensive specialized services and in favor of public houses with broad appeal. Some poorer licensees with partial licenses were able to compete successfully for profits within this competitive trade. Licensing policy was therefore as important as the realities of demand for drinking places in explaining the changing nature, as well as the changing size, of the tavern trade in colonial Philadelphia.

2

"Contrived for Entertainment"

Running a Tavern in
Colonial Philadelphia

THE MEN AND WOMEN WHO CONDUCTED Philadelphia's tavern trade came from various backgrounds, and each brought different resources to the trade. Some licensees had previous business experience, whereas others had none. Some publicans were cushioned by personal wealth from the ruinous consequences of business mistakes, while others were vulnerable to the slightest constriction in their cash flow. Most licensees rented the house in which they kept tavern, but a few publicans owned their public house. Some licensed premises were so small that the designation public "house" seems charitable; others were among the largest buildings in the city. Not all tavernkeepers were willing or able to offer the public any service more advanced than the purchase and consumption of liquor. Thus Penn's original intent, the creation of a stock of taverns providing identical, uniformly high-quality services, was never realized.

Moreover, in the first generation of settlement, Pennsylvania's legislators bowed to the realities of demand and created a distinction between full and partial licenses.[1] This decision gestured toward the distinction British custom and law made between alehouses and dramshops and taverns and inns. Yet, while licensees continued to bring a variety of resources to the business, and the stock of houses in which taverns were kept continued to vary in size, for most of the eighteenth century Philadelphia's taverns offered a broadly similar, and relatively narrow range, of services. Philadelphians could not place their taverns within the hierarchy of tone, ambition, and service to which British terminology, distinguishing alehouses from taverns, alluded. This was largely because in Philadelphia, unlike Britain, magistrates enforced a schedule that set maximum prices on the drinks and services sold in taverns.

Maximum prices were a feature of the very earliest licensing legislation in Pennsylvania, and subsequent magistrates and legislators continued to define and enforce such maxima. In 1718, for example, the assembly, noticing that it had become the practice of some publicans to charge "excessive rates," granted the justices of the peace power to set "reasonable" prices. Tavern prices were revised in 1731, and again as late as 1778.[2] William Moraley, an indentured servant whose published account of his life in Philadelphia and the Jersies has recently been rediscovered, testified to price controls being observed in Philadelphia in 1729. Moraley paid close attention to tavern prices, since he sometimes had to sell clothing and gifts in order to raise money to drink.[3] Nevertheless, the prices magistrates set, for example, twopence (later threepence) for a quart of beer, seem to have been low enough to ensure that most laboring Philadelphians could drink in any of the city's taverns but high enough to allow publicans the opportunity to realize a profit.

Using tavern ledgers and brewers' account books, we can examine the changing relationship between a tavern's services, usage, and profitability from the publican's perspective. Almost inevitably we know more about those services publicans offered self-consciously "respectable" residents and travelers than we do about services tailored for plebeian customers. However, the surviving business records illuminate the changing profitability of the trade as a whole and demonstrate the influence of maximum retail price codes. These maxima allowed publicans profit, but the margin of profit was not so great that publicans could afford to alienate some sectors of their potential market in order to cultivate others. Even a publican in a position to offer accommodation to overnight guests had an incentive to court the business of locals who simply wanted to drink a dram or mug in front of a fire. By the same token, a person licensed to sell only beer or spirits had an incentive to keep a house with as broad an appeal as possible. Successful licensees hustled for custom of all kinds. Despite the fact that the law distinguished between different types of license, the effect of codes setting maximum retail prices on the goods and services offered in public houses was to encourage licensees to be generalists rather than specialists.[4]

In March 1776, after a good dinner at an Oxfordshire inn, Dr. Johnson expatiated to James Boswell on England's taverns and inns: "There is no private house, (said he), in which people can enjoy themselves so well, as at a capital tavern. . . . No, Sir; there is nothing which has yet been contrived by man, by which so much happiness is produced as by a good tavern or inn."[5] The great lexicographer may have been aware of the precise distinction between a tavern and an inn, but he found it of little significance. Peter

Clark has shown that "inn," "tavern," and "alehouse" did not possess consistent or even particularly coherent meanings in late-seventeenth- and eighteenth-century England.[6] These terms supposedly identified legally defined distinctions of service; taverns, for example, served wine whereas alehouses did not. They also conjured distinctions of tone. Alehouses were associated with rural England and an agricultural workforce, taverns with England's cities and the middling elements of an urban population. But in reality English tavernkeepers sold beer as well as wine, innkeepers served locals as well as travelers, and some alehousekeepers would go out of their way to accommodate a gentleman willing to enter their house. Licensees, not licenses, created the distinctions of service that mattered most to English taverngoers. Some innkeepers paid close attention to the needs and desires of genteel travelers; others, especially in remote locations, offered only the bare essentials of service. Dr. Johnson would not have expected the designation "tavern" to guarantee enjoyment unavailable in an alehouse or inn. In Johnson's eyes a good tavern was one in which he and his friends were made welcome, while Scots, Whigs, Methodists, and patronizing noblemen were barred or at least kept out of earshot. Some tavernkeepers pandered to Johnson's tastes; others did not.[7] In Britain, as in colonial Philadelphia, the licensing distinction between inn, tavern, and alehouse was of less importance in determining the quality of a public house than the capabilities and attitude of the individual publican.

Philadelphia's tavern trade was competitive. Philadelphians always enjoyed a wide choice of public houses in which to drink. Publicans tried to attract customers by providing a site in which amenities available elsewhere were presented in a distinctive and appealing atmosphere. Some, but not all, of Philadelphia's publicans appealed to the ascriptive distinctions of the English tavern trade in an attempt to distinguish their house from the run-of-the-mill and to capitalize on perceived advantages. Some of the city's licensees declared themselves to be innkeepers in newspaper advertisements —and were recognized as such on tax lists—whereas others were content to be known as tavernkeepers or beerhousekeepers. Yet despite the fact some of Philadelphia's publicans called themselves innkeepers or dramshopkeepers, legislation distinguishing full from partial licenses did not have the effect of recreating old world distinctions of service within Philadelphia's tavern trade. A far more important influence on the trade's development was judicial regulation of the retail price of drinks and services sold in the city's taverns.

A Philadelphia licensee who styled himself an innkeeper, and advertised his willingness to provide gentlemen and travelers with genteel usage, committed himself to various expenses. He had to buy provisions for man and horse, provide bedding, pay for laundry, maintain fires, purchase candles, and maintain fixtures and furnishings. If the inn attracted overnight guests these outlays might be returned to him. However, the Philadelphia innkeeper was not free to put his own price on the labor of providing overnight accommodation. Nor could he mark up the price of drinks in an attempt to recoup his outlay. At fourpence per person per night, the permitted maximum rate for overnight lodging did not hold out the prospect of enormous profit to an aspiring innkeeper. If he attempted to cut costs—by washing bed linen infrequently or by refusing to provide firewood—he undermined the claim to distinction inherent in the decision to present his house as an inn. An inn was at its most profitable when its bedrooms contained travelers and its bar attracted contented regulars. But it required skill to balance the needs of visitors seeking safe and secure lodgings with those of regulars bent on breathing life into neighborhood loyalties. This skill was not the sole possession of rich, male, fully licensed innkeepers. Poorer tavern-, alehouse-, and dramshopkeepers of both sexes could attract both customers and profits by creating a secure or appealing atmosphere on their premises.

Ascriptive concepts like service, gentility, and security were of real economic importance for the tavernkeeper. The reputation, popularity, and hence profitability of a tavern could turn for the worse as quickly as a barrel of beer in a warm cellar. In order to maintain good relations with his customers, as well as with the wider community, the tavernkeeper frequently had to pursue business strategies designed to secure a competency rather than pursue maximum profit over the short term. For example, in order to maximize revenue and minimize risk, many publicans would have preferred to demand payment in advance for every service offered. But to do so meant risking alienating potential customers who, however untrustworthy, demanded credit as a mark of respect. A hard-pressed publican could have earned a few extra pennies by selling drinks after hours, but only at the risk of a prosecution instigated by a community that might include neighborhood customers. The tavernkeeper was dependent on the good opinion of an extraordinarily broad cross section of the community, whose views on the proper conduct of a tavern were expressed with an intensity entirely absent from their assessments of other trades. A goodly number of licensees made healthy profits from keeping public house, but equally many publicans were undone by the high financial and emotional overheads associated with this singular trade. A licensee's business acumen, patience, and especially his ability to bring a measure of finesse to the task of satisfying customers and suppliers were as important to his chances of success as the qualities of his house and the nature of his license. By trying harder than richer competitors to please customers and suppliers, a poor licensee keeping a small house could compete successfully for custom and profit.

The city's public houses were not identical, and this chapter describes the variety of services offered by them. Yet the city's schedule of maximum retail prices limited the profitability of the trade with the result that during the first two-thirds of the eighteenth century, Philadelphia's public houses were more alike than licensees' and tax assessors' eagerness to employ terms such as "tavern," "inn," and "alehouse" might suggest. Of course some of the city's dramshops traded on the margins of profitability, while some of the city's larger houses were among the most profitable business enterprises of their day. We inevitably know more about the latter than the former. But until the eve of the Revolution, the city's stock of public houses offered a relatively narrow range of services. The crucial determinant of profit was the personality and ability of the licensee.

*   *   *

Taverns came in all shapes and sizes. The number of rooms in the houses in which they were conducted helped determine one of the most basic distinctions within the city's stock of licensed premises, between houses that offered overnight accommodation and those that did not. It is not possible to construct a retrospective Michelin guide to the city's taverns. However, two billeting crises during the French and Indian war provide a means of drawing an aggregate picture of the quantity of lodgings available in the city's taverns and permit some speculation as to the quality of overnight accommodation they offered. In October 1756 Lord Loudon wrote to Governor Denny and the provincial council of Pennsylvania stating that Philadelphians would be required to billet, for the duration of the upcoming winter, one battalion of the Royal American Regiment.[8] The battalion had a complement of 547 officers and men. Philadelphia's mayor and aldermen contested the directive, yet, under pressure from the governor, eventually ordered the city's constables to conduct a survey of the number of beds available in the city's licensed houses. Despite the fact that they would be compelled to billet soldiers, the city's licensees were initially eager to comply with Loudon's directive. Encouraged by rumors that they would be paid a shilling per soldier per day (three times the going rate for accommodation and therefore adequate compensation for the disruption to their trade liable to occur as a result of tensions between soldiers and civilians), the city's publicans overstated their capacity. When complete, the constables' survey suggested that the city's stock of 101 taverns possessed four hundred beds.[9] If this estimate had been correct, and if we reckon that the battalion's 47 officers would have expected a bed to themselves while the other ranks would have been expected to double up, the city's taverns should have been able to accommodate the battalion's 547 members.[10]

However, when it became that clear that they would be asked to billet troops on credit, and for no more than the maximum rate laid out by the city's magistrates, Philadelphia's tavernkeepers came to a more realistic appraisal of their capacity to provide accommodation. By December the city's council was contesting Loudon's directive on practical as well as political grounds. "We find," they argued, "on the strictest enquiry into the circumstances of the keepers of such public houses, that many of them are so poor and indigent, that they are neither of ability to support the burden of providing for so great a number of troops, nor have proper houses and accommodations suitable for their comfortable reception."[11] Even when the soldiers, some of whom had smallpox, had been packed so tightly into the city's taverns that the regimental surgeon feared that "every house would be a hospital," Philadelphia's mayor reported that ninety-four men were in "very ill accommodation" and seventy-two men were without any billet.[12] In an attempt to resolve the problem, the regiment's billeting officer, Captain Tulliken, toured the city inspecting its drinking places. Comparing his survey to that undertaken by the city constables, it seems that 225 is a reasonable estimate of the number of beds available in the city's taverns in the winter of 1756. On a notionally equal distribution, each of the city's licensed premises would have offered two beds, or would perhaps have contained one room in which travelers might be accommodated. Yet, as Tulliken discovered, some drinking houses did not have a room to spare, while others had several. Tulliken's tour took him into several houses that appear to have been unlicensed dramshops.[13] He found that a handful of these unlicensed premises were large enough to be considered as sites for the billeting of troops. In contrast, other houses he visited were properly licensed but simply too small to offer accommodation. For example, Tulliken reported that the widow Gray claimed she could not offer a billet to troops at her tavern, the Bull's Head. Since the tavern was housed in a two-story building whose ground floor measured sixteen by twenty feet, and was being used by Gray as her

The Southeast Corner of Third and Market Streets. William Birch and Sons, Philadelphia, 1800. The Indian King tavern is shown on the extreme left of this street scene. In the Indian King's hey-day in the second quarter of the eighteenth century its amenities, its size and its brick construction were uncommon. The tavern was used as a meeting place by civic associations and by genteel travelers. Its keepers in this period, John and Sarah Biddle, also ran a store. They employed servants to cater for guests at their tavern.

residence, it seems reasonable to infer that her protest was justified.[14] Elsewhere in the city, publicans resisted turning over space to the regiment or did so with ill grace. Tulliken found that James Claxton, keeper of the Three Tuns, had deliberately underestimated the capacity of his house to the tune of four beds. Eight of the beds John Biddle was offering at the Indian King were "bad." The fact that these landlords were reluctant to turn over space to troops while payment for billeting was in doubt suggests that the provision of accommodation to paying customers was an integral part of their trade.[15]

The Indian King and the Three Tuns were among the largest public houses in the city. They had kitchens and stables and their keepers employed servants. But it is questionable whether these uncommonly equipped houses provided a distinctive service, unattainable by humbler competitors. When British army officers chose billets in Philadelphia's taverns, their choice fell consistently on those larger houses whose kitchens, stables, and levels of staffing set them apart from the general run of public houses and gave them claims to be considered prototypical hotels. So, for example, Captain White, of Forbes's regiment, which wintered in Philadelphia in 1758, put up at John Biddle's Indian King on High Street between Second and Third. It had, its keeper proudly announced, been "contrived for an inn of entertainment." The inn was built of brick and was three stories high. Fourteen of its eighteen rooms had their own fireplaces and the rooms seem to have had plastered walls.[16] The nearby Indian Queen was the lodging place of Forbes's regimental surgeon, Lieutenant Rogers. Perhaps more than any other public house in operation at the time, the Indian Queen was specifically designed to serve as an inn. An insurance survey conducted in 1767 described the Indian Queen as covering a ground area forty feet deep by twenty-one feet wide. Like the Indian King, the Indian Queen was brick-built and stood three stories tall. A newspaper advertisement described it as having five large rooms on the first floor to entertain "companies." Four of these rooms could be converted to form two even larger rooms capable of seating up to a hundred "gentlemen." The house was served by two large kitchens. It had sixteen lodging rooms on the second and third floors and four garret rooms for servants.[17] But it says something about Philadelphia's tavern trade that the majority of British army officers, a demanding group of customers, chose private boardinghouses even over public houses as well equipped as the Indian Queen. To be sure, officers and private soldiers could expect hostility, and even abuse, from the proprietors and patrons of the taverns where they billeted. However, they also received abuse as guests in private boardinghouses.[18] In 1758, when the officers of Forbes's Regiment chose billets, there were more than one hundred licensed premises in operation in the city. The fact that the regiment's officers chose billets in only nine of the city's public houses suggests that the vast majority of the city's taverns offered similar and very basic services.[19]

Officers and gentlemen looked above all for privacy in tavern accommodation. A room of one's own, away from the hustle and bustle of the bar room, gave spatial expression to the social distance between a gentleman and his inferiors. We might assume that the need and desire for privacy and service shared by genteel travelers of both sexes would have been more likely met in a large brick house, with plastered walls, equipped with a kitchen and servants, and "contrived for an inn of entertainment," than in a smaller, shabbier alehouse or tavern. But eighteenth-century customers judged the quality of a public house primarily by assessing the publican. If army officers stationed in Philadelphia had to stay in a tavern, they chose establishments like the Indian King and Indian Queen, but more than half of Forbes's regiment's officers stayed in boardinghouses. Mrs. Jones's boardinghouse was apparently at least as acceptable a billet as the Indian Queen, even though the Indian Queen was "contrived" for an inn. Given that Mrs. Jones's boardinghouse was almost certainly smaller than the Indian Queen, and unlikely to have been as well appointed, the regiment's officers were basing their choice on Mrs. Jones's character. In other words, contemporaries apparently believed that the service a gentleman might expect as the single guest of a suitably motivated private householder was as good as, if not better than, that he might receive as one of the many guests of a busy publican.

At least one Philadelphia innkeeper was prepared to concede this point. In 1755 a Virginian named Daniel Fisher undertook a lengthy sojourn in Philadelphia. He lodged at John and Sarah Biddle's Indian King and was impressed with the tone of the place. "Though this house is one of the greatest businesses in its way in the whole city," Fisher wrote in his journal, "everything is transacted with the utmost regularity and decorum." Fisher was less taken with the tavern's tangible assets—its plastered walls, eight bedrooms, and large kitchens and stables—than with its intangible atmosphere. He noted, for example, that each night at eleven by "invariable custom" a servant informed patrons civilly that the bar was closed. Fisher gave the credit for this atmosphere to John and Sarah Biddle. The Biddles were truly polite and "rationally benevolent." After Fisher had lodged at the tavern for ten days, Biddle took him aside and offered him a "dish" of tea. Fisher recorded the conversation:

At first [Biddle said] thou appear[ed] to us a stranger, and what is very agreeable to us, a sober one, for which reason we are apprehensive that it may not be so pleasing to thee to continue in a public house so hurried as ours sometimes is, tho[ugh] we do believe that ours is not the worst of the sort. If it is so, pray be free and let us know, for my wife in that case will readily enquire out a private lodging for thee in some reputable sober family in the neighborhood. Thee will be pleased to take notice that the desire of making things most easy and agreeable for thee is the occasion of this motion and if thee should like best to continue still with us only to dine at the ordinary then thee will be welcome, but before thee determinest thee consider thereupon.[20]

Fisher immediately replied that although the Indian King was the "most agreeable" public house he had ever stayed in, he preferred to move to a boardinghouse. For Fisher, the gentility of the Indian King rested in the fact that its keepers were honest enough to tell Fisher to look elsewhere for peace and quiet.

In light of testimony of this kind we ought to consider carefully the extent to which uncommon amenities provided in ambitious public houses set these self-proclaimed inns apart from humbler competitors. It would be an act of supreme historical condescension to presume that only well-off licensees like John Biddle were interested in, or capable of, acts of "refined" disinterest.[21] Men and women with few resources and with little or no experience in the trade announced, in almost obsequious terms, their willingness to act as servants of the public.[22] Those without the economic resources to furnish material grandeur made the prevalence of crime and confusion in and around public houses an occasion to advertise their honesty. Owen Humphreys informed the public that someone had left a box of valuable needles, spectacles, and other goods at his house. Humphreys undertook to return this box to anyone who could describe its marks and pay his expenses. John Knowles, keeper of the Boar's Head on High Street, took out an advertisement to advise the public that some unknown person had given him a note of "considerable value" to settle a bill of 1s. 6d. Knowles undertook to return the note to anyone who could describe it and pay Knowles's charges.[23] Neither Humphreys nor Knowles kept prominent houses. Virtually all we know of their careers comes from these isolated, and not entirely altruistic, announcements. Nonetheless, such advertisements are profoundly suggestive. Although not all publicans possessed the "rational benevolence" Daniel Fisher so admired in John Biddle, surely it was not absent among all those the tax assessors deemed alehousekeepers nor present among all those they deemed innkeepers. So long as at least a section of the taverngoing public believed that the character and capabilities of a licensee were more reliable determinants of the qualities of a house than its size and furnishings, a poor widow running a small house could compete for business with proto-hoteliers like the Biddles.

The role of servants and slaves in houses with pretentions to tone such as the Indian King, the George, and the Indian Queen ought to be considered in the same light.[24] On the face of it, a publican who purchased a slave girl to cook and wash was making a commitment to provide his customers with a level of service an impoverished widow running a dramshop or alehouse could not match. Yet a house like the Indian Queen *had* to utilize the labor of servants and slaves. Running its kitchens, stables, and bedrooms in the manner for which they were designed would have been beyond the capabilities of most families. Moreover, in many cases, tavernkeepers relied on the labor of servants and slaves because they had occupations and interests outside tavernkeeping. In addition to keeping the Indian King, John Biddle had a general store nearby. Biddle sold quality liquors, (including Herefordshire cider and Madeira), medicines (such as Jesuit's Bark), and linens and cloths.[25] Of 101 licensees on the 1756 tax list, thirty appear under occupations other than "tavernkeeper" or its synonyms, "mariner," "goldsmith," "saddler," and "bookbinder."[26] The presence of servants in a tavern, far from indicating a commitment to customer service, might well have signified a house in the care of a licensee too preoccupied with other concerns to worry over the "genteel" usage of his customers. Hence it is not entirely surprising that servants and slaves were to be found serving publicans and customers even in taverns with no claim to prominence as providers of board and lodgings.

When Philadelphia's clubs and societies chose tavern venues for feasts and celebrations, they too looked at the character of the landlord as well as the amenities of his house. One of the first civic associations in Philadelphia was the Society of Ancient Britons, whose members were predominantly Welsh. Philadelphia's Ancient Britons were at their most visible on March 1, when they held elaborate St. David's Day festivities. On St. David's Day 1732 members of the society gathered at the Indian King (run at that time by Owen Owen) and marched, wearing plumes of feathers in their hats, to St. Clement's Church. Following a service in the Welsh language, they called on the governor and brought him to the Indian King for an evening of "mirth and fellowship" that concluded with loyal toasts and the discharge of cannons. Something of the appeal of the event among the Welsh community of southeastern Pennsylvania can be gauged by the fact that the stewards for the festivities came from as far afield as Chester County.[27]

Festivities on this scale could not have been staged in a one-room alehouse. The Ancient Britons needed a tavern that could meet certain material requirements—a convenient location, plenty of plates and drinking vessels, a large table, and so on—and, at the same time, the aesthetic requirement that the event be conducted in what the Ancient Britons' stewards considered to be the best of order. They looked to Welshmen to house their festivities, but they also looked for value for money. Thus the profits to be made from festivities such as the Ancient Britons' St. David's Day parade did not flow automatically to whichever Welsh publican was lucky enough to be running the largest tavern in operation at the time. In 1729 tickets for a special St. David's Day sermon in Welsh were sold at Robert Davies's Queen's Head tavern on Water Street.[28] In 1730 tickets for the sermon were available at David Evans's tavern, the Crown, and the Crown hosted the Ancient Britons' celebratory banquet.[29] By 1732 the site of the festivities had been moved to Owen Owen's Indian King. Even though the Crown was smaller than the Indian King, and even after he had been snubbed by the Ancient Britons, David Evans continued to compete for this kind of business. In 1732, for example, he secured the provision of a "handsome entertainment" given by Thomas Penn to the wardens and vestry of Christ Church.[30] He continued to take custom away from larger competitors, organizing St. David's Day celebrations independent of the Ancient Britons in 1735. Although Evans was probably Welsh, he also courted the newly formed English Society.[31]

Other publicans had custom thrust upon them as a result of their social connections. John Shewbart, keeper of the London Coffeehouse, was connected by marriage to Philadelphia's innermost social circles. Shewbart's coffeehouse was the venue for a "very handsome entertainment" thrown by John Penn to honor the general assembly.[32] The first meetings of Franklin's Junto were held at Nicholas Scull's tavern, probably because Scull was a friend of Franklin's and a member of the organization. In a similar fashion, tavernkeepers who were Masons could garner the custom of Masonic lodges. The city's first Masonic lodge met at the Tun and the Indian King; both houses were kept at the time by Masons.[33] Henry Pratt, keeper of the Royal Standard, became senior grand warden of the city's St. John's Lodge. The St. John's, the second lodge founded in the city, held many of its meetings at the Royal Standard.[34]

Contemporaries, especially "respectable" taverngoers, assessed the reputation of a house by reference to the character of its keeper because legislation setting maximum prices for meals, lodgings, and drinks in taverns placed the publican who set out to court self-consciously genteel customers in a dilemma. Just as customers were presented with a choice of taverns, so licensees believed they were presented with a choice of customers. The keeper of a large house offering uncommon amenities and advertising itself as an inn attempted to court especially those customers who valued privacy, decorum, and service. Yet the regulatory regime set maximum retail prices for the provision of basic services and drinks low enough to make every house in the city economically accessible to the vast majority of the city's population and to restrict the profitability of offering uncommon services such as board and lodgings. Thus, while innkeepers set out to court travelers, they could not afford to ignore locals.

We can assess the impact of legislation setting maximum retail prices on the profitability of running a public house by examining transactions between the city's tavernkeepers and brewers. In the second decade of the eighteenth century, Joseph Taylor rented, and later owned, a brewery on Second Street. A ledger listing purchases from Taylor's brewery survives. Although this document does not assign occupations to the customers recorded in its pages, it is clear from other evidence that Taylor sold beer to private housekeepers and ships' captains as well as to licensees.[35] One of his licensed customers was Hannah Hubbard, who in 1715 was tenant of the Globe, a public house built by Samuel Carpenter. In a nine-month period between August 1715 and April 1716, Hubbard purchased sixty-three barrels of ale from Taylor at a cost of eighteen shillings per barrel, or a total of £56. Assuming Hubbard sold her beer to customers at tuppence per quart, she could expect to make six shillings profit on every barrel purchased. Her receipts from the sale of Taylor's beer during this period could have totaled no more than £74. She stood to realize a profit of £18 on her purchases from Taylor.[36]

Throughout the colonial period, brewers were prepared to sell sizable quantities of beer on credit to men and women licensees of all levels of taxable wealth.[37] It is difficult to assess the risk involved in purchasing beer on credit. Hubbard's orders with Taylor increased in the winter months, testimony perhaps to the difficulty of storing beer during a Philadelphia summer. If we assume that Hubbard tried to dispose of her stock at a uniform pace in order to minimize the risk of spoilage and interruptions to her cash flow, she would have needed to sell a little less than two barrels of beer a week, or ten gallons of beer a day. The account book of the tavern James West kept alongside his shipyard on Pegg's Creek, the Pennypot, suggests that it was not uncommon for a laborer to drink two or three quarts of beer a day.[38] Hubbard would have needed to serve fifteen such customers each day to dispose of her stock at the optimum rate. She presumably believed that she could sell beer at this rate, even though Owen Owen, keeper of the Indian King, a house with potentially wider appeal, placed slightly smaller orders with Taylor over a comparable period.[39] Hubbard may well have had other sources of income, but she would also have had a number of expenses, including the Globe's rent. In order to meet her repayments, Hubbard had to offer Taylor credits at her daughter's store as well as cash received over her bar.[40]

At least during the first fifty years of settlement, brewers were relatively understanding suppliers. Repayment arrangements such as Hannah Hubbard's are not uncommon in the pages of Joseph Taylor's ledger or in the Eight Partners' brewery account book dating from the 1730s. Collaborative rather than adversarial business relationships may have reflected the close links between Philadelphia's brewing and tavern trades that can be observed for much of the colonial period. During the first generation of settlement, many brewers, including William Frampton, Joshua Carpenter, John Whitpain, and Nathaniel Ible, also established taverns. The close association between the two trades continued into the second generation of settlement. A case in point concerning the Eight Partners brewery is worth examining in detail since it also illustrates the uncommon opportunities for women to take business decisions that the tavern and brewing trades could generate.

In March 1734, following the death of her husband, Elizabeth Cuff began what proved to be a nine-month term as manager of the Eight Partners brewery. The partners were not overjoyed. Peter Lloyd, one of the brewery's backers, wrote to another partner, Isaac Norris, Jr., that Peter Cuff's death was unfortunate because he had just brought the business into "good order" and acquired a "reputation both in this place and the West Indies." Lloyd explained that "the widow[,] who was really very assisting to him in the business[,] thinks she can carry it on at least for some time." To that end, wrote Lloyd, she had hired James Davis to assist her, "[and] if his conduct should prove agreeable to the skill he is allow[e]d to have in brewing [it is] possible we may continue in business[.] [B]ut I confess I have no opinion of him [and] was no ways instrumental to his being employ[e]d."[41] Lloyd explained that since it was vital that the brewery make use of its stock of malt and hops before the advent of hot weather, the partners had reluctantly agreed to place the brewery in the hands of Elizabeth Cuff and her assistant, James Davis. Despite their doubts as to her abilities, Elizabeth Cuff managed to secure from the partners the same salary as her late husband.[42]

Elizabeth Cuff's managerial decisions, beginning with her decision to hire James Davis, illustrate the links between brewing and tavernkeeping. Davis had been trained as a brewer in England. In 1722 he completed a term of servitude with the Philadelphia brewer Henry Badcock. Davis was then hired by George Campion. Campion ran a brewery and kept a tavern, first at the sign of the Plume of Feathers, later at the house Joshua Carpenter had founded, the Tun. Soon after Campion hired Davis he tried to force him to brand some barrels of Campion's beer destined for export with Henry Badcock's trademark. Davis refused and took out a newspaper advertisement denouncing Campion. When George Campion died in 1731, his widow, Mary, took over the Tun tavern.[43] As proprietor of the Tun, Mary Campion began performing small services for the Eight Partners brewery. When Elizabeth Cuff took over as the manager of the brewery, she continued existing links with the widow Campion at the Tun. For example, she subcontracted the preparation of the brewery workers' meals to Mary Campion. In return for providing this service Mary Campion received discounts on beer purchased from Elizabeth Cuff's brewery.[44] Cuff was doing Campion a favor by sending business her way. It is possible that in return Campion advised Cuff to take on Davis. Campion would after all have been particularly well placed to vouch for Davis's honesty and skill. The tavern and the brewery developed a complementary business relationship during the period in which they were managed by the two widows.

Tavernkeepers trading with the brewery run by Reuben Haines and Godfrey Twells at the close of the colonial period enjoyed rather less generous repayment terms than those offered by Joseph Taylor or the Eight Partners. Frederick Shryer managed to pay for two barrels of Haines and Twells's beer with what Haines and Twells's account book described as "dubious debts."[45] In general, however, Haines and Twells accepted only hard cash in payment for beer, and their account book suggests they were rather less likely than earlier brewers to advance beer to tavernkeepers on credit. This may have been because the profit margin on beer sales had been squeezed, cutting in turn tavernkeepers' takings.

Over the course of the eighteenth century, magistrates let the maximum retail price of a quart of beer rise from twopence to threepence, but the wholesale cost to publicans of a barrel of beer rose faster. A barrel of

Taylor's beer cost eighteen shillings while a barrel of Haines and Twells's cost thirty. Thirty-three percent of the wholesale cost of a barrel of Joseph Taylor's beer was returned to the publican via retail sales. In the 1770s only about 20 percent of the wholesale cost was returned, via retail sales, to publicans who purchased beer from the brewery run by Haines and Twells.[46]

Nevertheless, even at the close of the colonial period, poor publicans running small houses were ordering, and presumably selling, beer in quantities that dwarfed orders placed by the keepers of establishments such as the Indian King. John Knight, for example, paid for a license in 1767 and every subsequent year until 1771. A man of modest means (in 1769 his taxable estate was valued at £5), Knight rented a beerhouse near the market. Between September 1768 and December 1769, he purchased 2 butts, 114 hogsheads, and 42 barrels of beer from Haines and Twells at a cost of £414. He stood to make a profit of £82 on the retail sale of these purchases.[47] In 1769 Knight's near neighbor, the equally impoverished William Moore, paid for a license to keep public house.[48] Moore took over tenancy of the "noted beerhouse" owned by Samuel and Mary Murdoch located on the north side of Chestnut Street, a few doors west of Front Street. It was a two-story house, eighteen feet by twenty feet, with an "excellent vault."[49] Moore had reason to take advantage of these vaults. Over the course of a year, Moore purchased from the Haines and Twells brewery 48 barrels, 38 hogsheads, and 18 butts of beer at a cost of £267. If he sold every drop of this stock of 6,336 gallons at three pence a quart, Moore stood to make a profit of £49.[50] Moore was presumably selling, on average, 124 gallons of beer every week. In order to realize his profit, Moore would have had to sell nearly a gallon of beer each week for a year, to every one of the customers he was "entitled to" in a hypothetical equal share of the available market.

Perhaps, for once, we should take a real estate advertisement at face value. Moore's was a "noted" house because it was used by a wide variety of people. William Moore and John Knight kept beerhouses in the vicinity of the city's market. They were well placed to court casual customers, including men who ordinarily might regard a beerhouse as beneath their social station. But customers were presented with a choice of taverns in any particular location. Simply securing a convenient pitch by the market or near the docks did not guarantee business. To sell more than a hundred gallons of beer a week, publicans like William Moore or John Knight would have had to serve not only the men who drove pigs to market but also the men who bought and sold them. Just as the keeper of a tavern such as the Indian King, which offered an uncommonly wide range of services, had to open his door to all and sundry if he was to make a profit, so too a keeper specializing in a single service had to appeal to a broad range of customers. Rebecca Terry, for example, rented the Crooked Billet. Located at the north end of South Water Street, this house was only marginally farther from the city's market stalls than William Moore's beerhouse. Like Moore's beerhouse, the Crooked Billet was a "notable" house. It had been built in the 1690s by Alice Guest and was the "reputable" tavern to which Benjamin Franklin had been guided on his first trip to Philadelphia. Rebecca Terry and William Moore were both poor. But Moore purchased—and presumably sold—beer in quantities Terry simply could not match.[51] On the other hand, Elizabeth Clampfer, a wealthy licensee keeping a house some way from the city's market stalls, purchased far larger quantities of beer from Haines and Twells than Rebecca Terry did.[52] The difference in sales, and hence in profitability, between Elizabeth Clampfer's tavern, William Moore's beerhouse, and Rebecca Terry's Crooked Billet would seem to rest primarily in the licensees' differing ambitions and in their varying abilities to satisfy a wide range of customers within the cramped confines of a busy house.

An account book kept by Joseph Ogden allows us to view the profitability of the trade from the tavernkeeper's perspective. Between 1767 and 1771 Ogden kept the One Tun at the northeast corner of Third and Chestnut Streets.[53] We do not know why Joseph Ogden took out a tavern license. He owned a store and had been a retailer of dry goods for some years before he applied for his license. Perhaps he thought there were better profits to be made in tavernkeeping than in retailing. He rented the One Tun and let out his store during his tenancy at the tavern. In addition to his store on Chestnut Street, Ogden owned two cows and employed a servant. Ogden was wealthier than most licensees but a little poorer than the average shopkeeper. On the 1767 tax list his estate was valued at £30, in 1769 at £22.[54] When he left the One Tun in 1771 he became a ferrykeeper on the Schuylkill River.

The One Tun tavern was located within the block bounded by Third, High, Second, and Chestnut Streets, which was the most popular site for taverns in the city.[55] The tavern was housed in a building that had a frontage on Chestnut Street of twenty feet and a depth of forty feet. The ground floor was divided into front and back rooms. The tavern was equipped with a kitchen and stables. Ogden offered overnight accommodation; one night he managed to squeeze in sixteen paying guests. This was not a marginal dramshop or alehouse. On the other hand, it was not especially prominent. No stagecoach line stopped there, and Ogden did not tout for trade via newspaper advertisements. This was a house situated at the upper end of the middle of the city's stock of taverns.[56]

Most, but not all, of the transactions recorded in Joseph Ogden's tavern account book were initiated by customers who were "running a tab." The account book provides detailed, but not necessarily complete, information on the custom of overnight vistors. It offers even less information on Ogden's casual trade. More than one hand compiled the book. Sales are grouped within the ledger under the name of a customer and then by date. Within each date all kinds of items are jumbled up. The accounts of frequent visitors are scattered over several pages.[57] Some of the transactions recorded are as simple as John Doe purchasing a quart of beer or a peck of oats on account. In contrast, on any given date we might find the record of one person making use of virtually every service the tavern. A basic understanding of the volume of business conducted in the tavern can be formed by counting the number of transactions, of whatever complexity, initiated by an individual customer and recorded in the ledger. For instance, in October 1770 there were a total of 496 transactions at the One Tun. Some people used the tavern more than once in the month, so that the total of 496 transactions was generated by 183 individuals. The median number of appearances for each of these persons in the month of October was two. On average, for each day in October 1770, sixteen persons availed themselves of some part of the tavern's services in manner that made the use of the account book necessary.

Table 2 sets out Ogden's receipts from the provision of overnight accommodation in both October 1770 and during a five-month period of that year. Ogden sold lodgings at the rate of 4 d. per person per night, the prescribed legal maximum. Some customers came to the One Tun, stayed the night, and never returned. A handful of customers lodged for extended periods in the tavern. Men like John Trapnell, who either lodged or took his meals at the One Tun every day of October 1770, helped justify the expense and labor of providing board and accommodation. Trapnell incurred a debt of £2 4s. over the month for lodging alone.

The value of Ogden's trade in food and lodgings is impressive. In five months Ogden took in £140 8s. 11d. from the provision of lodgings and meals. Over the same period he received £105 10s. 6d. from stabling and the sale of hay and oats. In contrast, his receipts from the sale of liquor in the same period amounted to £102 9s. 1d. (Table 3). He took in a further £62 4d. from various services such as laundry, renting and shoeing horses, and lending cash. Ogden charged 1 s. for the provision of breakfast, supper, or what his account book describes as "eating." Dinner cost 1s. 6d. Ogden occasion-

TABLE 2   Receipts from Accommodations at the One Tun Tavern, 1770 (in shillings)

	October Sum	Five Months Sum	Mean
Lodging	85.57	417.62	83.52
Breakfast	160.58	615.23	123.04
Dinner	233.41	1108.41	221.82
Supper	126.47	636.79	127.35
Eating	8.06	30.81	10.27
Hay	326.39	1292.39	258.47
Oats	151.97	668.81	133.76
Stabling	77.58	149.23	29.84
	1,170.03	4,919.29	614.2
	(£58)	(£245)	(£30)

1 shilling=12d. 20 shillings=£1.
The five months analyzed in this table are June, July, October, November, and December.

ally amended his tariff for regular customers and he charged lesser rates for servants and slaves. For example, a servant's dinner was usually 1s. 3d. These prices were in line with those charged by other Pennsylvanian publicans and suggest that price controls were still being applied to the trade.[58] It seems that Ogden took his biggest profit on sales of hay and oats and charges for stabling. The price of hay and oats was not regulated by magistrates. Many customers purchased extremely small amounts of oats for their horses, an indication perhaps that they considered Ogden's prices too high.[59] Table 2 shows how lucrative was the provision of lodgings, food, and stabling for Ogden. He made more in one month from these services than publicans like William Moore did from a year's beer sales.

Although Ogden provided lodgings, meals, and stabling primarily for travelers, he profited from the use of these services by residents of Philadelphia. On October 13, 1770, Ogden let out the back parlor of his tavern to a group of eight men. These men drank four pints of wine and a bowl of punch and each of them took supper. A group described in the ledger as the city assessors were good customers. On October 30, 1770, they took Ogden's back room, spent 7s. 6d. on supper, 1s. 6d. on beer, and 4s. 6d. on punch. They met at Ogden's the next three nights. In return for providing a room and some basic victuals, Ogden took in £3 2s. 10d.

Table 3 lists Joseph Ogden's receipts from the sale of beer, wine, and

TABLE 3 Receipts from the Sale of Liquor at the One Tun Tavern, 1770

Liquor		October	Five Months	
		Sum	Sum	Mean
Beer	@ 3d.	60.22	275.87	55.17
Gin	@ 3d.	25.66	88.77	17.75
Toddy	@ 3d.	101.90	430.23	86.04
Wine		38.73	292.21	58.44
Grog	@ 2d.	7.20	53.61	10.72
Dram	@ 2d.	24.00	81.65	16.33
Spirits		0.25	7.85	1.57
Nostrum		2.25	24.99	4.99
Brandy		2.41	16.39	4.09
Punch	@ 1s. 6d.	82.41	499.55	99.91
Sling		6.23	12.83	2.47
Clubb		21.14	121.65	24.33
Cider	@ 2d.	5.11	46.09	9.21
Bitters	@ 2d.	3.47	27.04	5.40
Cordials	@ 2d.	8.24	62.69	12.53
Tea and Coffee		5.80	9.80	1.96
		395.02	2051.22	128.20
		(£19)	(£104)	(£6)

1 shilling=12d. 20 shillings=£1.
The five months analyzed are June, July, October, November, and December.

spirits. The account book records purchases made by customers who intended to pay when they had finished drinking or who were drinking on account. We do not know what type of trade Ogden did with men and women who paid in cash each time they went to the bar. Those customers who established some form of account certainly ordered wine and spirits more frequently than beer. They showed a particular preference for rum, though they ordered it mixed in varieties of punch and toddy rather than neat by the dram. Since beer, cider, and dram drinking were associated with plebeian lifestyles, and rum punch and wine were associated with gentility, one could infer that Ogden restricted credit to customers he considered "respectable."[60] On the other hand, he sold but modest quantities of those other indicators of genteel living; tea, coffee, bitters, and cordials. Over a five-month period in 1770, Ogden sold 1,720 measures of toddy but also 1,103 measures of beer. Thus although we do not know the size or nature of Ogden's cash trade, the account book suggests that Ogden's clientele was mixed. Laboring men probably bent elbows with respectable burghers in the One Tun tavern.

The account book gives an indication of the ways a tavernkeeper might have hustled to make a profit. Drawing on his background in trade, Ogden continued to sell goods on account while he kept the One Tun.[61] He made himself useful to his customers, buying, for example, a consignment of leather, cloth, and nails for one Lewis Trimble.[62] He placed advertisements in newspapers in Virginia and Maryland on behalf of his brother.[63] In April 1770 Ogden served a suit on Henry Butler on behalf of John Crosby, a frequent visitor to the One Tun.[64] More prosaically, Ogden accepted property into his keeping and returned property misplaced in the tavern. In November 1770 William Way placed in Ogden's safekeeping "some boxes large and small," a chest, a bed, and a parrot in a cage. In July 1770 Ogden sorted out the mix-up that resulted when Nicholas Way left with a whip belonging to Henry Ryley, Ryley left with a whip belonging to John Marshall, and Marshall left with Way's whip. When Patrick Travers left a beaver hat and some brass andirons at the tavern, Ogden entrusted Andrew Horndean to deliver these items to Travers in "the Carolinas." Where he could, Ogden charged for this kind of service, as, for example, when he "loaned" a horse (for £3) to John David in order that David might attend the fair.[65]

It is not easy to trace the sequence of debt and repayment through the account book. One point is clear: at any given moment, a sizable portion of Ogden's turnover was owed to him. In October 1770 the sum of money owed to Ogden on accounts not immediately settled totaled £13 5s. He rarely let unpaid accounts climb above £2, and only regular customers were permitted to reach this level of debt. In most cases, unpaid accounts amounted to shillings rather than pounds. Nevertheless, over the course of five months in 1770, accounts worth more than £68 were not immediately settled. This amounted to a little more than 15 percent of Ogden's total takings during this period. Yet it was a larger sum than the profit some publicans made from the sale of beer in a year.

Unlike most publicans, Ogden owned property elsewhere in the city and this cushioned him against bad debt and periods of slow trade.[66] Nevertheless, Ogden had a number of expenses to set against his gross income from the tavern trade. The most significant was the cost of renting the One Tun. In 1772 the yearly rent on the tavern was £80.[67] If we assume that Ogden paid £80 per annum in rent in 1770 and also that the margin of profit on every service and ware Ogden sold was the same as that on a barrel of beer—namely, 20 percent of the cost—Ogden would have made a tidy, but not spectacular, profit of £120 in 1770.[68]

As discussed in Chapter 1, Philadelphia's licensing authorities adopted a relatively tolerant licensing policy. The number of licenses issued in colonial Philadelphia was only slightly below the level of demand for them. With a large number of licensees engaged in competition for drinkers' pennies, no publican could afford to turn away customers. In addition, the effect of legislation governing the prices publicans could charge was to limit the profitability of specialized services to the point where publicans must have considered carefully whether their provision made economic sense. A comparison of Joseph Taylor's account book with that of the Haines and Twells brewery suggests that over the course of the colonial period publicans experienced a decline in the profit margin on the sale of beer.[69] Joseph Ogden's One Tun was probably bigger than William Moore's beerhouse, and Ogden probably offered a wider range of services, notably those relating to the needs of overnight guests. These differences surely contributed to a difference in net income. But both licensees had to hustle to make money; neither could afford to turn away potential customers. If sixteen people wanted rooms in the One Tun on the same night, Ogden squeezed them in rather than see their business go elsewhere. If a group of gentlemen wanted to hold a meeting in Ogden's back room, he accommodated them as best he could while appeasing his regulars.

There were, of course, differences between public houses; some were big, some were small, some were dirty, and some were clean. It would have been an amazing vindication of the ideals of Philadelphia's licensing policy if all taverns had been uniformly well appointed. However, the most telling differences between taverns stemmed from the keepers' personalities. What ensured the comparative success of Joseph Ogden, John Biddle, or William Moore was not personal wealth, a good location, or a decision to specialize in the provision of any one particular service, but the determination and ability to hustle up business and make a penny where it could be made. A determined, tactful, but relatively poor alehousekeeper could compete successfully for profits with a less able but relatively well-off tavernkeeper.

Philadelphia's publicans, trading within a legally enforced maximum retail price regime, encouraged social mixing in their taverns. A successful public house drew in a wide cross section of the public who made use of its facilities for various purposes. A publican's character or personality was crucial to the reputation of his house because the landlord was called upon not only to provide services but also to mediate between those who used them. The commitment, tact, and energy necessary to offer the public more than a simple drinking site were by no means exclusive to richer licensees running larger houses. (Indeed, as the Biddles all but admitted to Daniel Fisher, the more successful the keeper of a large house was in filling bedrooms and stables, seating people at the dinner table, justifying the need for servants, and catering for clubs and societies, the more he ran the risk of being too busy to provide the close personal attention customers, especially genteel customers, demanded.) Houses such as the Indian King and Indian Queen were clearly bigger than the majority of the city's licensed premises, but their size alone did not make them better. The uses to which Philadelphians put public houses demanded the successful publican be something of a diplomat and gave Philadelphia's tavern life its changing and unique character.

3

"Company Divided into Committees"

Taverngoing in Colonial Philadelphia

FROM THE FOUNDING OF PHILADELPHIA until the eve of the Revolution, diverse clienteles shared the city's public houses. During this period, rich male citizens, the city's aspiring patriciate and current judicature, used taverns. Their minions and personal secretaries—the men whose world Jacob Hiltzheimer recorded in his diary—also frequented taverns. Timeserving clerks, master craftsmen, artisans, laborers, and occasionally their wives and sweethearts visited taverns. They were joined by the sort of people eighteenth-century magistrates would have labeled "rogues" or "vagabonds." Philadelphia's elite, fearful of the licentiousness and immorality of the "lower orders," attempted to regulate the mixed company that gathered not only in taverns but also in other public spaces.[1] The hours during which a tavern might serve drink were strictly regulated. A whole range of popular pastimes were forbidden on licensed premises. Slaves, apprentices, and Indians were excluded by law from taverns. Even then, the role played by tavernkeepers in encouraging sailors, slaves, free blacks, servants, apprentices, and "wild boys" to "carouse" remained subjects of perennial concern.[2] While some sections of society were barred from public houses, others forswore tavern sociability voluntarily. Awakened Protestants and "respectable" women, for example, used taverns rarely, entering public houses on special occasions or when no other meeting place or site of accommodation was available. Nevertheless, personal letters and journals, tavern ledgers, and newspaper advertisements describing the attractions tavernkeepers offered the public suggest that at least until the eve of the Revolution a typical tavern company was socially and culturally heterogeneous. In varying combinations, rich, poor, and middling Philadelphians drank alongside one another in shared public houses.

As we have seen, the historical development of Philadelphia's tavern trade encouraged the creation of socially diverse clienteles. Licensing policy ensured that there were a goodly number of licensed tavernkeepers competing for customers. A regulatory regime that set maximum retail prices at a level most customers could afford, but limited the profits licensees made from the sale of goods and services, gave tavernkeepers an economic incentive to serve all and sundry. Moreover, many publicans took out licenses either in a desperate pursuit of a modest competency or as a means to supplement income from an unrelated trade. As a result, many, perhaps most, publicans had neither the time nor the inclination to attempt to serve customers according to emerging categories of social hierarchy. Moreover, in colonial Philadelphia's city wards, a typical city block was home to men and women of many different levels of wealth.[3] The "local" publican could therefore expect to serve an economically diverse group of customers. There is evidence to suggest that Philadelphians typically drank at more than one house. Thomas Penn, for example, spoke of Richard Hockley's practice of running up accounts, or "scores," at public houses.[4] Those Philadelphians who were permitted to visit taverns lawfully favored some houses over others, exercising elective affinities in taverngoing just as they did in other areas of sociability and consumption. But even if a taverngoer preferred to drink with men of a similar social standing, he also regularly visited taverns in which diverse companies might be found. Mingling with a socially mixed clientele was almost unavoidable in taverns that, during the colonial period, were usually too small to permit customers to enjoy the space or detachment their sense of self might have demanded. These factors provided the foundations for a degree of interaction between classes, cultures, and religions in taverns that later generations found unacceptable, even if they did not mean that a typical colonial tavern crowd always re-created in miniature a scale model of society at large.

Readers of Sam Bass Warner's influential study *The Private City* might argue that such a pattern of usage poses no great explanatory problem. If in colonial Philadelphia it was customary for men of different wealth and social status to meet one another face-to-face, one might improve upon Warner and argue that here was not just a "walking city" but a "talking city."[5] But the task of explaining and interpreting taverngoers' mores begins, rather than ends, with the understanding that for much of the colonial period Philadelphia's taverns were used by rich and poor alike. How did Philadelphians structure conversations across boundaries of status? How, and indeed why, did they talk with one another? Although colonial Philadelphians rubbed shoulders with people from different socioeconomic and cultural backgrounds to a degree unknown in the nineteenth, let alone the twentieth, century, this should not be taken to mean that they were supremely open-minded, tolerant, or adventurous. On the contrary, Philadelphia's taverngoers were opinionated, prejudiced, and hypocritical. Wealthy Philadelphians disliked drinking in the company of assertive laborers. The city's working poor loathed any expression of arrogance on the part of the "better sort" and often refused to defer to them in tavern encounters. Particular groups of taverngoers, identified by shared occupations, social standing, or interests, attempted to dominate particular taverns. But such attempts met with limited success. Taverns were shared spaces used by diverse clienteles, often for competing purposes. Recognizing this, Philadelphia's drinkers elaborated and employed cultural practices—including toasting, treating, and singing—designed to produce at least a temporary fellowship among mixed tavern companies. Yet precisely because Philadelphians put their taverns to a wide variety of uses, encouraged by the belief that their drinking rituals could draw men from many different backgrounds into relationships that were at least temporarily harmonious, the all-too-frequent product of tavern encounters was a dissonance that encouraged taverngoers to express reserve and detachment. Conflict *and* consensus were the hallmarks of tavern companies.

This raises a question I address in passing at the conclusion of the present chapter and at greater length in Chapter 4. Why, if taverns were the sites of contest, friction, and conflict between men drawn from a variety of backgrounds, was taverngoing so popular? But this question carries force only if it can be demonstrated that, at least until the eve of the Revolution, rich, poor, and middling did drink in one another's company in shared public houses. Accordingly, the main emphasis of the present chapter falls on establishing, by reference to Philadelphians' use of their public houses, that tavern sociability was shaped by cultural diversity.

I intend this argument to complement rather than challenge the work of those scholars who have investigated the origins of class-consciousness in early Philadelphia.[6] From first settlement to the conclusion of the French and Indian wars, Philadelphians consciously placed themselves in ranks, forming hierarchies of status in which men sought to establish who was immediately above or below them. At the margins, the difference in status between a leisured patrician and a disadvantaged laborer was relatively clear. But until the 1760s the city's economy, despite booms and slumps, offered a healthy and moderately hardworking laborer the chance to secure a competency. It also presented ambitious artisans with opportunities for economic and social advancement. In the Philadelphia which Franklin's *Autobiography* so lovingly recalled, a skilled artisan could make a living comparable to that of a professional or small-scale merchant. The city's economy in this period therefore imparted a fluidity to a rank-based system of social stratification absent in the class-based system that took shape in the final third of the eighteenth century. Ethnicity and culture further complicated the establishment of a clear-cut hierarchy of social status. Anglo-Welsh Quakers and Scots-Irish Presbyterians were reluctant to defer to one another, and each group sometimes patronized and at other times abused the city's German community.

Disputes over social status and esteem were, of course, sources of conflict and tension in everyday sociability. But, as David Shields has argued, Philadelphians also believed that civility—and civil discourse particularly—enabled a person to bridge distinctions of rank, profession, ethnicity, and calling.[7] Even as a journeyman printer, Franklin discoursed with the governor of Pennsylvania and local political leaders. The diarist Jacob Hiltzheimer numbered among his regular drinking companions men of varying wealth and cultural background. The uses to which socially diverse groups of Philadelphians put shared public houses reflected, and further promoted, a consciousness of the existence of hierarchies of wealth and status. But the act of drinking and conversing in shared premises implied a measure of equality between men upon which the mores of taverngoing in colonial Philadelphia sought, with some success, to elaborate and build. For most of the colonial period, the city's rank-based system of social stratification did not determine, and only partially informed, the uses to which Philadelphians put taverns. The rich did not drink solely in the company of other wealthy men, and they joined in tavern rituals and practices that brought them into a temporary fellowship with men of "lesser" standing uncommon in any other setting.

Toward the close of the colonial period, the changing structure of the city's economy, the growth of an enterprising spirit that sat ill with tavern sociability, and, ultimately, the growth of sharper economic inequality, political factionalism, and the collapse of controls on the maximum retail price of liquor encouraged changes in patterns of taverngoing and the creation of new types of public house by particular groups of taverngoers seeking to create harmonious but culturally specific forms of sociability. At the close of this chapter I describe the founding of William Bradford's Old London Coffeehouse, the first public house in Philadelphia built and operated with the needs and desires of a specific sector of the city's community in mind. First, however, I describe the uses to which Philadelphians put public houses in the first two-thirds of the eighteenth century and the cultural practices with accompanied drinking and conversation conducted by mixed clienteles in shared and cramped premises.

* * *

The only means we have of empirically testing the impression that taverns typically housed socially and culturally diverse companies that emerges from colonial diaries and journals is by reference to two extant tavern ledgers.[8] The ledger kept by James West, keeper of the Pennypot tavern in the 1690s, shows that Joshua Carpenter—the second richest man in the city—drank in the Pennypot alongside workers from West's shipyard. At the One Tun tavern, in 1770, Joseph Ogden served civic groups like the city assessors, a ship's captain, John West, and visiting gentlemen from as far away as the Carolinas, at the same time as the servants and maids of Ogden's numerous business associates.[9]

As discussed in Chapter 2, publicans like Joseph Ogden had an economic incentive to hustle for custom of all kinds. Philadelphia's publicans sought to draw in as many customers as possible, paying little regard to their social status. So, for example, the keepers of houses that claimed to offer accommodation for genteel travelers also sought to draw in local residents with attractions of broad appeal. In March 1737 Owen Owen, the keeper of the Indian King, placed the following advertisement in the *Mercury*: "On Monday last, a cat in the gaol of this city brought forth a living monster. It has one head, eight legs and two tails; from the navel downwards it has two bodies of the female kind. It weighs three ounces and a half, and is now dead, but is yet kept as a show, at the sign of the Indian King."[10] Over the years, keepers of the Indian King tempted the general public with similar sideshows. In 1740 Owen Owen promised "constant attendance" on any person wishing to see "a very wonderful and surprising creature . . . impossible to describe . . . a curiosity never before seen," the creature "known in scripture" as the camel. In 1749 John Bonnin invited the public to the Indian King to see his greatly admired prospects of Europe, which included depictions of Rome, Venice, Naples, and the siege of Barcelona.[11] The Indian King did not enjoy a monopoly on the promotion of this kind of entertainment. At the Coach and Horses, Henry Clark displayed a curious clockwork mechanism that represented Joseph's dreams. It could be seen for sixpence on any day except Sunday.[12] At the Crooked Billet, a clockwork mechanism that featured eight figures ringing changes on eight bells and a lady turning head over heels "like a mountebank" was displayed. The owner

boasted, "the likes of this was never heard of in *England*."[13] Richard Blackwell announced that the clockwork entertainment *he* was offering at the
Death of the Fox came directly from London.[14] Relatively decorous and
ingenious displays such as this had to compete for custom with cruder
displays. In 1767 Benjamin Davis invited the public to the Bull's Head to
gawk at a "wonderful" female child, or children, with "two heads, four arms,
four legs etc."[15]

While houses with pretentions to grandeur set out to draw in plebeian
customers, less ambitious establishments regularly drew in well-to-do customers. Over the course of the eighteenth century numerous taverns were
established along the Delaware riverfront. Their keepers hoped to profit
from the thirst of the city's stevedores, shipwrights, and sailors. Sailors
gravitated toward taverns to celebrate the completion of a voyage and to sign
up for their next job. Newspaper advertisements called upon sailors to sign
up for voyages in waterfront taverns, some with names like the Ship-A-
Ground or the Boatswain and Call, that advertised their association with
the sea.[16] But these waterfront taverns, intimately connected with the city's
maritime trade, also drew visits from ships' captains, merchants, super-
cargoes, clerks, and travelers with the money to take passage for faraway
places. In this way waterfront taverns were used by men with aspirations to
gentility as well as by local workers. Conversely, the owner of a vessel might
sit in a coffeehouse, thus drawing to him, and into the coffeehouse, sailors,
clerks, and laborers charged with delivering cargo.[17]

Vendues and auctions were held almost exclusively in the city's public
houses and drew diverse clienteles into taverns. The goods on offer at vendues ranged from job lots of dry goods to servants and slaves, ships, houses,
and even a plantation on the east side of the Schuylkill and an entire ironworks.[18] These events were often, but not always, staged in one of the city's
coffeehouses. Especially in cases such as sheriffs' sales, where auctions were
mandated, vendues were also held in any tavern in the vicinity of the property under the hammer. In this way, houses such as the Hen and Chickens,
which were not in other ways prominently involved in commerce, were
occasionally the sites of commercial activity.[19]

It was in the interest of the vendue-master to attract as wide a crowd as
possible to a sale. Even if there were very few in the crowd who could afford
to buy a house or ship, the sale of such items interested former neighbors
and shipmates, and their attendance could generate commercially valuable
excitement. Moreover, the actual form some sales took encouraged a certain
sense of drama and community involvement. In 1743, for example, James's

coffeehouse was the site of a sale by public outcry. Two lots on Society Hill were disposed of at Roberts's coffeehouse by an "inch-of-candle sale." Phillip John of the Rose and Crown sold a house by means of a lottery. In 1734 John Shewbart of the London tavern, in conjunction with the jeweler Mr. Woods, raffled a gold watch. Ten tickets were offered for sale to gentlemen at a cost of £6. On a Friday afternoon, at five o'clock precisely, the winning ticket was drawn.[20] This event and others like it must have been exciting even, or especially, for those who did not have tickets. The entertainment value of a sale by public outcry, an inch-of-candle sale, or a raffle should not be discounted, particularly as these events were often accompanied by treats of liquor. They drew crowds into coffeehouses, forcing merchants and traders to mingle with laborers.

The nature of some of the goods sold at public auction attracted wide community interest and involvement. For example, Reese Meredith invited the public to the George to view a "genteel riding horse . . . very gentle and sure footed," and to admire the horse's trotting and pacing. Jacob Hiltzheimer invited the public to the widow Gray's Bull's Head to view a bay gelding he was offering for sale. The horse could, Hiltzheimer claimed, "withstand fire and the beat of a drum." It is easy to imagine a tavern crowd putting that claim to the test. When a horse was led around a tavern yard for prospective buyers, public opinion on the quality of the horse and the price offered became no less integral to the transaction than the private thoughts of buyer and seller.[21]

Newspaper advertisements placed by business travelers suggest that they regarded taverns as places which served a broad range of people. In 1746 William Dawes informed readers of the *Gazette* that he was preparing to go to Europe and wanted to meet with his debtors. He gave notice that he would be available at the Three Tuns in the course of a journey that would take him to Queen Ann's and Kent Counties in Maryland, and Newcastle, Pennsylvania.[22] Joseph Ellis of Byberry, Pennsylvania, "intending for England," took lodgings at the Indian King to settle his accounts.[23] Henry Camm, from Upper Providence, Chester County, took rooms at the Indian King to meet with his creditors.[24] So did Adam Yager of Roxborough.[25] A periwigmaker, David Evans, took lodgings at the nearby Crown to settle demands against him.[26] Men who had to be seen to be making every effort to satisfy creditors used public, not private, houses to transact their business.

In addition to using residence in a tavern for the purpose of settling accounts, men of business used taverns to initiate transactions. The Three Tuns was the tavern chosen by Michael Brown for his regular trips to

Philadelphia. Brown was a silk dyer who promised "as much perfection" in the matter of dying gentleman's waistcoats as was to be found in London. He "gave attendance" at the Three Tuns on the first Friday and Saturday of every month.[27] Peter Partridge conducted a screenmaking and wireworks operation from lodgings at the Bull's Head on High Street.[28] In a very different vein, Jacob Ehrenzeller, who kept the Hand and Arm, hosted an evening school where gentlemen might be taught German in the best fashion. Ehrenzeller used his announcement of this venture to remind the public that he had a supply of universal fever pills that were very useful for persons who "could not take the bark." George Abington, who claimed to have trod the boards of the Theatre Royal, Drury Lane, invited all who wished to learn how to dance to treat with him at the Hendricks, or King of the Mohawks, tavern.[29] Michael Coleman Shaugnessey, a professor of Latin and French, took lodgings at the Queen's Head on Water Street. Shaugnessey, who had "but lately come to town," requested that those who desired instruction in the "universal languages" call on him at his "proper lodgings" at the Queen's Head.[30]

A startling testimony to faith in the malleability of tavern space (and its openness to people and activities of all kinds) can be seen in the actions of the Reverend Gabriel Nesman. Nesman was pastor of the Swedish Church at Wicaco. In the winter of 1749 he came to Philadelphia to ready himself for a return to Sweden. He had contracted some debts and "therefore, in order to discharge them, to support his family in the winter and to lay up something for the passage home, he intended to open a school in the learned languages, or of such philosophical and theological sciences as shall be desired." Nesman took rooms at the Indian King and organized his school from these quarters. Moreover, he undertook to preach a sermon in Swedish at the Indian King on the second and third Sundays of every month.[31]

Unfortunately, we do not know how many Swedish speakers came to the Indian King to hear Nesman's sermons, and we can only imagine what kind of response this use of tavern space drew from the Indian King's other customers. Although they conceived of taverns as being open to a wide range of customers and uses, taverngoers actually confronted with a mixed group of customers, each attempting to use the same space for different purposes, often expressed intolerant attitudes. For some, even the act of conversing around a common table produced tension.

Dr. Alexander Hamilton of Annapolis, Maryland, visited Philadelphia in the summer of 1744. He dined at a tavern on Chestnut Street (probably the Three Tuns) where he found:

a very mixed company of different nations and religions. There were Scots, English, Dutch, Germans, and Irish; there were Roman Catholics, Church men, Presbyterians, Quakers, Newlightmen, Methodists, Seventh day men, Moravians, Anabaptists, and one Jew. The whole company consisted of twenty-five planted round an oblong table in a great hall well stocked with flies. The company divided into committees in conversation; the prevailing topic was politics and conjectures of a French war. A knot of Quakers there talked only about selling of flour and the low price it bore. The[y] touched a little upon religion, and high words arose among some of the sectaries, but their blood was not hot enough to quarrel, or, to speak in the canting phrase, their zeal wanted fervency. A gentleman that sat next [to] me proposed a number of questions concerning Maryland, understanding I had come from thence. In my replies I was reserved, pretending to know little of the matter as being a person whose business did not lie in the way of history and politics.[32]

Hamilton's account captures the physical and emotional claustrophobia of a colonial tavern. The awareness that one's words were likely to be overheard and commented upon could in itself produce tension, while "high words" often followed from drink and talk conducted between men of different backgrounds and social rank.

The underlying source of friction in tavern encounters arose from the difficulties Philadelphians faced in reconciling their notions of a hierarchy of social status with the fact that drinking alongside, or in the company of, men of "inferior" or "superior" backgrounds implied in theory, and often required in practice, an equality of esteem. In the privacy of his travel journal, Hamilton could describe—or dismiss—his companions in a Philadelphia tavern thus: "I observed several comical, grotesque phizzes in the inn wher[e] I put up which would have afforded a variety of hints for a painter of Hogarth's turn. They talked there upon all subjects—politics, religion, and trade—some tolerably well, but most of them ignorantly. I discovered two or three chaps very inquisitive, asking my boy who I was, whence come, and whither bound."[33] Although Hamilton could admit, with surprise, that some members of the "lower orders" could discourse tolerably well on the topics of the day, he was reluctant to compromise his status as a gentleman of learning by entering into discussion with laborers and tradesmen. But any attempt by a gentleman to act upon the assumption that he was superior to the company he encountered in a Philadelphia tavern was liable to produce "high words." Fully aware of the assumptions that lay behind his pose of "reserve," those laboring Philadelphians Hamilton encountered in taverns badgered him, and his retinue, with questions.

There was little privacy in a colonial tavern. The single oblong table around which patrons of Three Tuns sat was typical of the furnishing of bar space in Philadelphia's taverns during the colonial period. For the first two-thirds of the eighteenth century, most taverns were conducted in buildings designed as private residences. During this period few taverns offered private meeting rooms. Booths and banquettes were unknown. As Benjamin Franklin found, the architecture of the city's taverns, as well as the curiosity of the city's taverngoers, meant that private conversations were liable to be overheard.

In June 1737 Franklin and two other men were appointed by the court of common pleas to resolve a dispute before the court. They agreed to meet in a tavern on High Street to discuss the matter. As Franklin waited for his colleagues in the tavern, someone told him a juicy story that was going around the town. This involved a mock Masonic initiation recently administered to a gullible apprentice named Daniel Rees. Rees had been induced to swear allegiance to Satan, drink a laxative "sacrament," and the like. Franklin was seen to offer "hearty laughter" at the tale. Several days later, in the course of a second "initiation," Rees died. The printer Andrew Bradford made this the occasion for an attack on the Masonic order, and a judicial investigation into Rees's death was launched. Franklin's laughter in the High Street tavern came back to haunt him. Known to be a Mason, Franklin felt compelled to issue a lengthy statement denying that the fact that he had been observed laughing at the story of the mock "initiation" indicated that he approved of, or was complicit in, the humiliation offered Rees. That Franklin issued such a statement illustrates both the permeability of supposedly private conversations and the importance Philadelphians attached to news, gossip, and observation gleaned from tavern encounters. If the whole town knew that Franklin had laughed at a story that happened to making the rounds, how much did it know about the substance of the discussions Franklin had visited the tavern to conduct?[34]

Much the same point could be made with reference to the use of taverns by clubs and societies. During the first half of the eighteenth century, Philadelphia's adult male population supported two fishing companies, as well as Welsh, Irish, Scottish, and English ethnic associations, a workingman's junto, a philosophical society, two Masonic lodges, and the "high-style" Governor's Club.[35] Smaller ad hoc associations, as for example those organising Christmas and New Year's revelry, or civic groups campaigning on a single issue, such as streetlighting in the city, also met in taverns.[36] Although conducted in the expectation of a greater degree of privacy than that normal in casual tavern conversation, club meetings were held in taverns that clubmen shared with other paying customers. The persistence with which Philadelphia's clubs, societies, and associations used public houses for activities which demanded a modicum of privacy is testimony to the value they placed on the peculiar space taverns enclosed.

By meeting outside the private home, men who formed clubs and societies could enjoy one another's company while testing and observing one another's character, free from the obligation to defer either to female company or to their host. William Black, a member of a deputation from Virginia that visited Philadelphia in 1744 to discuss matters relating to relations with Indian tribes in the colonies' shared backcountry, kept a journal in which he described in some detail the mores of taverngoing and sociability in Philadelphia.[37] He described his frustration at visiting a tavern with the genteel male friends he had made in Philadelphia and then going on to a private house for supper where he was trapped by a "Miss Talkative." Alexander Hamilton recorded in some detail the harangue concerning Presbyterianism he received from "a masculin[e] faced lady" over evening tea at his boardinghouse.[38] Both felt that they had to defer to their female conversational partners, but neither felt happy so doing. Black, Hamilton, and the well-to-do Philadelphians they met believed that some exchanges between men were best conducted outside the private home in male company. Clubmen attempted to justify this chauvinism by pointing to the quality of the conversation in such gatherings. In a series of visits to the Governor's Club, which met nightly in the Tun tavern, Hamilton discussed English poets, Cervantes, trade, war with Spain, and the expedition to seize Cartagena. He drank several toasts to the fairer sex with the clubmen.[39] However, Hamilton noted that even when the governor was present, "now and then some persons there showed a particular fondness for introducing gross smutty expressions which . . . did not altogether become a company of philosophers and men of sense."[40]

For many clubmen the primary attraction of the tavern setting was that in it they could drink to excess and talk without restraint. William Black was delighted to meet a friend in Philadelphia who kept "bachelor house" and could entertain therefore with a greater freedom than when a wife and children had to be "conformed to." Black was quite candid about the effect of this freedom, describing how he staggered his way home after a night spent at his friend's house.[41] An evening at the Governor's Club, he noted, might involve conversation over a "cheerful glass" or two, supper, and then lemon punch and further "fine wines." Not surprisingly, many men and women excluded from club sociability concluded that its primary purpose was heavy drinking.[42]

Those clubs and societies who used taverns for their meetings were aware that they might be disrupted by other customers, but hoped that publicans would find their patronage so valuable that they would help club-men insulate their activities from the bar room crowd. The willingness of tavernkeepers to accommodate clubmen who desired privacy varied accord-ing to both the physical dimensions of the house they kept and their estima-tion of the profit to be made by turning their bar over to one group of customers while excluding others. Some publicans were exceptionally coop-erative. William Black was invited to lunch with the gentlemen of the city's Beefsteak Club, which met at the Tun tavern. There he was treated by the members to twenty dishes in addition to beef "stakes."[43] It is hard to imagine that the Tun's keeper, James Mullan, could have served many other cus-tomers while this luncheon was in progress. William Black's fellow Virgin-ians were impressed with the Tun. Later in their visit, they decided to give an impromptu entertainment to the governor and the "other gentlemen of the city." At noon Black walked to the Tun and to ask them to prepare. At one o'clock the governor, his "levee," and the Virginians arrived at the Tun where "a little past two we sat down to a very grand table having upwards of fifteen dishes on it at once, which was succeeded by a very fine collation. Among the many dishes which made our dinner was a large turtle, sent as a present to Governor Thomas from a friend . . . we had the table replenished with all sorts of wine the tavern could afford, and that in great abundance."[44]

The Tun was particularly popular with clubmen. It was not an espe-cially large house, but it clearly had an uncommonly able kitchen staff and a reputation for providing fine food. However, the main reason James Mullan was willing to supply William Black with a banquet at short notice, or to house regular meetings of the Beefsteak Club, must have been that the profit he could make from entertaining such guests would make it worth his while to exclude other customers from the tavern while the gentlemen ate. No other publican seems to have followed Mullan's example. Hence, except in the Tun's heyday, clubs and societies used even pretentious taverns in the expectation that their private meetings would be liable to disruption from the bar room crowd. In 1769, for example, Mr. Gualdo announced to the "*Philharmonical* Merchants and others" that he was to hold a series of con-certs of vocal and instrumental music at Davenport's Bunch of Grapes tavern. He stressed that "decency, good manners, and silence" were to be regarded at all times and that only "sober and orderly" ticket holders would be admitted.[45] In 1772 a group of "young gentlemen" announced the forma-tion of a Free Debating Society. They implored those not motivated by the "advancement of knowledge" to stay away from an inaugural meeting at the

Philadelphia, November 21, 1769.

To the *Philharmonical*
Merchants, and others.

MR. GUALDO, having for divers Reasons postponed his going to *Europe* till next Spring, takes this Method to acquaint the Public, that during the present Winter Season, he (every other *Thursday*) intends to direct a CONCERT of *VOCAL* and *INSTRUMENTAL MUSIC* at Mr. *Davenport*'s, in *Third-street*, being the most convenient House for this Purpose, as any Gentleman can be private in the adjacent Room. Mr. *Gualdo*'s Views in this Undertaking, are to oblige his Acquaintances, and to compensate in some Measure those Losses, which, he has sustained in this Town, partly through his own Imprudences, and above all, through false Friends and Malevolents. He flatters himself to be capable of conducting a Concert to the general Satisfaction. Decency, good Manners, and Silence shall, at all Times, be regarded. The Season being too far advanced, Mr. *Gualdo* proposes to have only nine Concerts during this Winter Any Gentleman or Lady may purchase a Ticket for the nine Concerts for a Guinea, which, they may lend to any of their Acquaintances. Mr. *Gualdo* shall be obliged to any Gentleman or Lady for the Lend of new Music ; likewise, the Assistance of any Lover of Music, willing to exercise and improve himself, shall be gratefully acknowledged by their humble Servant

JOHN GUALDO.

N. B. The Door Keepers and other Attendants shall have positive Orders to give Admittance to none but sober and orderly Persons. Chairs will be placed in the best Part of the Room for the Ladies, and Benches for the Gentlemen. Tickets for the Season at a Guinea a Piece, to be had at Mr. *Gualdo*'s near the *Bank Meeting*, in *Front-street* ; half a Guinea to be paid on the Delivery of the Tickets, the other half in next *February*. Tickets for one Night at five Shillings a Piece, to be had of the Waiter of the *London Coffee-House*, and at Mr. *Davenport*'s. No Money will be received at the Concert Room, nor Admittance given without Tickets. The first Concert to be on *Thursday*, the *Thirtieth* of *November*, to begin at six o'Clock in the Evening.

[John Gualdo], "To the *Philharmonical* Merchants, and Others . . ." Broadside. Philadelphia, 1769. Library Company of Philadelphia. Even at the close of the colonial period, tavern space was shared by men and women who sought to put it to often incompatible uses. The precautions which Gualdo took to ensure that his concert series at Josiah Davenport's Bunch of Grapes tavern would not be disrupted by noisy plebeians, and Davenport's efforts to ensure the comfortable reception of a genteel audience, speak to an expectation that tavern companies were typically drawn from across the city's spectrum of wealth.

Indian Queen.[46] At the time both the Bunch of Grapes and the Indian
Queen had been converted in order to offer small groups a measure of
privacy. Yet even in exceptional houses clubs and societies could expect
eavesdropping and interruption from the other patrons of the taverns in
which they held their meetings. Tavern space was shared space, as newspaper advertisements asking only like-minded folk to attend club or society
gatherings make clear.

Although some publicans may have managed to insulate or screen
clubs from the intrusive, inquisitive sociability of their bar room clientele,
licensees found it difficult to provide individual customers with complete
privacy or protection. This was because licensees had a vested interest in
serving as many customers as possible. A good illustration of the dilemma
facing publicans can be found in their responses to crime. For some Philadelphians, the openness of the tavern was an invitation to commit crime.[47]
Taverngoers looked to tavernkeepers for protection. It was in the tavernkeeper's interest to make his customers feel secure, and some licensees did
make special efforts to protect their patrons from crime. For example, in a
pitch aimed at the men and women who came into Philadelphia for the
market, Samuel Austin announced that his Boat and Boy tavern had a
number of outhouses where goods could be locked up and a secure yard for
wagons.[48] However, few publicans went beyond passive measures in their
attempts to prevent crime. An exceptional incident, involving Richard
Brockden, owner of the Indian King, illustrates the problems crime in
taverns posed for publicans.

At seven o'clock on a Monday night in December 1732, a man walked
into the Indian King and presented what turned out to be a counterfeit
high-denomination note in payment for drinks for himself and two acquaintances. Something about this man, his acquaintances, or the note
aroused the suspicions of the Indian King's owner, Richard Brockden. Under pretense of getting change, Brockden ran out and contacted a friend, the
magistrate Andrew Hamilton. Brockden and Hamilton returned to the
tavern to interrogate their suspect. He claimed he had been given the note in
payment for some hogs he had sold at the market that day. Brockden and
Hamilton were not convinced and marched their suspect to the nearby
tavern in which he had taken lodgings. Hamilton and Brockden were
searching the man's bags for counterfeit notes when they were interrupted
by a woman who turned out to be the suspect's sister. They asked this
woman whether she had any pound notes and, observing the suspect wink-
ing at his sister, called in the tavern's female keeper to conduct a search of her

clothing. This revealed twenty-three counterfeit pound notes. The suspect then confessed that he had been drawn into a counterfeiting ring by a man named Watt, who had told him that there was no sin involved since it made money "plentier" among poor people.[49]

Several features of this story are interesting. The suspect apparently did not pass any notes at the tavern where he lodged but chose instead the Indian King. Presumably, in a compliment to the Indian King's reputation, he deduced that Brockden's was the type of establishment in which a rich stranger might pass a new note without inviting suspicion. Brockden went through the motions of accepting the note. He could not afford to be too fussy about the forms of payment he would accept without alienating customers. Yet something about the stranger's appearance and actions led Brockden, and Hamilton, to continue to doubt the suspect's explanation that he had received the note at the market. It was in Brockden's interest to question the customer, since he stood to be defrauded. But Brockden's willingness to take the matter further must have been based on the assumption that he could rely on Hamilton's cooperation. Surely Hamilton would not have been so accommodating to every small trader brazen enough to bother him of an evening. Brockden may also have calculated that Hamilton would provide some protection in the event that their accusations were proven false. In short, Brockden took action in this case because his interests were directly threatened and he felt that he could rely on protection and cooperation from a magistrate.

These factors seldom pertained in respect to the crimes that mattered most to customers. A publican might respond to the complaints of a man who had been robbed and cheated or to a woman who had been bothered by local customers, because a licensee who sought to attract overnight visitors could ill afford to run a house with a reputation for harrassing travelers in a city with as many taverns as Philadelphia. Yet there was little that licensees could do to prevent crime or impertinence on their premises without making a priori assumptions about the character of their customers that ran contrary to their need to serve as a wide a range of the public as possible in order to survive in business. Travelers understood this, although some victims of crime on tavern premises conjured visions of criminal conspiracies between a keeper and his regular customers.[50]

Women may have found the prevalence of crime in taverns, the inquisitive attitudes of drinkers and licensees, and the generally claustrophobic atmosphere that pervaded even Philadelphia's self-styled inns especially unappealing. The diarist Hannah Callender Sansom summarized the "disadvantages" under which a lone woman traveler labored. She had to regard every man she met as a wolf in sheep's clothing and accept that under the "guise of disinterestedness" lurked the "basest views."[51] Women traveling with men could still encounter an offensive suspicion. Charlotte Brown, who served as the matron of the English army's general hospital in America between 1754 and 1756, kept a journal describing her travels that is suggestive of the treatment that even gentlewomen received in colonial taverns. Brown was traveling in the company of a male colleague, Mr. Cherrington. She found that tavernkeepers and tavern customers assumed that they were man and wife. This is perhaps understandable. But Brown found that some publicans were reluctant to believe her explanations to the contrary or, worse, assumed that she was a kept woman. She had difficulty securing a room of her own. In one tavern, in order to secure two single beds rather than a double, Cherrington had to bluff the mistress of the house with the story that he and Brown were indeed man and wife but that Brown seldom favored him with space in her bed. When Brown and Cherrington arrived at the Indian King in Philadelphia in October 1756, "the people of the house" stared at her, speculating that Brown was Cherrington's mistress. The pair were eventually able to persuade the licensees—probably John and Sarah Biddle, whom Daniel Fisher had found so "rationally benevolent"—that Brown required a room of her own. But in order to protect her reputation while conducting business that necessitated meetings with both male and female callers, Brown found it necessary to take up lodgings in the city's hospital.[52]

Innkeepers needed to serve locals as well as strangers to stay in business. All licensees sought to serve as many customers as possible, sorting out the squabbles that arose from the shared use of cramped premises by men and women of differing social ranks as they went along. In practice the tone of many tavern gatherings was majoritarian. If a bar room crowd came to the conclusion that a female traveler was a kept woman, or that a male stranger was a runaway servant, or that a horse could not withstand the beat of a drum as advertised, their judgment took on an air of accepted wisdom that brooked little argument and to which licensees and skeptical patrons had to defer. But even men and women who did not share the values and prejudices of tavern talk made use of the network that supported it. For example, when Eliza Brooks's son was stung badly by poison ivy, she went into her local tavern to ask advice on treatments from a neighbor. A "studious man" who happened to be drinking there overheard Brooks's story and prescribed a concoction which eased her son's pain.[53] When political leaders wanted to gauge the mood of the town or canvass for support, they visited taverns and dispensed drinks in the knowledge that such activities carried at least as much influence with voters as a pamphlet manifesto. The great attraction of tavern talk for men of little formal education and modest social status lay in the fact that their contributions to it could, potentially, gain influence and notoriety. By the same token, the respect and influence afforded the views of men of little distinction or discernment in tavern talk was precisely what infuriated gentlemen of learning. One way in which Philadelphians sought to satisfy a demand for "elevated" conversation that was by no means the sole preserve of the gentry was by founding coffeehouses.

Coffee drinking and coffeehouses were at the peak of their vogue in England precisely as Philadelphia was being founded and settled. In England these new establishments courted the custom of a burgeoning urban gentry. As a Londoner put it, coffeehouses were "founded for the entertainment of gentlemen and merchants" to serve as "the theatres of news and politics." In *The Spectator* Addison and Steele celebrated the coffeehouse as the place where the "talk of the town" was initiated and weighed. But even in London, few coffeehouses could meet their celebrants' expectations. Those that did charged admission fees. By the early eighteenth century, London had so many establishments calling themselves coffeehouses that one Londoner sniffed that coffeehouses had "degenerated" into "mere alehouses."[54] Over the first half of the eighteenth century, at least four coffeehouses were founded in Philadelphia, two of them by widows.[55] Yet there were always periods in the development of colonial Philadelphia when the city possessed not a single coffeehouse. Moreover, until 1754 and the founding, by private subscription, of William Bradford's Old London Coffeehouse, Philadelphia lacked a coffeehouse that could claim to embody the values laid out in English grace literature.

The history of Philadelphia's first coffeehouse, built by Samuel Carpenter in the late seventeenth century, illustrates the difficulty of establishing an exclusive meeting place in a city with an assertive and undeferential population. The "vulgar" and "ignorant" demanded access to Carpenter's and, given the existence of controls on the maximum retail price of drinks, there was little that a coffeehousekeeper could do to keep them out short of applying commercially suicidal snobbery. Carpenter's coffeehouse was, to judge from its sale price of £450, certainly of a size fit to offer specialized service. One of its first keepers, Henry Flowers, attempted to make the business pay through the sale of coffee alone. He failed. Under Captain

Finney, a justice and former sheriff of Philadelphia, the house sold liquor as well as coffee. Finney was able to persuade the city's common council to hold meetings in his house.[56] But such patronage had no lasting effect on the level of debate and conversation in the coffeehouse. James Logan railed against the demagoguery of men who used the credulous crowd at Carpenter's coffeehouse to bolster their vanity.[57] Richard Peters, Pennsylvania's provincial secretary, complained: "The merest trifle in the world will be made into town talk . . . everything proper or improper, of a public or private nature, is constantly bandied about in the coffeehouse."[58] Such complaints echoed those of metropolitan critics. Philadelphia's first coffeehouses were simply too open, too vulnerable to the pedantry and prejudice of the vulgar, to claim to have any pretentions to live up to the ideal of uniquely well informed and distinctively sober public discussion. A coffeehousekeeper could refuse service to men he thought likely to be boring or pedantic, he could bar men who irritated regular customers like James Logan or Richard Peters, but only at the risk of diminishing his clientele to the point where the house ceased to be profitable.

Whether rich or poor, the men who patronized Carpenter's coffeehouse also frequented other, less modish public houses. The same pool of taverngoers who tried to breathe life into an idealized conception of coffeehouse conversation also supplied the clientele for coarser taverns. "Low" taverns—offering access to bawdy conversation, illegal gambling, billiard playing, and prostitution—attracted genteel Philadelphians throughout the colonial era. At the beginning of the eighteenth century William Penn, Jr., and John Evans, lieutenant governor of Pennsylvania, kept a riotous bachelor establishment at William Clark's tavern.[59] In 1761 a group of young "gentlemen" gathered regularly at a tavern on the southwest corner of Chestnut and Fourth before heading out onto the streets to slash women's skirts and petticoats with razors.[60] In 1770 Samuel Coates gave a gloomy account of the careers of twelve well-to-do young Quakers with whom he had attended school. Many of his former classmates were bankrupt, "poor P.S . . . drinks very hard," and "D.W." had been disowned by the meeting for keeping a gamecock valued at £25 and allegedly paying young girls £50 to strip naked before him.[61] At roughly the same time, Alexander Graydon was introduced to "the fascination of the billiard table" and "initiated into other seductive arenas of city dissipation" by Richard Bond, son of the prominent merchant Phineas Bond. Bond who showed Graydon "where beardless youth might find a lethe for its timidity, in the form of an execrable potion called wine, on the very reasonable terms of 2s. and 6d. a quart." Both lads were in their element when part of a "large bottle association," playing billiards, or watching horse races.[62]

Until the eve of the Revolution, most taverns in colonial Philadelphia were used by heterogeneous groups of customers. Well-to-do men demanded service in "low" taverns; laborers demanded a hearing in coffeehouses. Mixed tavern clienteles sought to use shared space for a variety of activities. The same small taproom might be the scene of one knot of customers getting drunk while another talked politics, one group of customers talking of flour prices while another discussed horse racing. Outside, in the tavern yard, a visitor might have found one person trying to bid up the price of a horse on sale, others arguing that the horse was worthless, and perhaps, in the corner, John Bonnin drumming up custom for his panoramic view of the siege of Barcelona. All accounts of the uses to which Philadelphians put taverns suggest some degree of frustration with the dissonance caused by the competing claims made on tavern space and the claustrophobia of bar room surroundings. Yet Philadelphia's taverns continued to find customers, even though many of those customers sought in a taverns a privacy that was frequently invaded. Alexander Hamilton continued to lodge at the Three Tuns, even though he found the company oppressive. Alexander Graydon continued to seek out "lethe for his timidity" in taverns, even though he knew that other patrons sought to use the same space for business transactions or quiet conversations. Throughout the eighteenth century, taverns were the site of meetings dedicated to various municipal affairs, despite the fact that news of supposedly private committee meetings held in taverns was likely to leak.[63]

Ironically, a major source of dispute within mixed companies was the employment of drinking practices, designed to produce a boozy fellowship among men who might hardly know one another, which made socially diverse tavern gatherings seem feasible in the first place. Taverngoers understood drinking to be a communal activity. In order to get along in tavern company one had to go along. When drinking and socializing in public, both gentlemen and laborers voluntarily placed themselves within group disciplines that had the effect of identifying and affirming mutual interests. The tone of many tavern drinking practices was recalled by Alexander Graydon:

Though without the slightest addiction to liquor, nothing was more delightful to me than to find myself a member of a large bottle association set in for serious drinking; the table officers appointed, the demi-johns filled, the bottles arranged with the other necessary dispositions for such engagements; and I put no inconsiderable value on myself for my supposed "potency in potting" or, in modern phrase, my being able to carry off a respectable quantity of wine. . . . As to those convivial qualifications, which are wont to set the table in a roar, I had never any pretensions to them, though few enjoyed them with more relish.[64]

The organization underlying the rituals of gentlemanly drinking, the "necessary dispositions" to which Graydon alluded, found their fullest expression in formal clubs but they were also a feature of ad hoc tavern assemblies.

Jacob Hiltzheimer's diary is one of the best surviving sources on the quality of social life in colonial Philadelphia. Hiltzheimer was a small trader, dealing chiefly in horses and cattle, who maintained ties with both German and British communities in Philadelphia. During the Revolution he served in a variety of relatively minor posts in congressional commissariats. Hiltzheimer's diary describes in detail with whom and on what occasion he drank. The key feature of the sociability his diary describes is its attention to reciprocity. For example, the killing of his steer "Roger" was for Hiltzheimer the social highlight of 1774. He invited his friends to see the beast dressed and weighed, and then hosted tavern parties that dined on Roger's steaks.[65] By organizing such events, Hiltzheimer repaid hospitality and prompted further invitations. A diary entry made on November 23, 1772, is typical: "This evening went to the Widow Spence's [tavern]; there supped on venison with the following gentlemen: Robert Erwin, William Jones, Richard Footman, Mr. Freeman, and Sutliff. Jacob Bates gave the supper on account of his leaving the city for Carolina."[66] Hiltzheimer's forms of appellation— poor "Sutliff" rated neither a first name nor a "Mr."—show that from Hiltzheimer's point of view the evening's guests were drawn from across the spectrum of social status. However, the shared consumption of food and

---

(*Facing page*) *The American Jest Book. Containing a Selection of Anecdotes, Bon Mots, Jests, Repartees, Stories, Etc. Etc.* Harrisburg, Pa.: Printed for Mathew Carey, 1796. Frontispiece. Library Company of Philadelphia. Throughout the colonial period Philadelphians who, like Alexander Graydon, lacked the facility to set a table roaring at displays of original wit could turn to anthologies of "refined" conversational adornments. The tone of the *American Jest Book* was smuttier than many of its competitors. Gatherings of clubmen, meeting for "serious drinking" sessions in taverns, provided a reliable market for such material in eighteenth-century Philadelphia. This illustration suggests how such works might have been used to bind drinking companies together. The well-to-do drinkers depicted here are viewed in a slightly satirical light. Their vaguely vulpine physiogonomies suggest that the humorous anecdote they are enjoying is of a risqué nature.

drink was understood, at least by Hiltzheimer, to take place on terms of temporary equality.

Hiltzheimer shared a little of Alexander Graydon's delight in "serious drinking." When he drank punch with his friend William Jones, a tavern-keeper, to celebrate Jones's second marriage, he wrote in his diary, "[I] got decently drunk[, the] groom could not be accused of the same fault."[67] On

the occasion of his third marriage, William Jones kept open house for four days. Hiltzheimer attended the first three days of this binge but confessed that he had to take a long ride "to wear off the effects of the punch and clear my head."[68] Hiltzheimer did not entirely approve of the drinking mores of his day, and none of the punch drinking he so assiduously recorded had the effect of erasing his sense of the social distance between himself and his fellow drinkers. However, he chose to participate in this style of drinking and was equipped with the kind of manners that allowed him to mix with serious drinkers from all classes and walks of life.

Where Graydon found fraternalism in large bottle associations and Hiltzheimer cultivated social connections in periodic celebrations, artisans found a similar sense of fellowship in drinking in and around the workplace. The pride that artisans took in the beauty and serviceability of the products they made, the idealization of Pennsylvania as "the best poor man's country," a belief that alcohol fueled strength, and the residual effects of an initial labor shortage all conspired to create an artisanal culture that took considerable pride in its abilities and jealously defended heavy drinking as a right and a privilege. In periods of all but the highest demand, the working day was punctuated by breaks for liquor and conversation.[69] Work-related drinking also positioned artisanal workers within the city's hierarchy of social status. For example, one of the perquisites of being a journeyman was the right to order apprentices to run over to the alehouse for beer.[70] In some trades artisans were "treated" by their employers. Builders and shipwrights expected treats of liquor at intervals during the construction of a house or ship and a party on completion. Although some owners gave gifts of money, most offered treats of alcohol. By doing so they legitimated the artisans' working methods.[71] Artisans also signaled their control over production by observing "Saint Monday."

In 1768 Franklin lamented that "Saint Monday is as duly kept by our working people as Sunday; the only difference is that instead of employing their time cheaply in church, they are wasting it expensively in the alehouse."[72] Franklin was right to point to the expense of Saint Monday, but conspicuous expenditure was central to its appeal and purpose. It was as important to an artisan as it was for Alexander Graydon or Jacob Hiltzheimer to be able to stand one's round and take one's place in communal drinking, and for similar reasons. Given the existence of periodic trade slumps and seasonal unemployment, a laborer in an artisanal trade had reason to develop a network of contacts. For the artisan as for the merchant, the link between social standing and fiscal credit was forged over beer or punch.

To argue that artisanal and genteel drinking practices had much in common is not to say that artisans and gentlemen mixed easily in tavern company. Gentlemen were not always welcome in artisans' drinking circles, and laborers might find themselves frozen out of gatherings presided over by the likes of Alexander Hamilton. Sometimes a gentleman found himself being asked to submit to the discipline of a group dominated by men he considered to be his inferiors; on other occasions a laborer might be asked to defer to drinking dispositions made by gentlemen. A drinker had to exercise a good deal of tact in such situations. Alexander Hamilton expressed contempt in his *Itinerarium* for the Hogarthian grotesques he found in many Philadelphia taverns. But he phrased his refusal to join in their circles in ways calculated to cause minimal provocation. He was "reserved" during his stay at the Three Tuns, keeping his views to himself, even to the point of maintaining a public silence. Hamilton drank and conversed with the members of the Governor's Club as well as with ordinary Philadelphians in modest taverns. He criticized tavern company as part of an attempt to emphasize the superiority of club life. However, it is significant that contemporary accounts of tavern sociability, including Hamilton's, suggest that taverngoers attempted to create "companies" rather than "committees." The reciprocal, clubbish drinking arrangements so enthusiastically described by Alexander Graydon and so assiduously nurtured by Jacob Hiltzheimer were also the goal of the typical tavern company.

Taverngoers employed two practices in particular—singing and toasting—in an attempt to draw into fellowship men and women from different cultural backgrounds and social stations. Neither practice was entirely effective, not least because a "typical" tavern company often contained men who did not want to be drawn into enforced intimacy with the dominant crowd. For this reason, the very forms by which taverngoers attempted to overcome their differences could also become the occasion of division and contest. The journal kept by the Lutheran minister Henry Muhlenberg provides several examples of the way mixed companies used songs to develop a sense of fellowship. Since Muhlenberg set himself apart from rituals of fellowship on principle, his journals also suggest the friction that accompanied the use of songs and other rituals of tavern fellowship. (On one occasion Muhlenberg had to bolt the door of his room to prevent interference from carousing Englishmen offended by his censorious attitude.)[73] In 1752 he traveled on the stage boat from Philadelphia to New York. On board the boat, and at a tavern in Bordentown, New Jersey, he was tormented by fellow passengers because he would not "join in." He reflected:

The English people have a kind of songs which are set to melodic music and describe all sorts of heroes and feats of arms on land and sea. Respectable people sing them as a pastime and regard it as a serious invasion of their liberty if one protests against these songs, etc. Now if one rebukes them on account of their amorous songs, they believe that they can justify themselves by referring to these songs about heroes. The musical setting and melodies of these songs of heroic deeds are very similar to those which our Germans use for church music.[74]

On this particular occasion, one of the members of the company who sang most lustily was a young Quaker.

Although they made use of public houses, Quakers, like Lutherans, generally stood aloof from the rituals of tavern fellowship. The contest of wills between a Quaker abstaining from "sinful revelry" and a tavern crowd bent on singing and dancing could be ferocious. Early in the eighteenth century, Elizabeth Ashbridge found herself in the unfortunate position of being "the spectacle and discourse of the Company" in a Philadelphia tavern. She was in the throes of conversion to Quaker belief. Her husband, believing that her newfound convictions had robbed her of a "livel[i]ness of temper" that was her natural state, removed his wife from Chester County in the hope that once away from Quakers she might be "cured" of their preaching. The Ashbridges journeyed on foot to Wilmington and thence by packet boat to Philadelphia, where they put up in a tavern. On arrival at this tavern her husband announced to the company that his wife was a Quaker and that he desired "if possible to find out some place where there was none." Mr. Ashbridge told the bar room crowd that she had once been a good dancer but that now "he could get [her] neither to dance nor sing." In a narrative of her spiritual travails she described what happened next:

upon which one of the [tavern] company stands up saying, "I'll go fetch my fiddle, and we'll have a dance," at which my husband was much pleased. The fiddle came, the sight of which put me in a sad condition for fear if I refused my husband would be in a great passion: however I [resolved not to comply] whatever be the consequence. He comes to me, takes me by the hand saying, "come my dear, shake off that gloom and let's have a civil dance; you would now and then when you was a good Churchwoman, and that's better than a stiff Quaker." I trembling desired to be excused; but he insisted on it, and knowing his temper to be exceeding cholerick, durst not say much, yet did not consent. He pluck[e]d me round the room till tears affected my eyes, at sight whereof the musician stop[ped] and said, "I'll play no more, let your wife alone."[75]

Presumably some of the customers in the Philadelphia tavern thought that Elizabeth Ashbridge's husband had gone too far and that he, rather than his wife, had made a spectacle of himself. But when the music ceased, Ashbridge and her husband remained in the bar. At least some of the tavern's customers, who might well have had their own experience of Quaker "stiffness," sympathized with Mr. Ashbridge. A man from Freehold, New Jersey, took Mr. Ashbridge's side, advising him that if he took Elizabeth to his town she would soon be "cured of her Quakerism." As this vignette illustrates, although singing and dancing could bind strangers in a tavern into a "company," there was always the danger that the very use of these forms could, by identifying and isolating customers who refused to conform, divide a company into potentially disputatious "committees."

Penn's first tavern regulations forbade toasting in taverns.[76] However, Philadelphia's taverngoers drank toasts despite the law and conscious of the fact that some of their number might find any toast, however innocuous, to constitute a form of oath taking and, therefore, blasphemy. It was incumbent on a tavern toaster to avoid sentiments that might offend the majority of the company in which he found himself. Toasting therefore consisted of the art of expressing relatively uncontroversial sentiments in a highly stylized manner. It promoted a style of drinking that identified and built upon what a company had in common, and created stylized conversational exchanges between men drawn from various ethnic, cultural, and social backgrounds. Particularly well phrased toasts were disseminated throughout the colonies by travelers and in published anthologies.[77] As with songs, sharing the sentiments of a toast and being able to join in bound a drinker to the group in which he drank and brought the stranger into fellowship with the regular. By the same token, toasting was a practice which could cause conflict by identifying and isolating men who refused to join in. When a man proposed a toast in tavern company, his companions were expected to drink to it and respond in kind. To refuse to drink a toast, or to propose a toast so obnoxious as to prompt refusal, led to fights.

The manner in which Philadelphians made use of taverns suggests curious paradoxes. Even men like Hamilton, Graydon, and Hiltzheimer, who understood and valued tavern fellowship, did not always join in the rituals by which it might be achieved. On the one hand, Philadelphians drank in ways that confirmed their sense of hierarchy and therefore divided them. On the other hand, they also attempted to drink in ways that emphasized mutualities, and espoused a rough and ready fraternalism that could have the effect of dissolving lines of status. Sometimes Jacob Hiltzheimer threw himself into the revelry at William Jones's tavern, and on other occasions he stood at one remove from the company he found. Contests between

customers often had their origin in the employment of precisely those ritualized forms of behavior such as toasting or singing designed to secure a convivial consensus.

Colonial Philadelphia's taverngoers were not masochists; taverngoing retained its popularity because taverngoers developed a rich symbolism through which they could suggest, and perhaps experience, pleasurable fellowship even within a competitive and often cruel milieu. Nevertheless, tavern sociability contained strong elements of contest. Aware that their conversation might be overheard, their wit or learning judged, many taverngoers felt pressure to shine in tavern exchanges. We have seen how, for example, even in old age Alexander Graydon felt the need to apologize for lacking the facility to set a table roaring with laughter. In his *Autobiography* Franklin felt it was necessary to explain away his failure to impress the company he encountered at the Crooked Billet on his first visit to Philadelphia. Gentlemen expected to be able to "win" conversational contests with their social inferiors. This assumption goes some way to explaining the willingness of a man like Alexander Hamilton to sit around a common table and drink with Hogarthian "grotesques." (Hamilton's self-confidence did not deter members of the "lower orders" from bearding him. However superior Hamilton may have felt, his interlocutors clearly felt they could put one over on him.) But even conversational exchanges conducted between men of broadly similar social station frequently possessed elements of contest. One night in 1702, James Logan was invited for a drink by Dr. Cox. Logan described the tone of their conversation in a letter to William Penn: "Upon his invitation, I was lately drinking a glass of wine with [Cox] at the White Hart. . . . Colonel Quary . . . came and joined us, after him J[ohn] Moore also, without invitation. Quary was familiar and pleasant, with much smoothness, but I gave him as many close rubs as I could have opportunity, which made him look rather more asquint than before."[78] Logan described with relish the "rubs" he gave the colonel because Quary and Moore, officials of the vice-admiralty court, were his political enemies.[79] The victory Logan wished

(*Facing page*) Toasting Glass. English manufacture. 1770? Philadelphia Museum of Art: Bequest of George Burford Lorimer. Philadelphia's taverngoers, rich and poor, offered toasts to one another in defiance of laws designed to suppress the practice. This glass, inscribed with images of the notorious Hellfire Club and the legend "Joseph M—, Master of Revels" was designed for (and celebrated) "serious drinking" sessions of the sort recalled fondly by Alexander Graydon.

Penn to admire consisted of Logan's apparent success in goading Quary without giving Quary the opportunity to claim that Logan had transcended the boundaries of politeness accepted by men of their social rank.

Drinking in taverns was often competitive. Alexander Graydon was proud of his fondly remembered "potency in potting." Thomas Apty adopted a similar approach to tavern drinking when he bet the customers of the Red Lion half a crown that he could down twelve pints of fortified cider in half an hour. (He did, but dropped dead before he could collect his money.) Taverngoers frequently got up races, sometimes between men, more often between horses.[80] Prior to the 1760s, the White Horse tavern was the unofficial headquarters of a horse-racing community in Philadelphia whose penchant for conducting its meetings on Sassafras Street resulted in the thoroughfare's becoming known as Race Street. Cockfighting found a home in taverns. The Pennsylvania Assembly legislated against cockfighting in 1700, 1711, 1779, and again in 1786. Such efforts were prompted by the huge popularity of the sport with people of all ranks of society. In 1735 Dr. William Shippen, a Presbyterian elder, wrote to a friend: "I have sent you a young game cock, to be depended upon—which I would advise you to put to a walk by himself with the hen I sent you before—I have not sent an old cock—our young cockers have contrived to kill and steal all I had."[81] Frances Hopkinson immortalized in verse the fight which took place in 1770 at Richardson's tavern, on the outskirts of the city, between (the birds of) James Delancey of New York and Timothy "Timmy Gaff" Matlack of Philadelphia. Matlack was a Quaker ne'er-do-well who had been disowned by the meeting for bankruptcy. At the time this fight took place, Matlack was on his way to becoming an influential radical. For this reason, and because he was fighting a New Yorker, Matlack received support from all ranks of Philadelphia society.[82]

Sometimes, of course, taverns were the sites not of black looks, harsh words, or symbolic contests but of actual fisticuffs. The Delancey-Matlack cockfight at Richardson's tavern ended in a mass brawl. The most infamous tavern brawl in the history of colonial Philadelphia involved William Penn's own son. William Penn, Jr., arrived in Philadelphia in February 1704. He had made the journey to the province on the same ship as the colony's new lieutenant governor, John Evans. The two young men had become friends on the voyage and, once ashore, decided to share quarters in William Clark's tavern. Evans had a reputation for heavy drinking, while Penn regarded his son as easily led and liable to fall into bad habits. Both men promised to behave themselves. But when James Logan paid a call on Evans one day soon after his arrival he found him disabled by "cholica pictorium," prompting Logan to conclude that Evans's reputation was justified.[83] Evans's actions in office did not improve his standing among Quaker city elders. He set about raising a militia, offering prospective recruits the incentive of exemption from the duty of serving on the city's watch. On the night of September 1, 1704, in Enoch Story's tavern, William Penn, Jr., made his opinion of the character of those who continued to choose to serve on the city watch known to some watchmen. A fight erupted in which the younger Penn received a beating.[84] Two months later, there was another "great fray" at Story's. Solomon Cresson, performing the office of watchman, came upon a crowd of after-hours drinkers at Story's. Since it was past midnight, Cresson bid the company disperse and beat those who were slow to leave. Apparently Cresson was unaware that Governor Evans was among the company. Evans in turn beat Cresson and tried to pack him off to prison. The mayor, recorder, and some of the city's aldermen came to Cresson's aid, trading blows with Evans and his cronies. Evans was among several persons injured before peace was restored.[85]

This brawl shocked Philadelphia and saddened Penn. Both John Evans and William Penn, Jr., left Philadelphia soon after these events. However, without resorting to a potentially anachronistic idealization of the behavior associated with the term "male bonding," it may be that tavern brawls dissolved, at least temporarily, the tensions that were their underlying cause. We should at least consider the possibility that eighteenth-century drinkers believed that a physical punch showed a man more respect than a verbal snub. Fighting implied a kind of equality whereas "reserve," of the kind Alexander Hamilton was so wont to demonstrate, suggested superiority. Alexander Graydon certainly seems to have believed something of this sort. Near the end of his life, he could still lovingly recall the antics of a member of the British military garrison, Captain Ogle. One day Ogle, while "bowz'd," set out to make sport of Quaker notions of brotherly love. He staggered into Bradford's Old London Coffeehouse. Throwing his arms around the first Quaker he saw there, Joshua Fisher, he said, "Ah, my dear Broadbrim, give me a kiss." He then began to "slaver" Fisher "most lovingly." An apothecary, Will Richards, intervened. Ogle challenged Richards, saying "Hah! My jolly fellow, give me a smack of your fat chops." To Ogle's surprise, Richards responded with a prolonged "kiss," which knocked Ogle to the floor and "sobered" the officer considerably. Richards and Ogle fell into conversation. Ogle, discovering that Richards was not a Quaker, treated him with new respect. Richards, for his part, concluded that "however [Ogle] might be disguised by intoxication, he well knew what belonged to the character of a gentleman."[86] Richards at least was willing to believe that such roughhousing allowed a taverngoer to identify new mutualities and associations. These, as the difference in status between an apothecary and an British army officer suggests, could cross lines of culture and class.

This incident had a significant denouement. When Ogle chose once again to make sport of the coffeehouse crowd, two aldermen in the coffee-house leapt up and began committal proceedings. With Ogle hanging over their shoulder they began to write up a warrant. Eventually Ogle said, "Aye, my father was a justice of the peace too, but he did not spell that word as you do. I remember perfectly well, that, instead of an 's' he always used to spell circumstance with a 'c.'" It was a shot heard around the town. As Graydon recalled nearly fifty years later, "this sarcastic thrust at the scribe" "disarmed the patrons [of the coffeehouse] of their resentment" and "turned the tide in favour of the rioters."[87]

The fact that committal proceedings against Ogle were instigated serves as a reminder that taverngoers' activities were a matter of legal con-cern. Taverns that became notorious as the site of fights and pranks were liable to be deemed disorderly, and closed. The assumption behind such actions was that if the community allowed Philadelphians to drink in loosely run public houses the incidence of offenses against the public order would increase. Tavernkeepers were beholden to a body of law that obliged them to prevent contests on their premises. Yet even if we agree that the law was correct in its assumption with regard to a likely increase in the number of public order offenses, what of their type? If Ogle had been committed for giving Will Richards a "smack on the chops" outside the statehouse rather than inside Bradford's coffeehouse, would the charge have been drunken-ness or assault? The available records do not allow us to reconstruct the manner in which courts interpreted the legal distinction between charges of drunken disorder and assault. However, it is at least possible that the kind of roughhousing and horseplay engaged in by Richards and Ogle was, so long as it was associated with taverns, a matter of being drunk and disorderly—a serious offense, but distinct from that of assault.

Some taverns seem to have been popular precisely because they were associated with contests and conflict. The Center House tavern serves as an example of this phenomenon. As its name implies, the Center House was located at the edge of Philadelphia's central commons, on the site of what is now City Hall Plaza. Although an integral part of the city's grid of streets and squares, this area was so sparsely populated in the colonial period that it was used for foxhunts, fairs, and militia musters. It became the site of the city's first purpose-built race course but was also a notorious haunt for highwaymen.[88] Given the Center House's geographical position, for most of the colonial period Philadelphians who drank there would have had a lengthy walk home. In the first generation of settlement, Hannah Penn urged her husband not to relicense the "ill red house" at center square.[89] However, a tavern was kept there throughout the colonial period. The Center House boasted the city's only bowling green and one of its few billiard tables.[90] These were popular amenities. A rakish British subaltern, Alexander Mackraby, who did not play billiards, attended the Center House precisely because he enjoyed the company of those who did. The tavern was not the sole preserve of the gentry. When two sailors from *Le Trembleur* wanted to fight, the entire crew marched out to the Center House.[91] Hannah Callender Sansom knew the Center House had a notorious reputation and that the well-to-do young men of her circle who went there to play billiards could expect "no distinction of company."[92] For moralists like Hannah Penn, the tavern continued in business because it had created an atmosphere where moral and civil laws were suspended. More likely, the tavern drew upon a different association. The commons were associated with contests, and such a site demanded not a first-aid station but a tavern.

It seems clear that Philadelphia's taverngoers did not find the potential for, or existence of, conflicts and contests in taverns antithetical to sociability. This raises the question, why, if taverngoers were inquisitive, argumentative, and combative, did so many Philadelphians use taverns so often? It seems that colonial taverngoers felt themselves to be possessed of a system of manners and procedures adequate to resolve any trouble that might arise from the use of the same house by men of different social backgrounds. Robust, and frequently chauvinistic, an egalitarianism that remained intolerant of dissent or even reserve seems to have emerged as the dominant tone of tavern intercourse for most of the colonial period. While this may sometimes have had the effect of dividing, in Alexander Hamilton's phrase, tavern companies into committees, it did not deter men like Hamilton from voluntarily visiting taverns. One would need to know more about how men in colonial Philadelphia thought about their gender and class before one could argue confidently that tavern contests, however symbolized, served to resolve or sublimate tensions between taverngoers. Nevertheless, precisely because the accustomed mores of taverngoing were valued, they were applied beyond purely social exchanges. This in turn led to fundamental changes in Philadelphians' attitudes toward taverngoing as well as in the design and operation of their taverns.

In retrospect it is hardly surprising that Philadelphia's merchants and traders built "their own" public house, William Bradford's Old London Coffeehouse. Merchants subscribed to this coffeehouse and encouraged daily attendance there, not because business dealings were unknown in existing taverns but because they were all too common. Philadelphians used, or attempted to use, taverns for a wide variety of exchanges, from the sale of a horse to discussion of the latest trade news. Quite apart from the difficulty of conducting transactions over the background noise of an inquisitive, opinionated, and often drunken tavern crowd, exchange activities involved concepts such as profit and loss, accuracy and speculation, justice and iniquity, which sat uneasily with the prevailing modes of tavern sociability. Why should a man, in return for a round of drams and the good opinion of a tavern company, accept a loss on the sale of a horse or a house when discussion in a more "rational" forum might bring him the price he desired? By the 1750s many Philadelphians involved in commerce, reacting against the slow and irregular conduct of business, and in accordance with the dictates of an "enterprizing spirit" that quickly transcended its basis in the precepts of evangelical Protestantism, began to conclude that tavern sociability was antithetical to efficient business activity.[93]

The eventual outcome of dissatisfaction with mixed tavern assemblages was that groups of Philadelphians founded, or laid claim to, taverns of their own. The story of the founding of William Bradford's Old London Coffeehouse illustrates this process. In 1754 Bradford, editor of the *Pennsylvania Journal*, set about converting a store on the southeastern corner of High and Front Streets in an innovative way. He gathered 234 subscribers, each of whom put up between twenty and thirty shillings to establish a merchants' exchange. The exchange then lent Bradford £259 to convert the store and start up operations.[94] No public house in Philadelphia had been built previously by private subscription; few taverns were run in purposely converted premises.

In a loftily phrased application for a license to sell spirituous liquors, Bradford set the tone for his establishment. "Having been advised," he wrote, "to keep a coffee house for the benefit of merchants and traders, and as some people may at times be desirous to be furnished with other liquors beside coffee, your petitioner apprehends it necessary to have the Governor's license."[95] The design of the Old London Coffeehouse reflected a desire to separate and distinguish trade from bar room conversation. The first floor was used as a tavern, while the second floor housed an "exchange" and coffeehouse. The real business of the place was conducted on the second

floor, protected from casual interruptions by the practice of referring in-
quiries to the ground-floor bar.[96] Complementing the architecture of the
house was the sense of ownership. Here was an establishment that belonged
to its primary clientele.

The bourgeois values of Bradford's clientele were captured in a letter
Edward Shippen wrote to his son soon after the coffeehouse opened. Shippen warned his son that the pursuit of pleasure was the sole preserve of
"crowned heads and other great men who have their incomes sleeping and
waking." Young Shippen should not throw luncheon parties for friends,
because such entertainments led to a day given over to drinking, the idle
sports of bowls and billiards, and late-night tavern suppers. Instead he
should follow the example set by his cousin who, though "opulent," got up,
worked hard, and then went on to the coffeehouse. His son should "by all
means" go daily to the coffeehouse but avoid the tavern. Attending the
coffeehouse was good for business; taverngoing was not. To drive home the
point, Shippen Sr. drew up a cost-benefit analysis of the expenses entailed in
living the fashionable life weighed against the potential benefits of sociability at the coffeehouse and exchange.[97]

William Bradford's coffeehouse was not everyone's cup of tea. Alexander Graydon grew up despising the values of the coffeehouse crowd. He
recalled that some of his childhood friends saw even a game of marbles as an
opportunity for accumulation. In contrast he claimed that "though I had no
dislike to money, it never impressed me as a primary good." According to
him, serious drinkers in a tavern company expressed a "high-minded contempt for the industrious and the plodding."[98] Nevertheless, a host of specialized business institutions evolved in the wake of Bradford's Old London
Coffeehouse. By the 1770s, the city boasted a merchants' exchange (built by
private subscription), wherein business was conducted in an atmosphere
detached from considerations of "leisure."[99] In 1774 James Hume opened an
"Intelligence Office" next door to the Old London Coffeehouse. Here ladies
and gentlemen could be registered for places of employment in any calling.[100]
At around the same time Matthew Clarkson opened an office near the
coffeehouse from which he issued loans and changed money. Richard Rundle
and John Jennings opened a specialized "Vendue House" in the same area,
while across the street from the coffeehouse William Goddard edited the
Pennsylvania Chronicle, a newspaper that prided itself on editorial independence.[101] As Elizabeth Grey Kogan Spera has shown, a central business
district began to take shape in Philadelphia toward the close of the eighteenth century.[102] The changed relationship between the city's taverns and its

William Bradford's Old London Coffeehouse. Illustration. (After Edward Munford?) *Annals of Philadelphia*, ed. John Fanning Watson. Philadelphia: E. L. Carey, 1830. Library Company of Philadelphia. (*Facing page*) The Old London Coffeehouse. Photograph. 1854. Library Company of Philadelphia. Two views of the first public house built by private subscription in Philadelphia. The Old London Coffeehouse stood on Front and Market Streets. The first floor contained a bar, the second the merchant's exchange it was built to house. Opened in 1754, the coffeehouse and merchant's exchange soon became a favored site of vendues and auctions. Slave sales, such as that depicted, were also held at taverns.

business life is captured neatly in an advertisement placed by Josiah Davenport, keeper of the Bunch of Grapes: "When it is considered that Third Street is becoming one of the grandest avenues in the city—that the house stands in the neighborhood of many principal merchants and capital stores—and also that it is very near the market, the propriety of a good inn in such a place will undoubtedly be admitted."[103] Whereas once taverns had housed a broad cross section of business activities within their walls, here was a tavern attempting to gain custom generated by business institutions whose very existence signified a fundamental dissatisfaction with tavern space.

The frustration Philadelphia's business community felt with the mores of tavern sociability was shared by some, but not all, of the taverngoing public. Men of varying levels of wealth and education contested the bour-

geois values enshrined in the design and use of Bradford's Old London Coffeehouse. As we have seen, Captain Ogle and men of his ilk made the crowd at the coffeehouse the butt of their revelry. Even drinkers who did not go so far as to beard the city's business community in its den were delighted to hear of Ogle's antics and put-downs and spread news of his japes around town. Men and women continued to masquerade, fight, drink to excess, and patronize taverns that sold no coffee in defiance of ever more confidently articulated "temperance" values. However, by the third quarter of the eighteenth century, it was becoming clear that distinct and fundamentally incompatible attitudes toward public behavior existed in Philadelphia. Some Philadelphians sought to abandon taverngoing altogether; many more chose where and with whom they drank with increasing care. Changing patterns of taverngoing threatened the economic viability of some public houses. Tavernkeepers responded in various ways. Josiah Davenport, for example, sought to woo customers who had abandoned the Bunch of Grapes by promising attentive service and good order on his premises. Other publicans booked novelties or special events in an attempt to draw in crowds. Still others attempted to follow William Bradford's lead by operating public houses that courted a part, rather than the whole, of the total taverngoing population. However, as long as the maximum retail price of drinks and services sold in taverns was set by the city's magistrates, publicans had to consider whether an exclusive public house could be made to pay. Establishments like Bradford's Old London Coffeehouse or the City Tavern, built by private subscription and opened in 1773, alienated a far greater number of Philadelphians than they attracted. The willingness of wealthy Philadelphians to subscribe funds to build a public house, as opposed to a meeting hall or private club, suggests that they continued to value speech and behavior in public. Nevertheless, the typical tavern assembly grew less heterogeneous in the final third of the eighteenth century, as "gentlemen" grew less willing to rub shoulders with artisans in the competitive, claustrophobic atmosphere previously typical of the city's taverns. By the eve of the Revolution, wealthy merchants usually drank in taverns of their own, in which the likes of shipyard workers were not welcome. This change in the way Philadelphians used public houses reflected, and to some extent promoted, changes in the very marrow of the city's cultural and political life.

4

"Of Great Presumption"

Public Houses, Public Culture, and the Political Life of Colonial Philadelphia

IN 1689 WILLIAM PENN WROTE TO THE provincial council of his fledging colony asking, "Whatever you do, I desire, beseech and charge you to avoid factions and parties, whisperings and reportings and all animosities, that putting your shoulder to ye public work, you may have the reward of good men and patriots."[1] He was too late. Almost from the moment the first Philadelphians stepped ashore, the city of brotherly love was embroiled in bitter factional disputes. These were reflected in, and to some degree prompted by, tavern talk. In 1683, for example, Nicholas More, president of the Free Society of Traders, took occasion in a tavern company to denounce the provincial council and assembly. More alleged that council and assembly were placing restrictions on the Society that contravened its charter and that as a result the entire colony would come to nothing. In his opinion the province's assembly and council deserved to be impeached, and would certainly be cursed by hundreds in England for their actions. As he intended, his words were overheard and reported to the provincial council. Brought before the council, More argued that he had spoken "rather by query than assertion." The councillors, however, found his "discourse . . . imprudent and unreasonable." He was let off with a warning not to repeat the offense.[2]

Other "whisperers" were not treated so leniently. In 1684 Thomas Hooton's public house was the setting for a meeting called by Anthony Weston. The meeting drew up a set of proposals that criticized Penn's plans for the development of Philadelphia. This meeting and the proposals it made profoundly angered Penn, who characterized them as being "of great presumption and contempt for this government and its authority." Weston was sentenced to three public floggings and all who had allegedly agreed with him were made to furnish bonds for their future good behavior.[3]

Although Penn championed freedom of conscience, "excessive" freedom of expression formed no part of his plan for the province. Pennsylvania was founded at a time when public speech in general, and tavern talk in particular, were viewed with suspicion and concern within the Anglo-American world. As Thomas Long reminded Englishmen in 1680, "We all know that murmurings were those winds which blew up and scattered those coals of jealous[y] which kept the whole nation in a flame twenty years . . . [ago and which] . . . now threaten a new conflagration. For as the learned Verulam observes, there is only this difference between seditious murmurings and seditious tumults, that the one is the Brother and the other the Sister."[4]

Long may have advised Englishmen to "meddle not with them that are given to change,"[5] but his advice was ignored. As Tim Harris has shown, the vibrant political culture of Restoration London was, from a Court perspective, "seditious" and profoundly feared.[6] A royal proclamation of 1672 noted an increase in "bold and licentious discourses" and argued that Britons had "assumed to themselves a liberty not only in coffeehouses but in other places and meetings both publi[c] and private to confuse and defame the proceedings of state by speaking evil of things they understand not."[7] The government contemplated the suppression of coffeehouses but in 1676 embarked on a policy of licensing public houses. In the case of coffeehouses, the licensee had to take an oath of allegiance and agree to "use his utmost endeavour to prevent and hinder all scandalous papers[,] books or libels concerning the government or the public ministers thereof from being brought into his house . . . and to prevent and hinder all and every person or persons from declaring uttering or divulging in his said house all manner of false and scandalous Reports of the government and ministers thereof."[8] It was in this climate that Penn drafted the laws governing public speech and behavior permissible in Pennsylvania. He stated explicitly that the laws "as to slanders, drunkenness, swearing, cursing, pride in apparel . . . shall be the same as in England [un]til altered by law in this province." Under Pennsylvania law it became a criminal offense to use a tavern to rail, scold, speak slightingly of a magistrate, utter "sedition," or spread rumors.[9]

For Penn and for Quaker idealists, false reports, tale telling, scolding, and the like were not only seditious but also sinful.[10] Those who persisted in telling tales and spreading rumors obstructed the object of achieving a broad reformation of morality within the holy experiment. And while Philadelphians might have enjoyed relating slanderous gossip, it did not follow that they enjoyed being the subject of rumor and tittle-tattle. For all these reasons the proposition that some restraint ought to be placed on speech and behavior in public enjoyed a measure of support and understanding in the province. There is something admirable about the serious attention Philadelphia's Quakers devoted to the question posed William Shewell: "If a false report be raised and spread abroad, received and entertained as a truth, being told so, and received so (as all false reports and tales are under the name of truth, which makes them the more mischievous) what course is best taken in such a case, that I may do all the right I can to the person concerned?"[11] However, Philadelphians were no better able to control the effects of their propensity for gossip, contention, and vituperation than their contemporaries elsewhere in the Anglo-American world. Indeed, despite prosecutions such as those brought against Nicholas More and Anthony Weston, a combination of factors ensured that Philadelphians enjoyed an uncommon freedom of expression.

As William Penn recognized, Pennsylvanians had come to America expecting more, not less, liberty.[12] While in theory it might have been possible to set strict limits on speech by drawing a distinction between freedom of conscience and freedom of expression, in practice, in the context of the religious and cultural diversity of Pennsylvania's burgeoning population, such a distinction proved untenable. Moreover, from the city's founding until the close of the French and Indian wars, Philadelphia was a city with a relatively even distribution of wealth, located within what many residents thought to be "the best poor man's country" yet settled. Many laborers made relatively good livings, and an ambitious artisan might rise to the status of master craftsman or merchant. The franchise was broader in Pennsylvania than in England or most of England's colonies. However, precisely because the city of Philadelphia flourished, Pennsylvania's governing bodies sought to limit its influence within provincial affairs by tightening franchise requirements for Philadelphians and by apportioning seats in the province's governing bodies without regard to the distribution of Pennsylvania's population.[13] Relative prosperity, coupled with threats to the city's voice in provincial affairs, encouraged Philadelphians to seek the fullest freedom of expression possible and militated against deferential social and political relations. Contemporary observers commented, not always favorably, on the climate of public expression that ensued. Gottlieb Mittelberger, for example, lamented the "excessive freedom" that made Philadelphia a paradise for artisans but a hell for officials and preachers. Jacob Duché thought that Philadelphians spoke and acted as though under the "immediate inspiration" of a singular "genius" of liberty.[14] Over time, the economic development of Philadelphia did generate a less equitable distribution of wealth and a self-conscious elite, but Philadelphia's emerging patriciate was never able to set firm boundaries of permissible public speech because divisions within, and between, the city's judicial, legislative, and social elites meant that no one group had the willpower or ability to significantly restrict the scope of expression. Notwithstanding early court actions, Quaker city fathers—heirs to a markedly anti-authoritarian tradition—were reluctant censors. They attempted to suppress only such "murmurings" as were, to them, particularly or egregiously seditious. They found that occasional prosecutions had a tendency to increase rather than diminish the incidence of "contemptuous" talk in taverns and other public places.

This chapter considers the links between the popularity of taverngoing and the conduct and content of political disputes in Philadelphia from first settlement until the eve of the Revolution. These links were forged in a climate of relatively free public expression. However, as modern Americans know only too well, a society in which individuals are free to speak their minds does not necessarily value such expression or find political significance in it. Moreover, even in the seventeenth-century city, there were places other than taverns where men gathered to discuss politics and religion. Nicholas More, Anthony Weston, and their friends and enemies could, and probably did, voice their opinions not only in taverns but also in meeting house and countinghouse, in letters, pamphlets, and private conversations. We therefore need to begin any investigation of the political influence of speech and action in taverns by asking why colonial Philadelphians believed that what they saw and heard in taverns was important.

The first half of this chapter analyzes the cultural assumptions colonial Philadelphians made about speech and behavior in taverns and other public places. Taverngoers paid extremely close attention to both their own speech and behavior and that of their drinking partners. They did so because they believed that the way a man spoke, behaved, and dressed presented vital clues as to his true character and worth. At the same time, Philadelphians believed that appearances could be deceptive. Just as seventeenth-century Calvinists believed that Satan sometimes assumed an innocent guise, so colonial taverngoers assumed that upstarts and tricksters sought to deceive the credulous. The great attraction of the tavern as a site of display and observation was that strangers and even long-time acquaintances might let slip an inadvertent comment or gesture indicative of their true character in exchanges conducted over drinks. If a man really was pious, learned, genteel, sinful, gauche, or crude, these characteristics would be revealed in his behavior among tavern company. However, the tavern setting magnified the tension that lay at the heart of Philadelphians' fascination with appearance. Abstract personal characteristics such as wit, gentility, or honesty lay in the eyes and ears of the beholder. What one man found funny or urbane, another found offensive or cynical. By whose standards should speech and behavior be judged? How could the man whose conversation was misjudged or misrepresented by tavern company achieve redress? In the singularly undeferential cultural climate that prevailed in colonial Philadelphia, these questions took on political connotations readily.

The assumption that every man possessed an opinion, and that each was as worthy of consideration as the next, held egalitarian implications that affronted the hierarchical organization of society and government. This raised inherently political questions. If laborers could not recognize gentility or learning when they saw it, why should their views on provincial affairs be afforded any weight? If, as many laborers believed, "haughty" gentlemen paid insufficient deference to the dignity of the laboring man in everyday encounters in taverns and other public places, was this not symptomatic of detestable and indefensible elitism in the councils of state? The second half of this chapter examines the ways in which speech and action in taverns not only reflected political debate originating in the formal spheres of government but also contributed to the form and content of such debate. I examine each of the major political crises in Pennsylvania's colonial history, arguing that, in each, the "small politics of everyday life" was conflated with the larger politics played out in the governing bodies of the province.

Within a climate of relatively free public expression, Philadelphians gathered in taverns to assess and judge men and their ideas, accepting that they, in turn, would be the subject of scrutiny. Taverngoers sought to form their judgments independently. As a result, the first two or three generations of Philadelphians fashioned from tavern talk and action a realm of discourse that existed outside the effective cultural control of both government and private or domestic authority. This realm was composed of private individuals who chose to assemble in taverns as self-consciously "public" figures. Within it, the taverngoer expressed a sense of citizenship and claimed the right to support or contest the pronouncements and predelictions of public government, free from that government's control and in the expectation that his opinions had a role in shaping government action.[15] In this way taverngoers contributed to the creation of a peculiarly "accessible" political culture in colonial Pennsylvania that had a marked influence on the conduct of politics in the province.

* * *

Philadelphia's public culture—that is, the cultural assumptions that governed the performance and interpretation of behavior in public in colonial Philadelphia—was formed, like a coral reef, from the accretion of continuing observations and judgments on the fit between private principles and public practice. Philadelphians, and their contemporaries elsewhere, believed that one's inner self, one's private or subjective identity, could be properly judged from, and ought properly to be displayed in, public behavior. As Robert Wiebe has argued, eighteenth-century Americans regarded character as perhaps their most precious commodity. What they strove to achieve was "a character"—as much the product of reputation as of self-fashioning—in which private principle was deemed to fit seamlessly with public practice.[16] In his *Autobiography* Benjamin Franklin showed how this could be done. Franklin described candidly how he came by a useful reputation for industry. It was his custom to stay late in his workshop, often working on projects for his own amusement but, nevertheless, engaged in toil "visible to our neighbors." One of these neighbors, Dr. Baird, was a member of a group Franklin identified as the "Merchant's-Every-night-Club." According to Franklin's account, Baird noticed Franklin at work at night when he returned from the club's meetings and each morning, as he went to his office, he saw Franklin at his bench. Baird brought these observations up with his fellow clubmen, presumably over punch at a tavern, and the club agreed that Franklin did indeed cut a most industrious figure. The result was that "credit and character" came Franklin's way.[17]

But as Franklin would have been among the first to admit, observations on the fit between principle and practice could have negative as well as positive outcomes. When, for example, Franklin sought to establish a joint venture with Hugh Meredith, it was threatened because their backers, who included Meredith's father, had on more than one occasion observed Meredith at tavern pursuits rather than at the workbench during the working day.[18] Philadelphians were as prepared to reprobate as they were to approbate on the basis of what they saw and heard of public behavior.

Philadelphians also had recourse to their public culture when assessing relationships between people of different backgrounds. They believed abstractions like "deference," "tolerance," "gentility," and "liberality" possessed an observable basis in behavior, and their public culture informed the expression and judgment of such qualities. One day Franklin was at work at Samuel Keimer's printing house when two "finely dressed" gentlemen called. They were the governor, Sir William Keith, and Colonel French. Keimer got himself ready to meet them. But as Franklin recalled in triumph: "The Governor enquired for me, came up, and with a condescension and politeness I had been quite unused to, made me many compliments . . . and would have me away with him to the tavern where he was going . . . to taste, as he said, some excellent Madeira. . . . Keimer stared like a pig poisoned."[19] Keith and Franklin both understood that they would be advertising a patronage relationship by sipping Madeira in public. By offering a drink, Keith was expressing a genteel liberality. Franklin, by accepting the offer, would be able to signify publicly his independence from Keimer.

Residents of the Quaker city shared an obsessive interest in posing questions of an individual's character by reference to his possessions, clothing, and appearance. If a man's neighbors possessed china bowls and silver spoons, could he remain in good standing with them if he in turn did not purchase such items? Benjamin Franklin's wife, Deborah, thought not.[20] If a man dressed in fine rather than in plain clothes, could he claim to be a pious Quaker? John Penn gave as one of his reasons for adopting the Anglican faith his frustration and impatience with "the little distinctions of dress" he associated with the Quakers.[21] During his travels, Alexander Hamilton, the doctor from Annapolis, witnessed an incident in which two Philadelphians were thrown off balance when they appeared at the dinner table wearing nightcaps, while the rest of the company wore wigs. The incident prompted Hamilton to reflect: "It is no mean jest that such worthless things as caps and wigs should disturb our tranquility and disorder our thoughts when we imagin[e] they are wor[n] out of season. I was my self very much in the same state of uneasiness with these Philadelphians, for I had got a great hole in the lappet of my coat, to hide which I employed so much of my thoughts in company that, for want of attention, I could not give a pertinent answer when I was spoke to."[22] Such description conveyed a sense of frustration—with which the reader was expected to empathize—at not having the means to present to the world a seamless fit between self and appearance. This frustration occasioned a prodigious expenditure of ink and paper on the production of grace literature in Philadelphia and the importation of yet more from Britain.[23]

Something like the full range of concerns contained within and generated by Philadelphia's public culture come together in Franklin's description of his first day in the city. Out of curiosity Franklin took up oars in the shallop that shuttled him ashore. Yet fear being thought poor, and cheap, led him to generously tip the boatmen. Franklin was "particular" in the details of what he was wearing and how he thought it would be perceived. His best clothes were at sea, so he stepped ashore wearing his working clothes. These were dirty from the journey. His pockets were stuffed with stockings and shirts. After a nap in the meeting house, Franklin met up with a Quaker whose "countenance I lik[e]d." The Quaker steered him away from the Three Mariners toward the "reputable" Crooked Billet. To Franklin's distress, the patrons of the Crooked Billet tavern quizzed him sharply on the assumption that he was a runaway servant.[24]

This account is built around an almost paranoid awareness of an ever present and deeply insightful public gaze. It also suggests that scrutiny of signifiers such as clothing preceded and perhaps preempted scrutiny of conduct and speech. His dirty clothes made the boatmen reluctant to accept his tip and led the company at the Crooked Billet to look askance at him. Yet Franklin himself paid equally close attention to the appearance of others. He waited to ask for advice on lodgings until he could question a man whose countenance indicated trustworthiness to him. At the end of a long and glittering career Franklin still felt compelled to set down the events of his first days in Philadelphia. He chose to do so in order that his readers might "compare such an unlikely beginning with the figure I have since made." Far from suggesting that appearances were of little importance if one's character was sound, Franklin's *Autobiography* suggests that a watching world will frequently misjudge inner character from outward appearance. In this sense the *Autobiography* reflects one of the dominant themes of Philadelphia's public culture, namely, that while outward appearances could provide important guides to inner character, they could also be deceptive.[25]

A contradiction lay at the very heart of Philadelphia's public culture. Philadelphians could agree that cultural rules governing public behavior existed, and that they ought to exist, but they could not agree on their precise nature or specific application. Although no one doubted that scrutiny of public behavior occurred, there was disagreement as to how accurate an instrument of assessment public scrutiny was or ought to be. This contradiction was felt most sharply within tavern companies. Precisely because they threw together men from all walks of life—in an atmosphere where liquor flowed freely and a man might, in his cups, let slip an indication of the true nature of the character that lay behind his public facade—taverns were the preeminent site of the scrutinizing public gaze. But "bowz'd" and "bur-dock'd" as they all too frequently were, taverngoers formulated and disseminated misjudgments and misapprehensions. Hence, through their actions tavern companies constantly brought up the issues of reputation, honor, and virtue that F. G. Bailey has usefully identified as constituting the "small politics" of everyday life.[26]

The inquisitiveness or, as some would have it, impertinence of tavern companies was widely remarked upon. As we saw in Chapter 3, Daniel Fisher was pressed to reveal his business by a fellow guest at the Indian King, Charlotte Brown's marital status was questioned by the crowd there, and Alexander Hamilton found himself being drawn out and sized up by the company he met at the Three Tuns. Hamilton concluded that Philadelphians "are inquisitive concerning strangers."[27] The manner in which Pennsylvanians handled such encounters reveals a consciousness of not only the small politics of respect and status but also larger political questions of authority and power. In November 1742, when the Reverend Henry Muhlenberg had been in the country for but a few days, he returned a horse to an inn in Philadelphia. "The innkeeper," Muhlenberg wrote, "took me into a room where were sitting a number of Englishmen, who put on airs of being men of condition. As soon as I came in, they asked me whether I was a Moravian, a Lutheran, a Calvinist or a Churchman. I gave them a reprimand and said they must learn better manners and not welcome strangers with such questions. They apologised."[28] Muhlenberg quickly formed the conclusion that the company he encountered was ill mannered and that they thereby forfeited any claim to his respect. He refused to specify the precise nature of his belief in order to preempt what he would have considered an improper critique of its content by men of lesser learning and lower status. At the same time, his refusal to bandy words with importunate Englishmen made a "higher" political point. German Lutherans in Pennsylvania were to be afforded the same civil and political rights claimed by Englishmen. Both Muhlenberg and his English tormentors understood that personal and provincial political themes were conflated in this encounter.

The tensions inherent in public encounters between men of widely varying political and religious views were not always so easily defused. Muhlenberg recalled an especially fraught confrontation on a packet-boat trip from New York to Philadelphia. In the safety of his journal he felt free to itemize the "dangerous company" he found on board. It consisted of "One, a daring fencing master, a ruined Irish nobleman who was an inveterate dueller. Two, the fencer's second. Three, a French gentleman who claimed to have been wrongly imprisoned in New York. Four, a gay peruke-maker. Five, an English female who has the outward appearance of piety but is probably a dangerous woman within. Six, a jovial young man whose ancestors were Swedes. Seven, I and Madame Koch together with her servants." On board the boat and at tavern stops along the way, this company, with the exception of its seventh component, sang, joked, and cursed, creating an uproar that reminded Muhlenberg of "Sodom and Gommorrah." Muhlenberg, acting on the assumption that his moral authority and Madame Koch's gentility would be compromised were he to allow this behavior to pass unchecked, remonstrated with the Irish dueler. The Irishman warned Muhlenberg, "do not act too pious." Muhlenberg replied, "There is no danger of our becoming too pious. But that you are godless is as clear as day." The dueler replied, "What right have you to give me orders you blackguard? Shut up with your crazy rubbish! I do not give a rap about God or the Bible or the King or the Pope. . . . Who are you anyway?"[29] Muhlenberg was a cross-grained man, unwilling to go along to get along. But he took the trouble to record this encounter in some detail because, as both his Irish tormentor and he recognized, at stake in this confrontation were inherently political issues involving both individual status and social authority. From Muhlenberg's point of view, his fellow passengers' behavior was symptomatic of the larger values of English society. Muhlenberg felt that if he could force the company to defer to him, he would not only score a small political point but also make a larger statement of values. He failed, not least because the company he encountered saw what he was about. For that reason Muhlenberg felt entirely justified in fashioning from criticism of an individual's behavior a critique of the culture he believed it represented.

Similar considerations, arising from an encounter with a barber who came to shave him in his room at the Three Tuns, hastened Alexander Hamilton's decision to leave Philadelphia. The barber "almost made me sick with his Irish brogue and stinking breath. He told me that he was very glad to see that I was after being of the right religion. I asked him how he came to know what religion I was of. 'Ohon! and sweet Jesus now!' said he, 'as if I had not seen your Honour at the Roman Catholic chapel coming upon Sunday last.' Then he ran out a blundering encomium concerning the Catholicks and their principles."[30] Hamilton was in fact a Presbyterian. From his point of view, the idea that a mere barber should dare to keep track of his movements, let alone beard him with unsolicited and misdirected opinions, was intolerable. Hamilton sought to avoid answering questions put to him by men he considered his social inferiors in order that he might affirm his gentility. Hamilton had grown up in Edinburgh and six years' residence in Annapolis, Maryland, had done little to diminish his sense that gentlemanly status conveyed privileges that Americans refused to honor.[31] It was precisely because Hamilton's wishes in matters arising from the small politics of everyday life were not consistently respected that he developed a bilious, conservative critique of American manners and government.

Almost inevitably, given the nature of the available record, we have a better sense of what self-consciously well-to-do men believed to be the larger political implications of behavior in companies of mixed social and cultural backgrounds than we have of the meanings laboring Philadelphians read into such encounters. It is difficult to tease out from the fragments of surviving evidence how plebeian Philadelphians felt and acted when confronted with what they regarded as unfair or unreasonable judgments based on scrutiny of their public speech and behavior. However, it seems that laboring Philadelphians, when in tavern company, contested their self-styled betters' claim to control the interpretation of public behavior. They regarded that claim as inherently unfair and also resented the injustice of some of the conclusions drawn from their speech and behavior by supposedly discerning gentlemen. Consider, for example, the basic thrust of advertisements warning against runaway servants, frauds, and tricksters. Such advertisements often described the suspect's conversation as well as his appearance. Philadelphians were warned to be on the lookout for John Jones, described as "a smooth tongued palavering fellow," and Henry Shafter, "an Englishman by birth, [who] has been on the expedition to Canada."[32] Employers placed such advertisements despite the fact that they believed laborers lacked discernment. They doubted that a plebeian tavern company could recognize gentility when they saw it, yet asked the same company to distinguish a "palavering" runaway servant from the gainfully employed but talkative workman in its midst.[33]

By offering rewards for the recapture of runaways, employers encouraged drinkers in taverns they themselves might have been reluctant to visit to suspect and even arrest strangers simply because of their speech or appearance. They were not particularly concerned about the damage a false accusation might do to the reputation and security of a talkative young man who happened to drink in a suspicious crowd. A poorly dressed former soldier of English birth, wrongly taken for a runaway because he happened to make a chance reference to Canada in a tavern, could expect little in the way of restitution upon discovery of the error. The indentured servant William Moraley, who was detained during the course of his travels on suspicion of being a runaway, understandably resented the experience. Yet when released from detention, a good breakfast and the satisfaction of picturing his captors' chagrin were the only sops offered to Moraley's injured pride. The experience of being falsely judged prompted the normally unreflective Moraley to broader, political speculations on the nature of servitude and justice, in much the same way as Alexander Hamilton's encounters with men he could conceive of only as Hogarthian grotesques promoted in his mind a larger political vision.[34]

Slander cases, which originated in small political concerns, could bring up larger political questions. The basis of slander presentments was that once formed, adverse public impressions and judgments were, like a stain, hard to remove. A good name could be restored if a court awarded the plaintiff in a slander case substantial damages. But while in theory a successful prosecution for slander or defamation held the prospect of satisfaction, in practice plaintiffs may have found that the operation of justice compounded the original slight. In 1695 a butcher, John Beacham, claimed £100 in damages for defamation he had allegedly received in the house of George Robeson. A jury found Robeson guilty of calling Beacham a "west country rogue," and of slandering Beacham by saying that he and his father were sheep-stealing rogues and dogs. Yet the magistrates awarded Beacham only one shilling in damages and the costs of the case. The value Beacham placed on his good name was not unusual. James Claypoole brought William Guest to court seeking £100 in damages for the slanderous and defamatory statement that Claypoole was a "knave and a rogue" uttered by Guest in William Frampton's public house. Claypoole received not a shilling.[35] We can imagine Beacham or Claypoole moaning and groaning about these judgments over a dram in a tavern. Had they done so, they would have risked a charge of railing against the magistracy. What kind of society, Beacham and Claypoole may well have asked, sanctioned such justice?

Tavern companies, the city's preeminent setting for the scrutiny of character, constantly generated issues within the small politics of everyday life. Was one's drinking partner affording one respect? Was tavern talk falsely impugning one's honor and reputation? These questions took on deeper significance because they engaged the broader, hierarchical organization of the city's social structure and political institutions. Did a barber have the right to insist on engaging a posturing swell in conversation? By what right did the few claim to privilege their assumptions about the practice and meaning of public behavior over those of the many? If a situation in which the good name of a butcher was measured in pennies while that of a merchant was measured in pounds were to pass unchallenged, would not the inevitable result be an abridgment of the rights and opportunities of the laboring man? Contests—whether between men from different or from similar social ranks—generated by the contradictions that lay at the heart of the city's public culture were not easily confined within the small politics of honor, reputation, and standing. They had the tendency to promote among those who were involved in them larger political considerations of justice and power.

At the same time, accustomed as they were to judging character from behavior, Philadelphians interpreted provincial policy by reference to the small politics of everyday life. Philadelphians believed that small politics shaped, and sometimes explained, high political policy. As a result, each of the great "high" political crises in the history of colonial Pennsylvania drew a measure of inspiration, and venom, from small political considerations. This tendency first became apparent during the political convulsions that followed George Keith's attack on the province's Quaker establishment.[36]

In 1689 Keith, a learned Quaker preacher who had been resident in America for four years, accepted an appointment as a tutor in Philadelphia's newly established Quaker school. In Keith's opinion Pennsylvania's Quakers were deviating from the discipline of the faith. Accordingly, he presented to the Philadelphia Yearly Meeting various proposals that would have had the effect of imparting an orthodoxy to the practice of Quaker belief in the province. Keith called for a "confession of faith" to be required of new members of the Society of Friends. He urged that deacons and elders be elected within each Monthly Meeting in order to counter the supposed influence of "raw and unseasoned" converts. Despite firm rebuffs, Keith continued to press his agenda and in 1691 was charged with heresy by the Yearly Meeting. Far from accepting this judgment, Keith in his turn alleged that the Meeting could no longer judge truth from error and had forfeited the right to discipline him. To Keith, Pennsylvania's Quakers were not simply lax; they were heretics who deserved epithets such as "silly fool," "idiot," "rotten ranter," "tyrant," "pope," and "heathen." He questioned their qualifications for government. Keith's Quaker opponents responded in kind, labeling Keith the "Brat of Babylon" and "Pope Primate of Pennsylvania."[37] Keith wore their scorn as a badge of honor. He prosecuted his polemic against Pennsylvanian Quakerism with a ferocity and vindictiveness his opponents felt honor-bound to match. This led to some bizarre and disturbing incidents. In 1693, for example, Keithians operating under cover of darkness attempted to erect a gallery from which they might exhort, or harangue, the worshipers inside the Philadelphia meeting house. Quakers attacked this structure with axes. Keithians responded by attempting to tear down the meeting house. The two sides eventually brawled in the street.[38]

The Keithian controversy did not originate in Philadelphia's public houses, and tavern companies may have expressed only limited interest in its theological particulars. However, Keith and his followers were able to present themselves, with a good deal of success, as champions of a "court of public opinion," which they cleverly idealized as the antithesis of an influence-ridden formal system of government. They argued that were the "facts" of Quaker hypocrisy and corruption to be laid before the public, Philadelphians rich or poor would see their Quaker leaders in their true light. They insisted that haughtiness displayed in personal relations infallibly betrayed oligarchic tendencies in the realm of provincial politics. By presenting their dispute with the Quaker establishment in these terms, Keithians sought to appeal to the interests and assumptions of the city's disgruntled tavern commentators. Hence the secular dimensions of the controversy reflected and drew upon the concerns of the city's public culture in a manner that demonstrates a conflation of the small politics of everyday life with larger provincial issues.

Precisely because they envisaged the merits of their case being judged by the public, Keithians tailored their critique of Quaker orthodoxy to take account of the key assumption of Philadelphia's public culture: that a man's private character could be judged from observation of his public behavior. Keith's contention was that Quaker worthies were improperly using the machinery of government to prevent the public from gauging the true extent of their corruption. This led them to conduct an extraordinarily vituperative pamphlet war. Samuel Jennings was a particular target of Keithian invective. A wealthy Quaker merchant, a magistrate, and a close friend of lieutenant governor Thomas Lloyd, Jennings struck Keithians as a man of "intolerable pride" who set himself "higher than the Lord Bishop of Delaware."[39] They set out to "humble" him on the grounds that "if [the Quakers] will stand upon the pinnacle above the level of the rest of mankind, or all who call themselves Christians, then they must expect to have their failings exposed."[40] George Keith reported with relish that this Quaker paragon was in fact a drunkard of such a pitiful stripe that when he talked up and lost a horse race with John Slocum, Slocum did not have the heart to claim as his prize the horse Jennings had wagered. Even worse, from Keith's perspective, Jennings had used his influence to have this story suppressed. According to Keith, a man named Peter Boss had been charged with uttering "scandalous, reproachful and malicious expressions" as a direct consequence of the fact that he had repeated the tale of Jennings's drunken wager in private letters as well as in public houses.[41] Keith alleged that a publican, John McComb, had been stripped of his tavern license for no other reason than that he had kept and distributed literature describing instances of misconduct such as Samuel Jennings's and additional attempts made by Quaker oligarchs to suppress free public discussion of their failings.[42] Keith used the prosecution of Peter Boss and John McComb to charge his Quaker opponents with corruption as well as hypocrisy. He told the public that the province's Quaker founding fathers were prepared to subvert good government to protect their reputations.

Court records confirm that Peter Boss was fined for railing against the magistracy but do not describe the testimony in the case. On Keith's account, Boss sought to defend himself against the charge by arguing that the allegedly scandalous expressions he uttered against Samuel Jennings were aimed at the man, not his office. The case was heard by Thomas Lloyd, who dismissed Boss's plea, ruling, according to Keith, "that [which] was spoke against Samuel Jennings, must needs relate to him as a magistrate, for take away Samuel Jennings, and where will the magistrate be?"[43] From Lloyd's perspective, "humbling" magistrates and elected officials undermined the public confidence upon which the workings of stable government were founded. It followed that public officials should be shielded from scurrilous assaults on their character lest, in the absence of proper deference to rank and office, the province be plunged into a "governmentish" anarchy. This position was arguably unjust in conception and certainly untenable in practice. The cultural context in which Philadelphians viewed public action and utterance assumed that even the meanest mechanic had a right and indeed a duty—which only an oligarch would seek to deny—to judge his neighbor's character from his behavior. Although we have no way of judging what conclusions "ordinary" Philadelphians—who, Keithian partisans believed, constituted the "court of public opinion" that would sit in judgment on Quaker public officials—drew from Keith's charges, the fact that Keith's position legitimated the public's right to judge its political leaders, by claiming that those leaders were denying the public the information and freedom it needed to form a judgment, must surely stand as the main factor explaining the longevity of the controversy. The public may not have believed any part of Keith's account of Samuel Jennings's debauched behavior. They may not have accepted Keith's account of the trial of Peter Boss. But they demanded the right to discuss these matters in tavern assemblies without fear of prosecution.

The manner in which the Keithian controversy was conducted illustrates three points. First, despite the existence of legislation limiting the exercise of free speech, and despite some sentiment in support of such laws, public speech in Philadelphia was, from an early date, free to a degree uncommon elsewhere in colonial America. Second, one can see in the Keithian controversy an idealization of the public realm. Keith sought public debate because he could not get his way in private forums (chiefly the Yearly Meeting). He thought he could win an appeal to the public by employing invective, disclosure, and demagoguery to encourage Philadelphians to judge their leaders' behavior in the same way they judged one another's. But if it was in Keith's interest to idealize the court of public opinion, this was because a large number of Philadelphians of all stripes did so already. Philadelphians could be moved to outrage by claims that their government was attempting to suppress the free flow of information upon which the public's ability to judge its leaders depended. This leads to a third point. Philadelphians might have regarded Keithian assaults on the reputation of their Quaker opponents as unfair or untrue. Nevertheless, "ordinary" citizens insisted that they were capable of judging their leaders and demanded the right to exercise their judgment in public discussion. These three factors continued to inform the cultural context within which the political history of the province was played out.

As Gary Nash has pointed out, elections in colonial Philadelphia did not typically generate much in the way of voter excitement.[44] A small number of families, mainly Quaker, controlled access to a provincial assembly in which the number of available seats consistently lagged behind the growth in the colony's population. Despite a broad franchise, the province's oligarchs united to prevent populist insurgents—"mushroom" politicians—from disturbing their control over the assembly and the powers that lay within its grant. Convinced that it alone could guard the colony's unique inheritance, the political establishment argued that laboring men should be "grateful," "quiet," and politically passive. But as Alan Tully has argued recently, although the formal structure of politics in colonial Pennsylvania remained stubbornly oligarchic, its political culture was singularly "accessible."[45] Pennsylvania's voters put up with an oligarchic system only so long as they retained access to the province's political leaders. It was in tavern discussion that Philadelphians' notions of "accessibility" found their fullest expression and development. Occasionally, indeed on more occasions than political leaders would have wished, Philadelphia's taverngoers could eavesdrop on their governors, or tax them man-to-man with their opinions. More generally, taverngoers insisted on the right to discuss the character of their leaders without deferring to their office. The very existence of a healthy public appetite for discussion of politicians and policies, and the turbulent tavern setting in which that appetite was assuaged, influenced the political history of the province by promoting among ordinary citizens a robustly populist political outlook. Despite the control provincial leaders exercised over the formal structures of provincial politics, they ignored the cultural assumptions Philadelphians made about the conduct of politics at their peril. Long after the details of George Keith's vendetta against the province's Quaker establishment had been forgotten, his tirades against the "haughtiness" of the province's political leaders continued to resonate with the electorate. As the political crises of the 1720s showed, when political leaders sought to deny or denigrate the public's right to judge its leaders and their policies, voters could become very excited indeed.

In the aftermath of the collapse of the South Sea Bubble, Pennsylvania was plunged into a depression exacerbated by a shortage of specie. Represented in the Pennsylvania assembly by Francis Rawle and David Lloyd, Philadelphia's artisans and middling merchants campaigned to secure a substantial issue of paper currency as a means of reviving internal trade and alleviating the depression. Philadelphia's wealthiest merchants, along with the bulk of the Quaker establishment, adopted a hard-money position. For reasons that cannot be considered entirely altruistic, Sir William Keith, then the lieutenant governor of Pennsylvania, threw his weight behind Lloyd and the assembly.[46] An initial issue of paper money did not resolve the crisis, and demands for a second occasioned an extremely vituperative campaign centered around conflicting interpretations of the frame of government of 1701. The niceties of Pennsylvania's frame of government probably held less interest for tavern commentators (and perhaps indeed for David Lloyd and Sir William Keith) than the rather more emotional questions of why and with what effect the provincial council, led by James Logan, was refusing to respond to laborers' demands.[47]

Anxious to establish himself as a champion of the common man, Sir William Keith developed innovative forms of political mobilization. In 1724 he formed two political clubs, the Gentleman's Club and the Tiff or Leather Apron Club, through which he doled out liquor and soothing words and gestures to the city's electorate. Sir William set out to present himself as a true English gentleman with a fine understanding of the proper relationship between rich and poor. In pamphlets and squibs, his partisans portrayed him as something of a saint, a man whose door was open to all, one who treated the meanest and the greatest in the city alike. The question of why, if

Keith was a friend of the common man, he organized separate clubs for his patrician and plebeian supporters was never asked because his opponents, James Logan and the provincial council, took dead aim at the right of the meanest sort of people to be involved in politics at all.

It was the pretentions to a formal political role claimed by "fireside champions" of butchers and bakers and candlestickmakers that enraged James Logan. If laborers were being pinched by recession, Logan asserted, the fault lay with their "luxury, Idleness, and Folly."[48] They should drink less, keep their minds off politics, and disabuse themselves of the notion that they had any right to criticize their rulers. He told John Wright that "we are now advancing to the highest pitch of scandal, when, by the vilest fiction and invented lies, in print and in forgeries exposed in public places, men's reputations are truly hunted down, and rendered the ridicule of the loosest spirits." Public discussion of Sir William Keith's polemics signified, he said, nothing more than extravagant licentiousness, consciously managed and fomented by organizations such as the Tiff Club.[49] Indeed, in tones that echoed Thomas Long's seventeenth-century warning to Englishmen against "murmuring," Logan warned that the involvement of laboring Philadelphians in matters they did not understand constituted an abuse of power. They had been deluded, Logan argued, into electing an assembly comparable to the Long Parliament and equally likely to produce lamentable excesses. Laboring men should be "grateful and quiet" and desist from "endeavouring to do better than very well."[50] Isaac Norris agreed. He thought Keith was bent on raising a "sinister army" of "new, vile people [who] may be truly called a mob."[51] This mob was being "halloo'd on" by what he referred to scornfully as a great number of "modern statesmen" who were making pernicious use of dramshops, alehouses, and taverns to draw the "lower orders" into the affairs of state.[52]

The form taken by an anti-proprietary pamphlet such as *The Observator's Trip to America* mirrored, even as it set out to guide, tavern talk. In this skillfully drawn squib, an English visitor to Pennsylvania is thrust into situations in which he comes to realize the true arrogance of the province's Quaker establishment. In a Philadelphia coffeehouse he overhears two fellows "prating" against Sir William Keith. He is puzzled, for he had thought Sir William was a friend of the common man. Later, in a tavern, he runs into a fellow Englishman named Roger and asks him how the people came to be so deluded. Roger, replying, "we are in a free English country with money in our pockets" and calling for "a mug of Mother Badcock's double beer" to prove it, regales the Observator with anti-Quaker feeling he has heard expressed in numerous tavern companies.[53]

That such conversations were actually taking place in Philadelphia's taverns was the presumption of the anonymous author of *A Dialogue Shewing What's Therein to Be Found*. This tirade against Sir William Keith railed at the "chatterings and vanity of our fireside champions, such as are generally . . . insignificant, or mere tools . . . who, over a dram or mug . . . make all the laws, and do all the business. And because they may have been genteelly bowed to, taken by the hand, or perhaps hugged and kissed, become inflated and imagine themselves of the greatest importance."[54] When, after the 1726 election, a mob set fire to the city's stocks and pillory, Patrick Gordon, the province's new lieutenant governor, called for a crackdown against public houses, which "too often prove the seminaries of vice."[55]

But by now the public's claim that its views, expressed preeminently in untrammeled tavern talk, had a role to play in the formal politics of the province was long-standing. The form and content of pamphlets such as *The Observator's Trip to America* or *A Dialogue Shewing What's Therein to Be Found* presumed the existence of a society in which men of different social and political backgrounds rubbed shoulders and talked politics in taverns. Meanwhile, an organization such as Sir William Keith's Tiff Club, as Keith's opponents realized with horror, recognised and sought to legitimate the presumptive right of "the public" to participate in high provincial politics.

Small political confrontations over drinks in the face-to-face world of the tavern changed the course of formal political events. A well-documented example concerns the assembly election of 1742, which was marked by a riot sparked by confrontations in and around Philadelphia's taverns. In 1739 the outbreak of war between Britain and Spain had reopened the question of what measures, if any, British colonies should adopt for their defense. In Pennsylvania, Governor Thomas proposed a scheme that would have drafted indentured servants into a militia for Philadelphia's defense. Quaker assemblymen, acting out of a mixture of pacifist principle and economic self-interest, stymied Thomas's attempt. The remnants of the Proprietary party, including Governor Thomas, most of the provincial council, and many Philadelphians with maritime connections, reacted angrily. The assembly elections of 1742 were particularly closely contested as a coalition favoring the creation of a militia sought to oust Quaker assemblymen. Partisans of Thomas' position circulated rumors that Quaker legislators were planning to allow hundreds of unnaturalized Germans to vote on behalf of their interest. The assemblymen responded in kind, spreading it about that the city recorder, William Allen, planned to unleash hundreds of sailors on the polling place on behalf of the Proprietary interest.[56]

The most energetic supporter of the assembly's position on election day was Israel Pemberton, Jr. At the time Pemberton was only twenty-four years old, but he demonstrated a well-matured sanctimony on polling day that antagonized many. On the morning of the election, three groups of sailors were discovered roaming the streets of Philadelphia. The immediate reaction of Pemberton and other panicked Quaker leaders was to demand that the mayor, Clement Plumstead, and William Allen personally confront the sailors. Mayor Plumstead, when roused from his bed by anxious Quakers, refused to break up a gathering of sailors saying: "Would you have me commit them on suspicion? They have as much right to be near the election as the Dutchmen you had last night at Reese Meredith's [the George tavern]."[57] Pemberton had greater success with William Allen, persuading him to confront one of the groups of sailors. Allen told the sailors to keep away from the election. They replied that they were taking advantage of a holiday given them by their captain and had no intention of disturbing the polling place. Allen accepted this assurance. But Pemberton was not placated, and he followed the sailors to Masters' Wharf. Here they hailed their mates on Captain Tough's ship *Industry*, at anchor in the river. Pemberton stepped forward to "caution" them. His presumption inflamed the sailors. Some shouted, "by God we will kill Pemberton." When the group began arming themselves with barrel staves from Nathaniel Allen's cooper's yard, Pemberton fled.[58] During this confrontation a certain Captain Mitchell emerged as the sailors' spokesman, and with Mitchell at their head the sailors marched back into town. They gathered at the Indian King. Here Thomas Lloyd heard Mitchell preparing the group for a confrontation at the polls by buying drinks and shouting, "every man his dram."[59]

Once again Pemberton pestered and harried the group. On James Morris's account Pemberton, joined by Thomas Lloyd, waded into the Indian King's crowded bar room to tell Mitchell that it was beneath his station to drink with sailors.[60] Exasperated, Mitchell demanded, "Damn You, what do you want with me?" Pemberton wanted Mitchell to disperse his men or run the risk of committal. Reaching for a cudgel, Mitchell shouted, "Damn You, commit me!"[61] Pemberton retreated but sought out the keeper of the Indian King, Peter Robinson, and told him to stop serving the sailors liquor as they appeared too "heated." Robinson told Pemberton that he ran a public house and would serve whomsoever he pleased, proving the point by presenting Captain Mitchell with a large glass of rum.[62] Once again Pemberton fled. Mitchell caught up with Pemberton later in the day, at which time the two exchanged heated insults and, finally, blows.[63] Later, at the city's polling station, windows were smashed, bricks and chairs thrown, heads broken, and fifty-four arrests made.[64]

At least one contemporary observer believed that this rioting had been sparked by small political considerations of respect, deference, and bravery. Joseph Turner testified that Israel Pemberton's haughty manner with Mitchell "had in a great manner occasioned the ensuing disorders of the day."[65] Whether by accident or design, Pemberton's charges—that Mitchell was engaged in demagoguery and that he should refrain from treating the sailors as equals or lose his status as a gentleman—were equally irritating to Mitchell and the sailors with whom he drank. As a ship's captain, Mitchell had obvious qualifications to lead a "parcell" of sailors, and in his actions he showed a fine understanding of what the men expected from what one of them described as a "frolic." They marched to the best tavern in town and Mitchell treated them to round after round of drinks. The style and tone of Pemberton's admonitions—the suspicion and contempt with which he viewed these specimens of the "lower orders" and those who associated with them—helped set the sailors against Pemberton and the assembly interest. Pemberton treated them as a brutish, unreasoning mob, whereas Captain Mitchell treated them as a gentleman should. Mitchell lost his temper with Pemberton for similar reasons: Pemberton was unjustly concluding from Mitchell's actions—drinking with a gang of sailors—that the assurances Mitchell had given William Allen counted for naught. Finally, of course, in the background, counting his takings as the dispute unfolded, stood Peter Robinson, keeper of the Indian King. As Robinson reminded the Quaker scion, taverns were businesses and he would serve whom he pleased.

Despite subsequent attempts by Quaker assemblymen to blame the day's events on the actions of a drunken and irrational mob of sailors, not all who came ashore took part in the riot. The crew of the *Industry*, for example, although doubtless excited by the appeals of their mates, were kept out of the riot by the actions of their captain. Captain Tough let his men leave the ship on condition that they accompanied him to the Turk's Head tavern. There, undisturbed by Israel Pemberton, captain and crew spent the day drinking peacefully. Moreover, even those sailors who menaced the court-house polling station could be dissuaded from violence by man-to-man appeals. Although he had been angered by the manner and implication of Pemberton's pleas that he "do something," William Allen did effectively interpose his authority at the courthouse. He waded into a group of sailors who were planning to break into the polling station and told them directly that they were a "parcel of villains." A "squat, full-faced, pock-fretten man" shouted, "Let's give Mr. Allen a Whorrah." Allen told them he didn't want any of their "Huzzas" and told the sailors to disperse.[66] They slunk away.

The events of the day hung on the conduct and outcome of such small political dramas. Crucially, William Allen, Captain Mitchell, and Captain Tough, by drinking with the sailors or arguing with them at the risk of a "whorrah," treated the sailors in ways that suggested some measure of respect for their feelings. The merchants James Morris, and John Bringhurst, by treating laborers like the cooper, Wight Massey, to drinks, showed a similar deference to the sensibilities of the plebeian elector.[67] In contrast, Israel Pemberton's actions were, as eyewitness Joseph Turner noted, inflammatory precisely because they nakedly suggested that he believed he had a right to expect deference from a "parcel" of sailors, their self-styled leader, and the tavernkeepers who humored them.[68] Many eyewitnesses believed that Pemberton, and other partisans of the assembly position, had simply not earned the right to deference. Richard Peters, an opponent of the assembly's position, penned a scornful account of the day's riot in which he alleged that "several magnanimous heroes" appeared from hiding only once order had been restored. "Young Israel Pemberton in particular," Peters continued, "ventured out of the court house chimney; and with him Isaac Griffiths, Samuel Norris and other young men of that stamp . . . [to help] drag the sailors to prison. To be sure [the sailors] deserved no pity; but to see those wretches, men of remarkable pusillanimity, lording it over the journeymen, who were pinioned and in the custody of Constables who called their victims by the most vile names and beat them unmercifully, there was no man but what thought worse of Israel and his followers than of the rioters."[69]

As we have seen, the course of everyday tavern encounters in Philadelphia regularly provoked confrontations such as that between Israel Pemberton and Captain Mitchell in which both participants and observers sought to establish and assess honor, respect, and reputation. Patrician and plebeian, Quaker and Presbyterian, stranger and local alike read a wealth of meaning into public action and utterance. Yet, at the same time, Philadelphians were conscious of the fact that some men sought to dissimulate. All agreed that behavior and speech indicated character, but they divided on the question of who was the best judge of behavior. Both the appetite Philadelphians possessed for judging behavior and the terms upon which they made their assessment therefore carried an enormous potential to generate conflict. Where such conflict erupted, as, for example, when a young pup like Israel Pemberton asserted that it was ungentlemanly to consort with sailors, the small politics of character—the disrespect this showed to Mitchell and his men—was conflated with the larger politics of the province. To Mitchell's way of thinking, Pemberton's behavior was not simply disrespectful but symptomatic of the larger political values and outlook of the Quaker establishment.

Of course most encounters between patrician and plebeian, German and Briton did not end in fistfights or court cases, let alone contested elections. As we saw in Chapter 3, Philadelphians developed a various practices through which they could express their willingness, especially in tavern company, to agree to disagree. Alexander Hamilton sometimes kept his own counsel in taverns, and in time even the Reverend Henry Muhlenberg learned to refrain from criticizing all but the most vexatious behavior he encountered in the course of his ministry. Laborers in Philadelphia sometimes chose to defer to leaders—for example, by joining organizations such as Sir William Keith's Tiff Club—if the terms offered acknowledged their sense of worth. Frolicking sailors accepted a warning from William Allen but ignored the threats of Israel Pemberton because Allen confronted them directly, acknowledging their sense of how relations between men of different classes ought to be conducted. The various accommodations by which Philadelphians avoided living in a state of perpetual conflict with their neighbors created a unique political culture. Philadelphians demanded the right both to judge their political leaders and to confront them directly when they felt their interests were being ignored. It was in tavern companies that the "governmentishness" of Pennsylvania's mixed and multitudinous population found its fullest—and often its ugliest—expression.

We might regard the proposition that the public has a right to judge as well as elect their political leaders as laudable, but much about the application of this principle in colonial Philadelphia was unpleasant and destructive. A polity in which Keithians championed the rights of the public by means of vicious ad hominem campaigns as manipulative as the oligarchic practices they sought to expose and destroy might be characterized as flawed. A polity in which Quakers who opposed a militia on principle found their arguments dismissed by proprietary opponents as symptomatic of personal cowardice or hypocrisy could be said to have possessed an impoverished vocabulary of political debate. Many of his contemporaries would have agreed with Gottlieb Mittelberger's claim that Pennsylvania was an absolute hell for elected officials even if it was a paradise for laborers. The problem was that for much of the colonial era many men outside the charmed circle of Pennsylvanian officeholders, especially in the under-represented city of Philadelphia, regarded their robustly undeferential political culture as a source of civic pride. Although they may have chosen to use it in negative and vicious campaigning, Philadelphians enjoyed a singular freedom of political expression and uncommon access to their political leaders.

Pennsylvania's officeholders were never comfortable with the populist assumptions of the province's political culture. During the Keithian controversy Thomas Lloyd had advanced the proposition that if the public retained an unabridged entitlement to speculate on the personal character of provincial officials the public interest would be damaged by a decline in respect for authority and an increase in malicious and atavistic gossip. Later James Logan made the point that tavern pundits, far from forming their opinions after independent reflection, were in fact "halloo'd on" by "fireside champions." To the ordinary taverngoer these positions smacked of patrician contempt for plebeian intelligence and assertiveness. Israel Pemberton, Jr., suffered during the 1742 election riot for making explicit what laboring men took to be implicit in official critiques of tavern discourse. However, although some well-to-do Philadelphians concluded that Pemberton brought a beating upon himself, there was by midcentury a growing sense among provincial leaders that the high politics of the province ought not to be conducted within, or with reference to, the personal and passionate realm of the tavern.

The extent to which tavern companies arrived independently at opinions that had claims on the attention of provincial officials became an issue in the last great political crisis of the provincial era. The 1764 election, which came hard on the heels of the Paxton Boy's march from the backcountry to the outskirts of Philadelphia, was the most hotly contested in the history of the colonial assembly. Benjamin Franklin and Joseph Galloway led a coalition of interests that sought, for various reasons, to establish Pennsylvania as a royal colony. As elections approached, Franklin and Galloway employed time-honored tactics to muster support for their attack on proprietary government. They kept open house at a Philadelphia tavern. There, over drinks, the merchant Thomas Wharton was seen denouncing proprietary government in the company of "one Knowles, a barber."[70] William Franklin, governor of New Jersey, came over to a Germantown tavern to dole out drinks to supporters of his father's "Old Ticket." John Penn wondered, "is this conduct becoming a King's Governor?"[71] The question carried force because Old

Ticket partisans employed personalized and demotic insults, as well as arguments from principle, to attack the proprietary interest and its supporters. Isaac Hunt, for example, coined the term "Piss-brute-tarian" to describe the Penn family's chief section of support within the electorate.[72] Not surprisingly, Franklin and Galloway's opponents responded in kind. The Philadelphia merchant Samuel Purviance, Jr., a Presbyterian, organized a "New Ticket" to contest Franklin and Galloway's scheme to transform Pennsylvania into a royal colony. New Ticket partisans circulated ad hominem attacks on Franklin and Galloway, on the grounds that if the leaders of the Old Ticket were not reelected "the rest would be like a body without a head" and the campaign for royal government would be stymied.[73]

As in the Keithian controversy of the 1690s, the assumption behind venomous election pamphlets such as *An Answer to the Plot* was that "the public," those voters both parties tried to woo through treating sessions held in public houses, had a right, and something of an obligation, to judge the nature of an abstract proposal, such as changing the basis of provincial government, by reference to the personal character of those who either supported or opposed it. Hugh Williamson was the New Ticket's most effective hack propagandist. From his point of view, lines of doggerel that mirrored, and attempted to prompt, tavern humor made a political as well as a personal point:

F——n, tho' plagu'd with fumbling Age,
Needs nothing to excite him.
But is too ready to engage
When younger Arms invite him.[74]

Williamson would have claimed that it was in the public's interest to know that Franklin had an amorous nature, stole other scientists' discoveries and fathered illegitimate children, or that Galloway was a haughty, ambitious office seeker.[75] Apprised of this "information," the public would come to the correct verdict on Franklin and Galloway's plans. Given this climate of debate, it was no easier in the 1760s than in the 1690s for those politicians who, like John Dickinson, argued that state policy should be judged on its merit alone, to separate the politics of personal reputation from the politics of provincial affairs. In the run up to the 1764 election Dickinson and Galloway challenged one another's integrity in speeches before the Pennsylvania assembly and ultimately traded punches in the street outside.[76]

By 1764, on the eve of the transformation that would be wrought in

THE PAXTON EXPEDITION. Inscribed to the Author of the FARCE, by HD.

Henry Dawkins. *The Paxton Expedition. Inscribed to the Author of the Farce.* Cartoon. Philadelphia. 1764. Library Company of Philadelphia. In 1763 backcountry settlers in Paxton and Donegal attacked peaceful Conestoga Indians resident in Lancaster County, Pennsylvania. When the Pennsylvania assembly ordered the ringleaders of the violence arrested, an armed mob (the Paxton Boys) marched east on Philadelphia to demand that Quaker assemblymen offer more support to white settlers in backcountry regions.

Pennsylvania's politics by the questions raised by British imperial initiatives, Philadelphia's singularly accessible political culture threatened to create a style of electioneering that, to many contemporaries, replicated the worst features of British practice. Philadelphia was developing an embryonic Grub Street, its voters were being wooed with treats of liquor and at all levels of political involvement a thorough-going conflation of the small politics of honor, reputation, and character with the large politics of state policy could be observed. Commenting on the conduct of the 1764 election, Benjamin Newcomb has observed, "it was a great loss to colonial American history that no Hogarth was available to paint the royal governor of New Jersey . . . passing out punch and beer to thirsty German 'boors'" in a Germantown tavern.[77] In fact, unlike any other election campaign in the history of colonial Philadelphia, that of 1764 did inspire prints in the Hogarthian spirit. In these and other commentaries on developments in electioneering, the electorate's judgment and the role of drink and of tavern treating in forming their judgment were viewed with a skeptical eye.

In 1764 Henry Dawkins published in Philadelphia *The Paxton Expedition: Inscribed to the Author of the Farce.*[78] Here Dawkins depicted the chaos witnessed in Philadelphia as the authorities tried to assemble a force to repel the Paxton Boys in 1763. The print favored Franklin and Galloway's Old Ticket in the 1764 election by contrasting Franklin's success in brokering a peaceful settlement of the crisis with the inept preparation made by proprietary officials and assemblymen. In the top left-hand corner of the print, cowardly soldiers call for grog from a passing rum vendor. Elsewhere, bemused citizens, drawn from across the city's class spectrum, witness and pass comment on instances of hubris and personal cowardice. *The Election Medley*, a cartoon published in 1764, presents a darker view of electioneering. In the foreground, slightly to the right of center, a diabolic figure asks a gentleman, "How goes matters now?" The cartoon answers this question by depicting a group of White Oaks, highly skilled and comparatively wealthy ships' carpenters who supported Franklin and the Old Ticket, passing out preprinted ballot papers to a group of bovine German voters. A Presbyterian minister at the foot of the steps offers forlornly "Saving Grace for a Vote." Elsewhere in the cartoon, men clustered in conversation betray their principles in favor of party. In the center a magistrate demands of a deferential figure, "Your vote, or lose your license." The man, presumably a publican, answers, "Interest before honour."[79]

Despite the fact that he involved his son William in time-honored tavern treating and political mobilization, Benjamin Franklin shared Henry

THE ELECTION A MEDLEY. *Humbly Inscrib'd to Squire Lilliput Professor of Scurrility.*

Henry Dawkins. *The Election Medley,* detail. Broadside. Philadelphia. 1764. Library Company of Philadelphia. Dawkins depicts Philadelphia voters participating in an assembly election.

Dawkins's sense that it was not in the province's best interest for tavern companies to exert so great an influence on the conduct and content of political debate as that observed in the 1764 election. In the run up to that election Franklin began to develop a line of argument that ultimately drove a wedge between Philadelphia's tavern culture and Pennsylvania's political culture. Franklin blamed the number and poor quality of taverns in Pennsylvania on government corruption. He charged that "Many bills have been presented to late Governors to lessen the number, and to regulate those nurseries of idleness and debauchery, but without success, from whence it seems evident, that so long as the Proprietaries are interested in our ruin, ruined we must be: for no deputy [governor] will dare to regulate this mischief because it will lessen the revenue; nor accept a compensation for this revenue, as it will affect his successor; nor even accept a greater annuity, because, it may in time, increase into a higher sum."[80] Charles Thomson agreed. He laid debauchery, enervation, and business failures brought on by a shortage of specie at the door of the tavern and backed Franklin's campaign to limit their number. In classical republican rhetoric Thomson asked Franklin to remember the story of the way in which Cyrus "took to break the spirit and soften the war-like disposition of the Lydians and render them the most abject slaves by erecting bagnios and public inns. . . . I will not say [that this] is the design of our Great Ones. But it is true that in almost every tavernkeeper the Proprietors have a warm advocate and the more effeminate and debauched the people are, the more they are fitted for an absolute and tyrannical government."[81] If, as Franklin and Thomson argued, licensing policy was corrupt, then it followed that the views of taverngoers could be discounted because they were poisoned at source. Moreover, if an oligarchic proprietor had poisoned the well of public opinion, then the views of those men who did not form their political opinions in beery, face-to-face tavern contests but chose instead more rational and "independent" assemblies—for example, William Bradford's Old London Coffeehouse and Merchant's Exchange—might be said to be worthy of special consideration.

Yet, despite evidence of a growing sense that electioneering and political mobilization ought to be distanced from the demotic language and personal antagonism associated with the tavern setting, the practical business of politics continued to retain strong links with the tavern. For example, in 1765 an unknown artist, in all likelihood Henry Dawkins, *A New Song Suitable to the Season, to the Tune of "Good English Beer"* on behalf of the Old Ticket.[82] This broadside reproduced, under an illustration of well-to-do

[Henry Dawkins?] *A New Song Suitable to the Season, to the Tune of "Good English Beer."* Broadside Ballad. Philadelphia. 1765. Library Company of Philadelphia. The punch-drinking gentlemen proclaim their support for the Old Ticket. To the right, a slave boy, whose speech is rendered in patois, appears to be crying, "This is fine fun, God bless [the] Old Ticket." To the left a devil declares, "These fellows are too honest for me," and indicates his support for "McMurder" (the predominantly Presbyterian New Ticket). By 1765 Pennsylvania's political culture had developed an uncompromisingly partisan style which led factional leaders and critical observers to seek to detach political discussion and mobilization from the tavern milieu even as they continued to use it to canvass for support, treat voters, and organize demonstrations.

Philadelphians offering "huzzas" for the Old Ticket over drinks (and a diabolic figure indicating his support for the mainly Presbyterian New Ticket), an electioneering song whose chorus ran:

> Then, to them Crown our Bowls,
> Our Plenteous Brown Bowls;
> And toss them of[f] Clever; to all true British Souls,
> to all true White Oaks Souls [and] Old Ticket, Old Ticket for ever
> Huzza Old Ticket, Huzza Old Ticket.

The song's reference to the White Oaks points to one of the peculiarities of Pennsylvania's political alignments in the waning years of proprietary government. In the decade preceding independence many well-to-do Philadelphians displayed increasing impatience with the accustomed mores of tavern sociability and began to patronize exclusive establishments such as William Bradford's Old London Coffeehouse and the City Tavern in which even wealthy laborers were not especially welcome. At the same time, and for similar reasons, political leaders and observers critical of Pennsylvania's accessible political culture began to consider how they might detach political discussion and mobilization from the tavern milieu. Yet the collapse of the movement for royal government, coupled with the crisis provoked by the Stamp Act, produced a peculiar political climate in which political leaders reached out for the support of Philadelphia tavern companies such as the White Oaks even as they privately doubted the propriety of such political organization.

In the immediate aftermath of the Stamp Act crisis, the leaders of each of Pennsylvania's three main political groupings were, for different reasons, seeking to build in Philadelphia alliances that cut across divisions of wealth and status. The coalition through which Benjamin Franklin, Joseph Galloway, and Charles Thomson had orchestrated their campaign to bring royal government to Pennsylvania had been discredited and divided by its initial support for the Stamp Act. Nevertheless, the remnants of the coalition, convinced that they might yet replace proprietary with royal government, pursued what James Hutson has called a "politics of ingratiation." The guiding spirits of this faction, concerned to avoid offending British ministers, reached out to organizations of workingmen such as the Hearts of Oak and White Oaks in an attempt to suppress popular agitation against British measures. Meanwhile, assemblymen and councillors wanting to preserve proprietary rule sought to appeal to the loyalties of laboring Philadelphians in order that they might control and limit demonstrations liable to give offense to Parliament and thereby ward off parliamentary scrutiny of the viability of continued proprietary rule. Finally, a third grouping—which Hutson labels the "independents"—cultivated the support of Philadelphia's laborers to make its opposition to measures of the ministry meaningful.[83] As the imperial relationship began to founder, considerations of political strategy gave the leaders of each of Pennsylvania's political factions a vested interest in attempting to control and channel the activities of at least some politically conscious artisanal tavern companies.

The events following the announcement in Philadelphia of the fall of Grenville's ministry illustrate the influence of tavern gatherings on the practical conduct of politics and the day-to-day business of organizing and sustaining the political activity that eventually led to independence. Samuel Wharton told Franklin that when news of the Grenville ministry's fall reached Philadelphia, Chief Justice William Allen hurried to Bradford's Old London Coffeehouse to applaud one of the happiest events in the history of America. The day was thereafter spent "in congratulations on a revolution." Franklin's opponents in the proprietary interest celebrated with a grand dinner at the coffeehouse. While the gentlemen dined inside, the lower orders were treated to tubs of grog outside.[84] A mob gathered and talked up the project of razing the houses of Franklin and Galloway in retribution for their initial support of the hated Stamp Act. As Wharton recalled, "this behavior aroused our friends, [the White Oaks] who met at Widow Gray's tavern" and "associated for the preservation of peace in the city." Once it became clear that the White Oaks were ready to defend Franklin's house, "the abettors to the pulling down of our houses began to dread that the same might be executed upon theirs."[85] Trouble continued to rumble through the city. In a subsequent disturbance John Hughes (Franklin's nominee for the post of collector of the stamp duty in Philadelphia) was hanged in effigy, and a mob threatened to destroy his house. Joseph Galloway spent that night at the Indian King tavern, where, as he told William Franklin, "I had a full opportunity of advising our friends and there proposed a Union for the preservation of the peace of the city, several of the White Oaks and the Hearts of Oak were there—they all declared they would be ready."[86]

By using tavern companies like the White Oaks and the Hearts of Oak to manage political developments, men like Galloway invested the political beliefs expressed by laborers gathered in taverns with a measure of legitimacy. Yet Galloway, and indeed William Franklin, doubted that tavern drinkers expressed any political opinion worthy of note precisely because, in successive election campaigns, they had successfully employed treats of liquor and scurrilous election pamphlets to shape the will of "ordinary" men they regarded as being fundamentally credulous. Benjamin Franklin and Charles Thomson were equally familiar with the tricks of the electioneering trade. They too began to doubt that drinkers in taverns expressed any opinions other than those planted artfully by incendiaries, demagogues, or a designing proprietary interest. Yet, like their opponents, the leaders of the coalition that would bring independence to the city of Philadelphia continued to rely on tavern companies to supply support for their cause.

The growing sense that the tavern was an inappropriate and even pernicious setting for political discussion and action (a sense inspired by changing patterns of taverngoing as well as by developments in provincial and imperial politics) had a profound effect on the conduct of the American Revolution in Philadelphia. Yet even after independence Philadelphia's taverngoers continued to use the peculiar space of the public house to give voice to political prejudices and to plan and undertake political actions. They continued to believe that action and speech in the public realm were indicative of man's inner character. The revolutionary generation's almost obsessive concern with identifying and promoting virtue, while discovering and eradicating corruption, built upon a conflation between the small politics of everyday life and the large politics of province and empire that had been established within years of the city's founding almost a century earlier. Moreover, in the revolutionary era laborers and artisans continued to assert their right to speak to religious and political issues without deferring to social or political authority. A European visitor to Philadelphia in 1783 commented: "People think, act, and speak here as it prompts them; the poorest day-laborer on the bank of the Delaware holds it his right to advance his opinion, in religious as well as political matters, with as much freedom as the gentleman."[87] Nevertheless, by the close of the eighteenth century, tavern talk—the talk of the town—stood removed from the formal workings of government. Despite the fact that Philadelphians of all social classes continued to discuss politics in public settings and to read political significance into public behavior and speech, the political culture of the newly independent democratic state was less accessible than that of the oligarchic proprietary colony. By the 1780s alienated militiamen were reduced to demonstrating outside exclusive sites like the City Tavern, in the hopes of exerting a direct influence over their rulers that earlier generations of laboring men had claimed as their right in intensely personal and sometimes drunken encounters inside taverns that typically served mixed clienteles. In short, during the final third of the eighteenth century, the work and decision making of governmental bodies grew ever more distant from that previous locus of public discussion in Philadelphia—the tavern—even as those bodies made ever more elegant claims to be agencies constituted of, by, and for the people.

5
"Councils of State"

Philadelphia's Taverns and the American Revolution

IN THE FINAL THIRD OF THE EIGHTEENTH century, Philadelphians of all ranks and backgrounds grew disillusioned with the mixed company previously typical of their city's taverns. Although taverngoing retained its popularity, and although Philadelphians continued to discern and contest social and political meaning in public speech and action, taverngoers expressed through their custom an increasing preference for sociability among men of similar background and opinion. At the same time, sections of the taverngoing public demanded the more efficient provision of specific services. The city's tavernkeepers attempted to respond to both of these developments.

Travelers' demands for ever safer and more reliable stage and packet-boat services led some publicans to advertise their willingness to transport passengers and luggage personally. A handful of public houses became the termini for regularly scheduled stage services. In 1764, for example, John Buckingham, keeper of the Coach and Horses on Third Street, advised "all gentlemen and ladies that incline to travel by land rather than by water" that he ran a coach service to Bordentown, New Jersey.[1] By 1794 four coach and boat lines conducted daily services from Philadelphia to New York and the city was served by two triweekly services to Baltimore, a biweekly departure to Lancaster, and weekly services to Reading and Harrisburg.[2] The George on Arch Street, one of the city's oldest taverns, became particularly associated with stagecoach business. In 1789 its keeper, John Inskeep, brokered the amalgamation of two competing lines serving New York.[3] Anthony Fortune was one of many licensees who made a bid for the custom of the city's resident elite. In 1771 he advised the public that his Three Tuns now had a "long room" suitable for the reception of juries, or any set of "gentlemen," to the number of sixty or more, on "private or public" business.[4]

The Old Plough Tavern. C. 1885. The Free Library of Philadelphia. This tavern, on the south side of Pine and the east side of Second Street, was founded in the third quarter of the eighteenth century. Shown on the right are the tavern's stables and the door leading into the tavern's public rooms. The sheds of the city's second market, established in 1742, are visible through the archway. The Plough competed for custom with the Pennsylvania Farmer at Second and Lombard Streets. Both taverns, as their names suggest, wooed farmers who came to town to trade at the city's new market.

However, before the collapse soon after 1778 of controls on the maximum price of goods and services sold in taverns, the willingness of self-consciously respectable members of the city's mercantile and legal elites to subscribe funds to build taverns of "their own" was the most visible manifestation of a growing appetite for selective and exclusive forms of sociability shared by patrician and plebeian alike.[5] The most influential house built by private subscription was the City Tavern, founded in 1773 at a cost of more than £3,000.[6] An equally significant although less costly indicator of change in the tavern trade was the new sign outside a modest tavern on Sixth Street. The sign of the Four Alls depicted four figures: a king on the steps of his palace and the motto "I govern all"; a general in full dress, "I fight for all"; a minister, "I pray for all"; and a laborer, "I pay for all."[7] The tavern's sign announced that what "A Lover of Liberty" dubbed the "impudence" of men who believed that "mechanics were of no consequence" would not be tolerated inside.[8]

The first half of this chapter describes and explains the emergence in the 1760s and 1770s of public houses like the City Tavern and the Four Alls that were designed and operated with the intention of making some potential customers feel more welcome than others. In this section I locate taverngoers' emerging appetite for sociability among like-minded men in the ways in which Philadelphians made sense of economic change and political division in the final third of the eighteenth century. Whatever the difference in social status between regulars at the City Tavern, the Four Alls, or James Byrne's Tenth Street tavern (the favored haunt of militiamen), these houses owed their existence to a desire to exchange and discuss news and information, and to form and amend character judgments by reference to speech and appearance. During the revolutionary era Philadelphians, whether rich or poor, continued to believe that speech and action in public—especially in taverns—held singular significance as likely indicators of the true value of men and ideas. Why else would laboring men strapped for the necessities of life have continued to frequent taverns? Why else would the subscribers who funded the City Tavern have contributed considerable sums to build and frequent a licensed imitation of their own homes?

The city's mercantile and legal elite could have followed the example set by the city's carpenters and built a meeting hall or auditorium for themselves. They chose to build a tavern instead, thereby symbolizing their continuing belief that speech and behavior observed and enacted in the singular setting of the tavern gave unique insights into the true character of men and ideas. Yet although wealthy merchant and distressed artisan alike continued to insist on their right to make, and act upon, judgments of public speech and behavior observed in the tavern, they could not agree on the standards that ought to inform their judgment of public life. Neither possessed a monopoly on truth, but each believed such a monopoly might be achievable. The stubborn certainty that their standards, and theirs alone, were objective, coupled with a refusal to compromise that was reinforced by the economic changes and ideological ferment of the last third of the eighteenth century, began to drive Philadelphians away from tavern settings in which competing values jostled for preeminence and toward settings like the City Tavern in which they hoped only one set of cultural values would be recognized and affirmed. In this sense it is not the specific nature of the economic changes and political issues of the revolutionary era but rather the ways in which Philadelphians made sense of these developments that account for changing patterns of taverngoing.

The exclusivity of establishments like the City Tavern and the hostility of drinkers to opinions that challenged the bar room consensus produced a sea change in the accustomed context of political debate in Philadelphia. As we saw in Chapter 4, in each of the political crises of the colonial era, Philadelphians confronted their rulers in direct, personal, public encounters. They demanded that political debate be conducted in accordance with the assumption that the public's right to pronounce upon provincial policy was recognized. As Pennsylvania's political leaders adopted patterns of sociability that diminished the frequency with which they encountered the lower orders in the cramped confines of a public house, many of them also abandoned even the pretense of interest in the political opinions of laboring men. Safe inside the coffeehouse, one Philadelphia merchant felt free to denounce radical artisans opposed to resuming trade with Britain in 1770 as a "rabble" who had no right to an opinion on the matter.[9] Drinkers in sites like the Four Alls, Byrne's Tenth Street tavern, or the newly renamed "Wilkes and Liberty" (formerly the Arch Street Ferry) might have expressed equally pungent denunciations of the political pretentions of the "better sort."[10] The decreasing frequency with which rich and poor discussed politics face-to-face, coupled with the uncompromising spirit in which even tavern gatherings composed of men of roughly equal social rank approached political discussion, had the effect of undermining the behavioral foundations upon which the province's uniquely "accessible" political culture had previously rested.[11] This change in the context of political discussion began to inform some part of the content of politics, because it occurred even as republican ideology and the peculiarities of provincial politics in the last years of proprietary rule were conspiring to produce the most democratic state constitution in America. The second half of this chapter examines key moments in the prosecution of the American Revolution in America's largest city, demonstrating the influence that the changing context of public political discussion exerted on the manner in which these were played out.

*   *   *

In 1783 Captain Erkuries Beatty celebrated St. Patrick's Day in a manner few other men of his class would have been prepared to emulate. He described his experiences in a letter to his brother:

A few reduced Continental officers, captains of ships, Irish volunteers, hatters' apprentices, including as many other trades of the same likeness as there was people almost—sexton, bell-ringer, psalm singer . . . clerk of Christ Church and doctor's mates on stages, damn[e]d droll sinners to be sure—in such mixed company did I spend the evening in a dirty, noisy tavern low down in Water Street—where we held out 'til one o'clock and behaved exactly in character. . . . A picked and select company it was too—I was obliged to think myself highly honored in getting introduced into it about eight o'clock—but say nothing, I am now very thankful I am clear of it without my head being broke.[12]

Beatty asked his brother to marvel at his chutzpah in celebrating St. Patrick's Day in the company of "reduced Continental officers" and apprentice boys. Yet a generation before, a drinking bout in the company of men he clearly considered to be his inferiors would not have had the flavor of adventure Beatty gave it. His letter testifies to the heightened political and social antagonism that crept into tavern sociability in the closing years of the eighteenth century. Although, on occasion, rich and poor continued to find themselves in one another's company, Beatty's letter suggests that by the 1780s they were happier drinking among their own kind.

The origin and influence of the growing desire for select and exclusive sociability that Beatty's letter captures are encapsulated in the history of the founding and use of the City Tavern. In 1772 Samuel Powell conveyed a sizable lot on the north-west corner of Second Street and Walnut Streets to a group of seven wealthy citizens. These men in turn solicited from each of fifty-two friends subscriptions of £25 to finance the construction of what became the City Tavern. The project was managed on behalf of the subscribers by a board of trustees. John Cadwalader, the trustees' treasurer, took a hand in the tavern's design and stipulated that the finest materials be used in its construction.[13] As a result, building costs escalated and the trustees were forced to call upon John Penn for a loan of £1,000 to augment the funds raised by subscription and donation. The finished building cost more than £3,000.[14]

In August 1773 the trustees announced to both prospective tenants and the public that "As the Proprietors have built this tavern without any view of profit, but merely for the convenience and credit of the city, the terms will, of consequence, be made easy to the tenant: the extensiveness of the undertaking, in superintending so capital a tavern as this is proposed to be, requires some stock beforehand, as well as an active obliging disposition. A person so qualified, it is imagined, will find it in his interest to engage in it."[15] Daniel Smith was probably the first American ever to be interviewed for a position as tavernkeeper. When he announced his good fortune in being chosen as the first keeper of the City Tavern, he pointed out his accomplishments, while not neglecting to puff those of the subscribers. He told the public that the "gentlemen proprietors" had chosen him as a "proper person" to keep the City Tavern:

in consequence of which he has furnished it, and at a very great expence has laid in every article of the first quality, perfectly in the style of a London tavern; and in order the better to accommodate strangers he has filled up several elegant bedrooms, detached from noise and as private as a lodging-house. He has also fitted up a genteel coffee room, well attended and properly supplied with English and American newspapers. The City Tavern was erected at great expence by a voluntary subscription of the principal gentlemen of the city for the convenience of the public, and is much the largest and most elegant house occupied in this way in America.[16]

More than was often the case in such advertisements, the City Tavern justified the enthusiasm of its celebrants. Inside and out, the City Tavern's design strove to emulate the spirit of such fashionable London haunts as Tom's Coffeehouse and the Grecian Rooms.

The City Tavern was a substantial brick building, with a frontage of fifty feet and a depth of forty-six feet. All the windows had shutters, all the walls were plastered, and the house was floored throughout with yellow pine boards. Patrons entered via a sweeping set of stone steps, whose effect was enhanced by the fact that the tavern was set back twenty feet from Second Street. On the first floor, on either side of a central hall and staircase, were two rooms that ran the whole depth of the building. Apart from a chair rail, and cupboards on either side of the chimney breast, these rooms contained no decorative architecture. Each could be divided in two by movable screens for private dinners or meetings.

The second floor contained the tavern's most famous feature. Running the width of the back of the building was the City Tavern's "Large Room," or long gallery. This gallery, like the rooms below, could be divided in two if necessary. The point of division was marked with "fluted pilasters," "pedistals," and "frett cornice." The gallery's ceiling was "lofty." Opposite the windows in this large room were "boxes," subtly lit, which afforded privacy.[17] This gallery was used for grand civic dinners, events staged by the city's Dancing Assembly, and extraordinary political meetings. Two smaller rooms on either side of the stairs occupied the street side of the second floor. When the tavern hosted balls and banquets these rooms could be employed for serving or preparing food, for gaming, or as quiet areas for rest and recuperation. On the third and fourth floors were guest bedrooms. A garret met the needs of servants, while the kitchen and storerooms were housed in ancillary buildings.[18]

In 1773 Philadelphia's first gossip columnist, "Polinurus Pepper, Esq.," wrote that he expected the "political, commercial, literary and religious interests of the province" to be "learnedly discussed by many a knot of grave and sensible freeholders" at the City Tavern.[19] Neither Pepper nor the patricians who flocked to the City Tavern believed that learned discussion of provincial affairs was a regular feature of exchanges in most, if any, of Philadelphia's existing taverns. Well-to-do Philadelphians subscribed to the new tavern precisely because they were dissatisfied with the conversation, and much else, on offer in the rest of the city's public houses. The "grave and sensible freeholders" who patronized the City Tavern consciously sought to create a visible and audible discursive distinction between the supposedly dispassionate, rational, independent, and objective social behavior and observation conducted in their house and passionate, irrational, and dependent speech and behavior encountered in the city's other public houses. The City Tavern's patrons sought to establish that their discussions were of different, higher quality than those found in other, lesser houses. As they sought to breathe life into their expectations, patrons of the City Tavern made use of the one advantage they had over patrons of the Four Alls: their access to state and congressional leaders.

On the very day that John Adams arrived in Philadelphia to take up his seat in the First Continental Congress, he was met by a delegation of prominent Philadelphians and whisked away to the City Tavern. Here he received "a fresh welcome to the city" and further introductory conversation. Adams and his fellow delegates were eventually treated to a supper "as elegant as ever was laid upon a table."[20] Adams was quick to pronounce the City Tavern the most genteel establishment of its kind in America and became a regular patron. Like Adams, George Washington chose to "sup" at the City Tavern on the very evening of his arrival, before he had even visited his lodgings.[21] Other congressional delegates, including many who later fulminated against the supposed influence afforded to dramshop orators by Pennsylvania's first state constitution, used the City Tavern as an informal clubhouse. As early as May 1775, George Read noted, "a few of us have established a regular table for each day in the week save Saturday when there is a general dinner—our daily table is formed by the following persons . . . Randolph, Lee, Washington . . . Harrison, Alsop . . . Chase and Rodney."[22]

The Merry-Fellows Companion. Harrisburg, Pa.: for Mathew Carey, 1797. Frontispiece. Library Company of Philadelphia. The gentlemen who subscribed funds to build Philadelphia's City Tavern hoped that it would house convivial and yet learned discussion among "knots of grave and sensible freeholders." In practice, the men who patronized the City Tavern were no better able than drinkers in a run-of-the-mill establishment to control the divisive effects of political discussion in revolutionary Philadelphia. Gatherings such as that depicted here held an enduring appeal for well-to-do Philadelphians in the last quarter of the eighteenth century.

The prospect of access to the chatter produced by such gatherings prompted Joseph Galloway, an opponent of independence, to welcome the decision to convene a Continental Congress grudgingly. "Having these gentlemen at the scene of action," he wrote, "we shall no longer be misled by newspaper accounts and private letters, but shall proceed on solid information and principles of safety."[23] Similar considerations led local and national committees to choose the City Tavern as a site for their meetings. In 1775 the Pennsylvania subcommittee of the Congressional Committee of Observation, Inspection, and Correspondence began regular meetings at the City Tavern. They were joined in February 1776 by the standing committee of five charged with superintending the congressional treasury. Such committee business, along with the custom of state and national politicians and officers, returned to the City Tavern following the British evacuation of Philadelphia in 1778, despite the fact that the tavern had continued trading during the occupation.[24] So close was the tavern's continuing association with the workings of government that the visiting French marquis de Chastellux could comment in 1780, "it must be understood that the delegates [to the Continental Congress] . . . have a tavern to themselves."[25]

Despite the City Tavern's prominence in the 1770s, the house lost its place in the affections of the city's gentry in the 1780s. In 1785 the tavern's unique trust agreement was dissolved. The trustees sold the building to Samuel Powell, who leased it to Edward Moyston. Moyston became the first of numerous tenants to confront the fact that the building's design and reputation as a tavern had begun to discourage gentlemanly custom. Gentlemen were no better able to prevent public political discussion from generating feuds, fistfights, and even duels than were laborers.[26] Precisely because they continued to value and closely interrogate speech and behavior observed in public settings, the genteel patrons of the City Tavern readily conflated small political questions—especially those revolving around honor and respect—with the much larger issues of independence and state governance. Despite the fact that it was used almost exclusively by visiting politicians and Philadelphia's resident patriciate, contention was as difficult to accommodate within sociability at the City Tavern as in any other tavern.

During the Revolution, the tavern's patrons went out of their way to stifle dissent and enforce political consensus. For example, the congressional dining circles at the City Tavern noted by George Read in 1775 and the marquis de Chastellux in 1780, reflected sectional divisions. But even after obvious opponents of independence had been banished from the tavern, social events were threatened by arguments over commitment to America's cause. In 1781 the managers of Philadelphia's Dancing Assembly, which then met in the City Tavern's long gallery, appealed to lukewarm patriots to stay away from their dances:

It is expected that no man who has not taken a decisive part in favor of American independence will, in future, intrude on the Dancing Assembly of this city: such characters are either too detestable or too insignificant for Whig Society. The company of those who were so insensible of the rights of mankind and of personal honor, as to join the enemies of their country in the most gloomy moment of the revolution, cannot be admitted. The subscription paper, thro[ugh] accident, has been handed to some characters of this description.[27]

The marquis de Chastellux attended an assembly dance at the City Tavern in the course of a visit to Philadelphia in 1780. He was surprised to find that "like the 'toasts' one drinks at table" the dances had "a marked connection with politics." The managers named one dance "the success of the campaign"; another, "Burgoyne's defeat." Chastellux was not alone in finding that effort made by the assembly's managers to ensure one, and only one, meaning would be read into the evening's program made for "methodical" amusement.[28] By 1785 pleasure gardens, parks, and purpose-built assembly rooms had begun to supplant the City Tavern's long gallery as the place to see and be seen, as Philadelphians, rich and middling, searched for a sociability among company that would refrain from pouncing on the political significance of every last detail of speech and deportment. Moreover, by the 1790s purpose-built and economically viable hotels offered "respectable" citizens more in the way of space, privacy, and propriety than lodgings at the City Tavern while exclusive and specialised mercantile exchanges and bureaus offered ever more reliable or valuable information. In short, the well-documented history of the rise and fall of this one tavern offers a microcosm of the major developments affecting the trade as a whole in the last quarter of the eighteenth century.

The affinities and antipathies that drove Philadelphians to seek out and patronize exclusive public spaces like the City Tavern and the Four Alls were rooted in growing economic inequality and insecurity and given focus by the political crises of the American Revolution. However, it is not so much the exact nature of economic and political dislocation in the final third of the century as the ways in which Philadelphians made sense of these developments that accounts for change in Philadelphians' patterns of taverngoing.

As Billy Smith and Gary Nash have shown, in the final third of the eighteenth century Philadelphia's economy underwent a profound transformation whose effects were felt first at either end of the city's spectrum of wealth.[29] In the years after the French and Indian wars, Philadelphia's rich became even richer, while, by relative and absolute measures, the city's poor became poorer. By 1774 the richest 4 percent of the city's population laid claim to 55 percent of the city's taxable wealth, while the poorest 30 percent held but 1 percent.[30] This redistribution of wealth was accompanied by unprecedented threats to the economic security of the gainfully employed. Many Philadelphians, especially those "middling men" whose ranks included artisans and craftsmen who were underemployed, under threat, but, for the moment, one step ahead of utter destitution, hoped that the new state government would enact an economic program designed to return to laborers the access to economic security that had characterized the best poor man's country.[31] The erosion of both living standards and the value of capital assets produced by the great inflation that accompanied the closing years of the Revolutionary War dashed hopes of a recovery and brought home to middling men the scale and intractability of the economic transformation afoot. During the 1790s many laboring men recaptured a prosperity that held out the promise of a return to the more fluid rank-based system of social stratification that had characterized the colonial city. Nevertheless, with hindsight we can see that in the final third of the eighteenth century Philadelphia's economy produced enduring divisions of wealth that became the basis of a class-based system of social stratification.

However these developments do not themselves explain changing patterns of taverngoing. There had always been rich and poor in the city. Philadelphians had experienced the effects of trade slumps long before the crisis in America's relationship with Britain developed. During the first two-thirds of the eighteenth century genteel Philadelphians had tolerated tavern gatherings in which they drank and conversed in close proximity, if not warm fraternity, with men of lowly estates and contrary opinions. It is the ways in which Philadelphians explained new economic realities to themselves, and to their neighbors, that fostered change in the choices they made about where and with whom they would drink.

The role played by economic change in encouraging some taverngoers to reject inclusive or accommodating mores of sociability turns on one of the great ironies eighteenth-century Philadelphia's cultural history. Precisely because so many Philadelphians had for so long accepted a relative moral equality grounded in healthy economic prospects, they tended to understand mounting economic inequality in absolute moral terms.[32] In 1736, when Pennsylvania could claim to be the best poor man's country, John Webbe told readers of the *Pennsylvania Gazette* that since men were born equal it was "impudence to tell another animal like myself that I came into the world his superior; none is born with a right to control another."[33] Building on this claim, Pennsylvanians created a hell for aristocrats, government officials, and clerics. Men like Alexander Hamilton, Israel Pemberton, Jr., and the Reverend Henry Muhlenberg had to learn to tolerate a familiarity in social interactions that was born out of this sense of equality.

As we have seen, it was in the tavern that Pennsylvanians' views on equality received perhaps their purest affirmation. Men entered William Moore's beerhouse or John Biddle's Indian King as merchants, craftsmen, or servants and they left, slightly drunker, possessed of the same station in life. But while actually in tavern company, men drank and conversed in ways that presumed, or attempted to create, a notional and temporary equality. Heavy drinking, toasting, and singing reduced, or elevated, rich and poor participants to a common moral plane. Taverngoers who were uncomfortable with this sociability contributed to its egalitarian tone by refraining from direct criticism of its assumptions. They did so partly out of fear; a bullying, intolerant majoritarianism characterized many tavern companies. Yet even a snob like Alexander Hamilton, no friend of egalitarian assumptions, willingly "played along" in mixed tavern company. He believed that such company could serve as a mirror in which to project his own self-image; he presumed that within such company he might glimpse an insight into his neighbors' character inadvertently revealed; and he hoped that he might pick up interesting or useful snippets of conversation. In short, the accustomed mores of tavern sociability in colonial Philadelphia, which were built around the willingness of rich and poor to listen to or at least observe one another, militated against the application of absolute moral judgments in everyday encounters.

In contrast, the rhetoric of contempt and condemnation that developed out of Philadelphians' attempts to come to terms with the economic changes of the late eighteenth century drew upon uncompromising moral perspectives that were incompatible with the inclusive assumptions Philadelphians had previously brought to tavern sociability. Within a city in which rich and poor still lived cheek by jowl, both the trappings of wealth—big houses, fancy carriages, elegant entertainments—and the stigmata of poverty—malnutrition, threadbare clothes, rum swilling—were clearly visible. But what did extreme wealth or poverty say about a man? If townhouses, carriages, and fine clothes signified a morally and politically reprehensible "opulence" or "luxury," why should the less well-off acknowledge any claims to "superiority" made by their possessors? Indeed, was it not the duty of the virtuous man to resist the "arrogance" of such claims? If, on the other hand, laboring men lacked even that modest stake in society afforded by a competency, what claim on the attentions of a gentleman of discernment could their opinions and grievances, let alone their company, possess?

During the final quarter of the eighteenth century, Philadelphians applied ever more uncompromising value judgments to the visible effects of economic change. The application of pejorative characterizations of wealth or poverty was often triggered by perceptions of drinking behavior. By the 1780s the keepers of the city almshouse had become convinced that the destitution they witnessed in the men and women they knew as "customers" betokened a completely flawed and thoroughly objectionable morality. Isaac Millenar was "nearly blind, but never misses finding rum." Joseph Paulin, a tailor who sought assistance at the almshouse, was admitted with the comments "drunken" and "worthless." Robert Aitkens was a "worthless, drunken, laughing barber," while the "old hangman" James Boy was "vile, drunken" and "long known here."[34] Such terminology suggested an economic and spiritual destitution so profound as to put its possessors beyond the pale of civilized society. And yet, to the puzzlement and frustration of the overseers and their respectable backers, these specimens actually possessed reputations and contacts in the community at large. Michael McDonald, who, the overseers noted with disgust, was so drunk when admitted that he "rolled" into the almshouse incapable of standing, had a nickname: "Joe King's Mick." So did John McClure—"King of America"—and Robert Fritz—"Crazy" or "Foolish Bob."[35] These men were no angels. Few Philadelphians, rich or poor, would have enjoyed an evening in the company of a vile hangman or a verminous alcoholic. "Joe King's Mick" was not a particularly affectionate moniker. But, like the very rich, the city's poorest residents lived at, but within, the margins of city life. Hugh O'Harra was a "frequent worthless" customer who made a practice of recuperating in the almshouse before running off, selling his almshouse clothes, and drinking the proceeds.[36] O'Harra knew Philadelphians prepared to buy his clothes and he knew of publicans prepared to serve him. He may not have been well liked, but those who came in contact with him may have been slower than the guardians of the poor to condemn his habits and lifestyle. For if the intemperance and "insolence" of the destitute was as visible as it was objectionable, so too was that of the rich.

Alexander Graydon served in the city's "silk stocking" militia company and left this description of their musters: "the place of rendezvous [was] the house of the Captain [John Cadwalader], where capacious demi-johns of Madeira were constantly set out in the yard where we formed, for our refreshment before marching out to exercise. The ample fortunes of Mr. Cadwalader had enabled him to fill his cellars with the choicest liquors; and it must be admitted that he doled them out with the most gentlemanly liberality."[37] By publicly treating the company this way, Cadwalader established his claim to leadership and at the same time softened the impact of the company's necessarily unequal military rank. Such rituals also signified, at least to those who partook of them, a common gentility based on a level of wealth that put its possessors beyond the compulsion to work for a living. Yet the all-too-frequent result of such gatherings was a boorish drunkenness that undermined the superior image the "better sort" attempted to present. On December 1, 1778, the Supreme Executive Council of Pennsylvania and the state assembly threw themselves a dinner at the City Tavern that cost over £2,000. A "most gentlemanly liberality" was the order of the day as 270 diners drank 522 bottles of Madeira, 116 large bowls of punch, 9 of toddy, 6 of "Sangaree," and 24 bottles of port. Some indication of how the evening ended is provided by a bill for damages of more than £100. The diners destroyed ninety-six wine glasses, five decanters, and one "large inkstand."[38]

The expense and excess of such evenings attracted criticism even from those who attended them. Major General Nathanael Greene was one of numerous military and political leaders to complain of the prevalence of "luxury and dissipation" in Philadelphia.[39] In 1778 Massachusetts congressional delegate Samuel Holton refused an invitation to a lavish ball thrown by a "society of French gentlemen," saying "I think it is not the proper time to attend balls when our country is in such distress."[40] Even greater was the indignation among those who knew that they would never be invited to such festivities. In 1775 the city's elite proposed welcoming Martha Washington to Philadelphia with a grand ball at the City Tavern. Radical artisans, arguing that such an entertainment contravened the association agreed by the Continental Congress, and angered by the implication that their objections showed an uncouth attitude toward the fairer sex, threatened to tear down the City Tavern if the ball went ahead. This particular event was canceled, on the grounds that "commotion" would be "very disagreeable at this melancholy time."[41] Nevertheless, the city's elite continued to propose and stage events whose expense and pretentions troubled less exalted observers and led them to question patrician values. In May 1781, for example, a mild-mannered clerk, George Nelson, noted in his diary that

Continental currency had depreciated by 175 percent, that country folk were refusing to accept Continental bills, and that two grand receptions aboard a visiting French frigate were to be held as planned despite the fact that the poor could not procure the "simple necessities" of life.[42]

George Nelson was a middling man of Baptist convictions. Applying the secular precepts of Protestantism to everyday sociability, Nelson and many other Philadelphians adopted abstemious lifestyles in the final quarter of the eighteenth century.[43] Yet, like many of his contemporaries, Nelson found that the dictates of sociability, and the need to maintain vital patronage relationships, tested his commitment to sobriety. In October 1780 Robert Erwin insisted that Nelson, Nelson's mentor Jacob Hiltzheimer, and the rest of their circle celebrate Erwin's sale of a string of horses by taking punch at Captain Matthew's tavern. Nelson went along reluctantly and sat uncomfortably among the punch drinkers. He was horrified when a foursome within their party fell to card playing. The evening had become "very disagreeable" and Nelson left as soon as he "decently could."[44] In light of persistently high levels of alcohol consumption and the continuing appeal of taverns, even advocates of temperate values sometimes found it necessary to socialize in surroundings whose excess they felt able to criticize only within the privacy of journals or diaries. Exposure to such gatherings left men like Nelson all the more determined to avoid tavern sociability where they could.

Nelson believed, and the available data suggests, that the revolutionary crisis saw no marked decrease in the purchase and consumption of drink among the population as a whole. On the contrary, Philadelphians played their part in creating what W. J. Rorabaugh has described as early national America's "great alcoholic binge."[45] Yet whereas drinking behavior had once helped bring men from all ranks of society together, Hugh O'Harra's dramshop debauches, John Cadwalader's "genteel" punch parties, and George Nelson's distaste for all forms of alcoholic excess symbolized and exacerbated the social, economic, and cultural gulf that grew between classes in the final quarter of the eighteenth century. Philadelphians were fully conscious of emerging class distinctions; indeed by employing pejorative characterizations of their neighbors' drinking they distanced themselves still further from one another. For example, patrician conservatives dismissed Pennsylvania's militia leader Stephen Simpson, secretary of the committee of privates and a former chairman of the Cordwainers' Fire Company, as nothing but a "drunken shoemaker."[46] To the keepers of the almshouse, the "noted old cobbler" George Hewes was doubly damned as "drunken and political."[47] Slightly less offensive but equally uncompromising was a newspaper essay, espousing the interests of the laboring man, which leveled the charge that the city's merchants were engrossing "monsters" "unworthy of the fellowship of society."[48] The supposed "arrogance" of wealth, exemplified in the intemperate, "riotous, lounging" lifestyle of those "who are so complaisant to each other as to call themselves the better sort of people" led a writer in the *Pennsylvania Evening Post* to compare unfavorably the leisured rich with the gainfully employed. The latter were "a set of honest sober men, who mind[ed] their own business" and yet lived under constant threat from patrician speculators as well as plebeian thieves.[49]

The ways in which Philadelphians understood economic change and the increasing willingness of rich and poor to employ characterizations of one another so pejorative as to justify withdrawal from one another's company greatly influenced the ways in which taverngoers made sense of the great political issues of the late eighteenth century. Here again, it is not so much the nature of the political issues that faced Philadelphians (although these were serious) but how Philadelphians treated differences of political opinion when they encountered them in everyday sociability that accounts for changing patterns of taverngoing.

We might argue that questions such as whether America should be independent or whether Pennsylvania's radical state constitution was viable or just, were inherently more divisive than the questions that dominated the political history of colonial Philadelphia, such as whether the city should furnish a militia. But even if this were the case, Philadelphians could still have prevented the issues of the revolutionary era from disturbing time-honored patterns of tavern sociability by simply agreeing not to discuss politics in tavern gatherings. The Philadelphia merchant John Ross raised a laugh by declaring on the eve of independence that he was for neutrality because he knew that whoever ruled America, it was his destiny to be a subject. Alexander Graydon remembered this years after the event because its pose of resignation was so rarely encountered in daily sociability.[50] Unlike Ross, most of Philadelphia's taverngoers, rich and poor, chose to continue to discuss politics in tavern gatherings in the final quarter of the eighteenth century despite, and perhaps because, political discussion in public houses divided even men otherwise possessed of shared interests, backgrounds or personal fortunes. For them, silence, or conversational neutrality, were suspicious.

In common with other Americans, most residents of the Quaker City believed that the key concepts of republican ideology had, and ought to possess, an observable basis in behavior. Within a system of thought that postulated an almost paranoid certainty that designing men waiting for an opportunity to subvert the virtuous lurked in every community, it was incumbent on the patriotic citizen to observe and judge his neighbor's speech, deportment, and appearance. Loyalists cast an equally suspicious eye over public speech and behavior in an attempt to detect the "incendiaries" and demagogues they believed lay behind the crisis in imperial relations.[51] According to this logic, only dissemblers or agents provocateurs hid or censored their political beliefs in order to foster apparently sociable exchanges with men of different opinions and backgrounds. The man of principle spoke his mind in public even, indeed especially, when he found himself in company that did not share his beliefs. Where a man could not persuade the company in which he found himself of the virtues of his particular political opinion, he had almost a duty to withdraw, lest his own political integrity be tainted.

However, ultimately virtue, patriotism, sedition, and treason lay, like gentility, thrift, and sobriety, in the eye of the beholder. The behavioral forms by which Philadelphians attempted to enact, ascribe, and discern ideological positions became the subject of contestation that originated in a problem long familiar to taverngoers—by whose lights should virtuous behavior, patriotic commitment to America's cause, or intolerable attachment to the Crown, be recognized, applauded, or punished? The emergence of more pronounced and seemingly permanent divisions of wealth exacerbated this problem of judgment. If laborers could not recognize gentility, how could they be trusted to define patriotism? If the well-to-do could not understand the plight of the workingman, why should laborers accept patrician definitions of virtue?

The assumptions which Philadelphians made about how political issues, once raised, should be discussed were inherently divisive. This can be seen at its most striking in the schisms that befell civic associations built around shared interests. As early as 1765 Franklin was writing to his friend Hugh Roberts in an attempt to prevent the effects of "public political misunderstandings" from destroying his cherished debating society, the Junto.[52] Each of the city's two fishing clubs was ultimately torn apart by the political passions of the period.[53] The members of Philadelphia's Hibernian Society felt compelled to expel countryman Thomas Batt for "taking a formal part against the attitudes of America."[54] On taking up his place in the Continental Congress, John Adams noted with approval that events had forced the Philadelphia's English benevolent association, the St. George's Society, into schism. One faction—composed of "staunch Americans"—met at the

City Tavern, another—"staunch Britons"—met out of town, and yet a third
—"halfway men"—met at the Bunch of Grapes.[55]

In the years immediately preceding independence, each of the city's
political factions attempted to lay claim to taverns of their own, houses in
which their—and only their—political opinions would be welcome. For
understandable reasons, Philadelphia's Loyalist community was particularly
eager to meet in sites in which their views would not be challenged and
misrepresented by other taverngoers. In July 1776 the Pennsylvania Committee of Safety conducted a major investigation of rumors of organized
opposition to independence in the city of Philadelphia. Isaac Atwood, a
comb maker born in England but resident in Philadelphia since 1773, provided the committee with a detailed account of the city's Tory community.
According to Atwood, "Jones, the tavern keeper by the Dock," was "a
principal hand" at meetings of Tories that drew together tradesmen and
merchants in a number of the city's taverns but especially at the widow
Ball's. At these meetings Jones urged armed opposition to independence.
Wealthier, and generally more cautious Loyalists, like Joseph Stansbury and
John Kearsley, argued against Jones while continuing to meet with him.[56]
Isaac Atwood, who was a lukewarm opponent of independence, kept his
own counsel in these gatherings before turning his former conspirators over
to the authorities. That same summer, Daniel Smith, keeper of the City
Tavern, and Robert Saunders, the tavern's barman, were forced to admit to
Philadelphia's Committee of Safety, which held its meetings at the City
Tavern, that some of their tavern's regular customers were in fact Loyalists.
Smith told the committee that in the fall of 1775 a company of some fifteen
gentlemen, including the prominent Philadelphia merchant Joseph Stansbury, had begun holding regular meetings in one of the City Tavern's private
rooms. Smith, convinced that he had heard this group singing "God Save
the King" and "Rule Britannia," eventually barred them from his house.
Smith's barman testified that he heard the group singing Loyalist songs but
could provide no further details because they "stopped their conversation"
when he came in to serve them.[57]

The radical master craftsmen and lesser merchants who formed the
backbone of the network of committees that directed Philadelphia's independence movement adopted William Bradford's Old London Coffeehouse as their unofficial headquarters. At least one prominent conservative
—William Allen, the former chief justice of Pennsylvania—continued to use
Bradford's coffeehouse even after the house had become associated with the
cause of independence. When Allen baited the crowd there with his will-

ingness to shed his blood (and theirs) in opposition to independence, Bradford felt compelled to inform the city's Committee of Safety of the abuse offered to the public by Allen's words.[58] Yet despite William Bradford's willingness to bar customers who expressed hostility to independence, his patrons continued to disagree on the progress of their cause. On May 15, 1776, William Allen's kinsman, the lawyer James Allen, was present at the coffeehouse when Bradford read out the congressional resolution instructing the colonies to assume all powers of government. Allen thought it significant that the resolution was "ill-received," with only one man present offering a "huzza." But because he had declared "my aversion to their principles" on previous visits to the coffeehouse, Allen found that he had become "obnoxious" to the "independents" who gathered there. On this occasion, he kept his own counsel.[59] Other patrons were not so restrained. Partisan dispute and division continued to accompany political and mercantile discussions at Bradford's coffeehouse. In 1783 Eleazar Oswald announced that he was reopening the coffeehouse "on its original plan." He "earnestly entreated" "those gentlemen that have . . . from its first establishment considered it a[n] [ex]change for commercial transactions" to "return to their old accustomed place without regard to party distinction."[60]

If Philadelphians could not avoid the divisive effects of political discussion in civic associations built upon shared interests or in public houses, such as the City Tavern or Bradford's coffeehouse, which catered to a restricted range of cultural affinities and presuppositions, the uncompromising spirit in which they approached such discussion had effects even more pronounced in randomly selected tavern gatherings. Since they believed that they were living through a distinctive epoch in human history, it proved very difficult for Philadelphia's taverngoers to agree to disagree on political questions. This raised two issues that, especially after 1774, began to assume central importance in the high politics of revolutionary Pennsylvania: what right, if any, did men who disagreed with the political sentiments of the majority have to express their opinion and how, if at all, should state government suppress political dissent?

As Barbara Clark Smith has pointed out, the Association of Nonimportation, Nonexportation and Nonconsumption adopted by Congress on October 20, 1774, amounted to far more than a declaration of economic warfare against Britain. The association laid out an ethical program for America through which patriots "expressed social ideas and sought social change."[61] The association was the most confident and ambitious prescription of republican values enacted during the revolutionary era. It attempted to lay out forms and standards of behavior against which all friends of America might judge virtue and patriotism. From Philadelphia, word went out to the colonies that a true friend of American liberty should forego "every species of extravagance and dissipation." Prescriptions designed to inculcate virtuous behavior applied to public appearance—the good republican ought to adopt homespun garments, forego lavish expenditure on funerals, and abandon cockfights and theatergoing—as well as the consumption of various goods in domestic settings. Of course these prescriptions applied to all Americans, regardless of their opinion of the justice of America's cause.

Many Philadelphians thought America should be seeking conciliation, not confrontation, with Britain. Even some of those Philadelphians more or less convinced of the necessity of a break with Britain were alienated by the association's spartan republicanism. Yet the association assumed that its prescriptions provided the one and only way a host of abstract concepts could and should be correctly judged and enacted in public. It was very easy, once the association had been adopted, for uncompromising partisans to claim that, for example, refusal to wear homespun clothing or to illuminate one's windows on a republican feast day constituted an infallible sign of hostility to America's cause. By the same token, it became ever harder for men like John Dickinson, author of "Letters from a Farmer in Pennsylvania," to argue that Americans had a wider range of choices than joining in a movement for independence or perishing under tyranny. The Continental Congress declined to identify those members of the community best suited to the task of defining the limits of the permissible. Responsibility for enforcing the association was left in the hands of local committees. In Pennsylvania, these committees operated without a mandate from existing agencies of government; in the city of Philadelphia the committees that enforced the association were dominated by master craftsmen, small traders, middling merchants, and radical artisans. Men who had not previously wielded political power in the city now defied the authority of officeholders who had grown accustomed to thinking of themselves as society's natural leaders.

The adoption of the association most directly affected patterns of taverngoing by exacerbating a preexisting tension within tavern sociability; what right, if any, had an individual to express in public views that dissented from the opinion of the company in which he found himself? Should a man who proposed a Loyalist toast to a gathering of patriots be lynched, imprisoned, or simply dismissed as an eccentric?[62] There was, in all probability, a measure of consensus that the more obnoxious displays of loyalty to the Crown ought to be suppressed. Alexander Mackraby, an officer in the British army, celebrated St. George's Day 1770 by meeting some twenty other native-born Englishmen in a Philadelphia tavern, dining on roast beef and plum pudding, and getting drunk "pour l'honneur de St. George." This crew then paraded through the streets to the playhouse, where they made the audience chorus "God Save the King," "Rule Britannia," and "Britons Strike Home."[63] Most Philadelphians, including perhaps many Loyalists, would have supported the suppression of such provocative expressions of hostility to the American cause. But Philadelphians disagreed sharply as to whether individuals expressing personal beliefs, however misguided, ought to be made subject to rituals designed to coerce conformity.

On September 6, 1775, a group of "gentlemen" later described as "far from being mobbish or mobbishly inclined" seized the conservative lawyer Isaac Hunt.[64] Hunt had defended a trader charged with breaking the association by questioning the authority of the Committee of One Hundred set up in Philadelphia to enforce it. Following a reprimand from the committee, Hunt had withdrawn his remarks and agreed to offer a public apology. The gentlemen who abducted Hunt intended to ensure that his apology took a proper form. They placed him in a cart and paraded him around the city's streets. Hunt, standing in the back of the cart, expressed what eyewitnesses concluded was a becoming contrition. The protesters chose a route that took them past the house of a staunch Tory, Dr. John Kearsley. Kearsley, fearing that he might be tarred and feathered, barricaded himself in his home. When the unruly procession appeared, he declared that he would not be taken alive and fired a pistol shot at the demonstrators in an attempt to disperse them. The associators dragged Kearsley from his house by a ground-floor window. Offering Hunt a safe-conduct home, they now paraded Kearsley through the streets. Kearsley had been cut and bruised in the melee and presented a "most shocking appearance." Nevertheless, as the procession moved on through the city's streets to the Old London Coffeehouse, Kearsley roared out "God Save the King" and hurled imprecations at Congress and the cause of independence. At Bradford's coffeehouse, in what was by now an accustomed ritual, Kearsley was "exhibited as a spectacle to a great number of respectable citizens."[65] Although disheveled, Kearsley refused to retract or amend his Loyalist statements. The mood grew so ugly that Samuel Rhoads, mayor of Philadelphia, called for militia to protect Kearsley and the Old London Coffeehouse from mob violence. The associators were forced to escort Kearsley back to his house to prevent his being lynched.

Those who organized such ceremonies of humiliation presumed that witnesses would agree with their definitions of sedition and treason, contrition and remorse. Yet staged rituals of humiliation, apology, and reintegration inspired a variety of conclusions among witnesses. Charles Biddle, for example, did not share Dr. Kearsley's political views, but he had a grudging admiration for the bravery with which he expressed them under duress. Crowd actions against dissenters inspired premonitions of what Jefferson later termed the "tyranny of majority," with many respectable citizens concluding that rituals in which political dissenters were publicly humiliated or made to recant their views were as intolerable as the oafish antics of Alexander Mackraby. James Allen was deeply troubled by what he took to be mob excesses. "I love the cause of liberty," he wrote, "but cannot heartily join the prosecution of measures totally foreign to the original plan of resistance. . . . The madness of the multitude is but one degree better than submission to the Tea Act."[66] Allen was dismayed that the efforts of radical committees to enforce a conformity of outlook on a complicated body of political issues stifled and suppressed the freedom of expression that allowed a discerning observer of public life to judge men and ideas and, in turn, enact his sense of citizenship. But when he expressed his reservations about the use of coercion to stifle dissent in sites like Bradford's Old London Coffeehouse, Allen became "obnoxious" to the radical committeemen who gathered there. In many patriot's eyes, the committee of safety acted entirely correctly when, in the spring of 1776, it imprisoned Dr. Alexander Kearsley to prevent him misleading "weak and credulous persons" thereby endangering the "public cause."[67]

James Allen struggled for longer than most of his peers to avoid the easy conclusion that plebeian committeemen were, simply by virtue of their station in life, incapable of understanding, let alone defending, the principles of free and reasoned debate. Yet ultimately Allen concluded that some men possessed better judgment, discernment, and understanding than others. Such men, a minority of the population, had a duty to guide the deliberations of the less able majority. It was in conformity with these principles that Allen chose to serve as a militia private. As he put it: "I choose to have a musket on my shoulders, to be on a par with them . . . [I] believe discrete people mixing with them, may keep them in order."[68] Charles Thomson, the moderately successful merchant who orchestrated the network of committees that pushed Philadelphia toward an acceptance of independence and later served as secretary to the Continental Congress, believed, like Allen, that the rules and conduct of public debate ought to be set by men who had demonstrated discernment and restraint.[69] He too was troubled by some aspects of the conduct of the committees set up to enforce the association. Describing Philadelphia's Committee of One Hundred, he wrote, "Many of the members of this body who were suddenly raised to power, and who exercised an uncontrolled authority over their fellow-citizens, were impatient of any kind of opposition. . . . Instead therefore, of cooperating to keep down parties, they were laboring to raise and foment them."[70] Thomson's qualifications are significant. Traders, master craftsmen, and artisans were not necessarily incapable of reasoned debate and judicious political action, but they were inexperienced, impatient, and inappropriately passionate. Nevertheless, for Thomson and Allen, as well as for disillusioned radicals like Benjamin Rush and chauvinistic conservatives, the substance of politics in revolutionary Philadelphia came to revolve around the ways in which the policies of an independent state government could be made subject to the influence of men of discernment and protected from the passions and energies of the less able.

Patrician complaints about plebeian assertiveness had been heard before. In the aftermath of the 1742 election riot one disgruntled patrician approvingly cited *Cato's Letters* to the effect that "when impious men bear sway, the post of honor is a private station."[71] Yet in the 1770s gentlemen did not retire to the "private station"; they retreated instead to exclusive public houses—building them from scratch if necessary. Men like James Allen, Charles Thomson, or even Benjamin Rush did not seek to withdraw from public life; they craved a different type of public space. James Allen was a trustee of the City Tavern. His willingness to become involved in the project originated in a sense that it ought to be possible for a man to discuss politics with neighbors in an atmosphere in which men took one another's views seriously but could agree to disagree. Some of the men who drank at the City Tavern echoed Benjamin Rush's bilious denunciations of Pennsylvania's state government, while other patrons, perhaps equally fearful of anarchy, adopted a world-weary fatalism summed up by the merchant John Ross. Some of the men who drank at the City Tavern avoided militia service; some, like James Allen, took their chances in regular militia units; others served in the city's silk stocking company. These differences colored the uses to which the City Tavern's patrons put their house. Political discussion at the City Tavern was just as rational, or irrational, and fully as passionate as that conducted in less exalted sites.

Merchants and lawyers claimed that the judgments reached in their tavern colloquies were weightier than those reached in sites such as the Four Alls. They took as a self-evident truth the notion that intelligence, open-mindedness, and reliable information were not equally distributed among the city's tavern companies but were instead found almost exclusively within their circles. Yet, as the crowd at the Four Alls or Byrne's Tenth Street tavern was well aware, the City Tavern's patrons arrived at their opinions in much the same way as the crowd at any laborers' tavern. In both settings men attempted to judge the truth of reports received by referring to the character of the messenger. In both settings men sought to discern and impute motive and outlook on the basis of behavior. Political discussion was as likely to produce high words and heavy drinking at the City Tavern as at the Four Alls. At the City Tavern, as in other houses, taverngoers wove personal considerations of honor or respect into the fabric of their discussion of such larger concepts as virtue or justice.

It is not necessary to believe the varying claims Philadelphians made on behalf of their tavern to accept that by making them, Philadelphians changed the context of public discussion. By their very existence cultural sites like the City Tavern, Bradford's Old London Coffeehouse, and Byrne's tavern helped change the context in which politics was discussed in the city. At the same time, economic change and ideological ferment exacerbated preexisting tensions within the cultural assumptions of taverngoing. As the number of sites in which a man might encounter mixed company declined, as neighbors grew ever more intolerant of dissent, and as the behavioral foundations of the province's previously "accessible" political culture crumbled, two competing models of tavern sociability began to emerge. In one, a man was expected to drink and converse only in company that shared and confirmed his opinions. In the other, a man achieved a measure of harmony and accord in conversation by resisting the temptation to launch polemical attacks on the company in which he found himself. The second model could tolerate a diversity of opinion and background in tavern gatherings; the first could not. Since these competing conceptions of public sociability could not coexist within shared space, Philadelphians were driven to establish new and exclusive sites. By doing so they helped foster the illusion that a discursive distinction between rational and irrational, passionate and dispassionate, artificial and forthright, reasonable and unreasonable public speech and behavior could actually be observed in a comparison between sites like the City Tavern and the Four Alls.

These developments changed the context of political discussion in the city in ways contemporaries recognized. In 1776 Joseph Reed, an opponent of the state constitution struggling to detach political decision making from bar room debate, described himself as being in the midst of a "wordy war."[72] Reed was fighting to ground the public opinion that ought legitimately to inform the deliberations and decisions of a democratic assembly in one, and only one, discursive context: rational discussion conducted among self-consciously moderate and dispassionate men. His metaphor captures nicely the manner in which, beginning in 1774 with the adoption of the association, the context or nature of public political discussion began to form some part of the content or substance of politics in Philadelphia.

The first shots in Reed's wordy war were fired in the spring of 1774 when Paul Revere arrived in Philadelphia bringing news of the passage of the Boston Port Bill, the dispatch of HMS *Lively*, and an appeal for support from Boston's Committee of Correspondence.[73] Revere also brought with him private letters from John Hancock and Sam Adams, addressed to Joseph Reed and Thomas Mifflin, in which the Bostonians pleaded for support from their allies in Philadelphia. Reed, Mifflin, and Charles Thomson, coordinators of the network of radical committees in Philadelphia, were determined to mobilize support for Boston. They knew that a variety of moderate and conservative factions stood opposed to precipitate action while, at the same time, the radical artisans were demanding more resolute opposition to Britain. Reed and Thomson left frank accounts of how they set out to stage-manage the city's response to Boston's request. Mifflin, Reed, and Thomson called for a "public meeting" to be held at the City Tavern on May 20, two days after Revere arrived in town. The three men met in advance and decided that the best tactical response to Boston's request that could be secured was an expression of support for Boston and an agreement to correspond with other colonial legislatures on further measures of resistance. In order to secure this outcome, Mifflin, Reed, and Thomson agreed that their proposals ought to be put to a public meeting by John Dickinson, the city's most influential moderate. On the day, the three leaders lunched with Dickinson at his home and hatched a plan designed to secure the outcome they desired. Reed, Mifflin, and Thomson would address the meeting in turn, and each would propose ever more radical responses to Boston's request. Thomson would propose a unilateral boycott of British goods, a measure he knew would create uproar. At this point, having created what Thomson frankly described as "an *apparent* dispute,"[74] Dickinson would address the meeting and lay before it, as if in the spirit of spontaneous compromise, the measures the four had agreed on in advance. Dickinson agreed to play his part, with the proviso that the meeting appoint a committee to petition Governor Penn to convene a special session of the Pennsylvania assembly. Their plans finalized, the four men left Dickinson's house separately lest observers conclude that they had been plotting.

On May 20, 1774, more than two hundred "gentlemen" packed into the long gallery of the City Tavern. Reed read out the Bostonians request for assistance. Mifflin, and then Thomson, proposed a boycott of British trade. At the conclusion of his fiery speech, Thomson fainted and the meeting "fell into uproar." Dickinson stepped forward and proposed, as agreed, an apparently spontaneously conceived package of compromise measures. These products of an apparent dispute were later explained to the populace at a mass meeting in front of the statehouse.

The assumptions that made such a stage-managed discussion seem feasible and attractive to Thomson and his coconspirators are profoundly significant. Granted, the balance of political power and opinion in the city was such that Thomson had good reason to believe that any response to the British measures against Boston that might find favor with both radical laborers and conservative merchants could be achieved only by a preemptive seizure of the high ground of public debate. Nevertheless, the City Tavern's long gallery was the sanctum sanctorum of a self-consciously rational and exclusive sociability. It was the institutional home of the socially conservative and supposedly disinterested elite that Thomson sought to woo. Thomson and his colleagues knew that the context in which such an important meeting was held would exert a powerful influence on its outcome. By choosing to stage a public meeting in such a private setting, they sought to legitimate the political views of one segment of Philadelphia's population by reference to the appearance of fully public discussion. When described in newspaper accounts in other colonies, it would appear that Philadelphians had conducted something like a town meeting. Thus outsiders, and perhaps even some Philadelphians, would believe that public opinion in Philadelphia was synonymous with the views of a relatively narrow segment of society: those dispassionate men of discernment who met in exclusive public houses like the City Tavern.

Thomson, like Reed, Mifflin, and Dickinson, would not have been unduly worried if one effect of their carefully stage-managed response to Boston's plea for assistance was the formation of an impression that radical measures proposed by laboring men were not truly representative of rational or dispassionate opinion in Philadelphia. During the 1764 election campaign Thomson had argued that taverns were corrupting the electorate and sapping their capacity to resist an autocratic provincial government. Even before the adoption of the association, Thomson was prone to believe that since intelligence and experience were not evenly distributed throughout the population, the discerning few rather than the misguided multitude ought to set the rules of public political debate. But Philadelphia's radicalized laboring men could not be entirely excluded from the debate over independence and state government. Confronting an obstinately moderate assembly and a proprietary interest bent on protecting its perquisites by displaying obedience to the Crown, the alliance of radical merchants, traders, and lawyers that brought independence to Pennsylvania, and dominated the drafting of the state's first constitution, enlisted the support of both craft organizations such as the White Oaks and Hearts of Oak and rank-and-file militiamen. Although the likes of Charles Thomson sought to keep alienated laborers and militiamen at one remove from the central decision making of this alliance, conservatives believed that its operation paid altogether too great a deference to the political pretentions of the "lower orders." Even in old age Alexander Graydon betrayed a distinct uneasiness as he recalled the context in which independence had been achieved. As he put it, "the spirit of liberty and resistance being so generally diffused, it seems scarcely necessary to mention that it drew into its vortex the mechanic interest, as well as that numerous portion of the community styled in a republic 'The People.'"[75] Men who frequented houses like Bradford's or the City Tavern precisely out of a desire to avoid the "mechanic interest" found it almost impossible to judge the merits of independence or the terms of the first state constitution in isolation from their distaste for the manner in which these decisions were debated, enacted, and enforced. Joseph Reed's "wordy war" can be seen at its bitterest in the aftermath of the radical laborer's greatest victory in the American Revolution: the adoption of Pennsylvania's first state constitution.

During Pennsylvania's first state constitutional convention, the delegate Thomas Smith wailed, "our principle seems to be this: that any man, even the most illiterate, is as capable of any office as a person who has had the benefit of education; that education perverts the understanding, eradicates common honesty, and has been productive of all the evils that have happened in the world."[76] Worse was to come for Smith. In the event, the state constitution paid handsome tribute to the diffusion of the spirit of

liberty among "that . . . portion of the community styled . . . 'The People.'"
Chief among these, to judge by the contemporary outcry against it, was
section fifteen of the state constitution's frame of government.

In addition to publishing its proceedings and opening its sessions to
members of the public, Pennsylvania's new unicameral assembly was required to suspend the enactment of legislation until the bill in question had
been made available for public perusal. Adoption was contingent on the
passage of a formal motion of approval in a subsequent assembly session. An
informed public would therefore have the opportunity to express their views
on each and every piece of legislation passed by their assemblymen. This
procedure, which the first state assembly attempted to follow by printing its
bills and posting them in taverns and other public places, was designed to
encourage "mature consideration" of government policy.[77] Conservative
critics of the state constitution worried that this provision sanctioned an
utterly improper or immature discursive context. The notion that tap room
philosophers might be allowed—let alone encouraged—to approbate government policy was anathema. Alexander Graydon accused republican
leaders of a "hypocritical love for the people."[78] The essayist Camillus railed
against the "absurdity" of a "new system of government [which] gives a part
of the people, particularly those who frequent public houses where the laws
are always posted up for consideration, a negative upon the proceedings of
the whole state."[79] Visitors were also troubled by this encapsulation of Pennsylvania's singularly democratic conception of statecraft. Taking up his seat
in 1776, the North Carolinian delegate to the Continental Congress William
Hooper described Philadelphia's taverns and dramshops as the "councils to
which the laws of this state are . . . referred for approbation before they
possess a binding influence."[80] By formalizing the presumptive right of "the
people" to instruct their elected leaders, the constitution imparted a quasi-
constitutional function to political discussion in taverns, a function many
Philadelphians thought it ought not have and which, by the century's close,
it did not possess.

When radical tribunes spoke of the "impudence" of the city's elite, they
had in mind the attempt by the "better sort" to privilege the setting and style
of political discussion in sites like the City Tavern over that conducted in
houses favored by laborers. The political pretentions of the crowd at the
City Tavern were bitterly resented, and contested, by laboring men. Yet
precisely because visitors, congressmen, and state assemblymen regarded
exclusive venues such as the City Tavern as sites of wholesome political
debate, plebeian radicals—while they vehemently denounced the arrogance

demonstrated by wealthy social conservatives—recognized the power and influence of the conversation that went on inside exclusive public houses by making sites such as the City Tavern the target of demonstrations. Paradoxically, by demonstrating outside the City Tavern laboring men contributed to the very arrogance and presumption they sought to contest. When laboring men threatened Bradford's Old London Coffeehouse with destruction or when they vowed to tear down the City Tavern if a ball to honor Martha Washington went ahead, they contributed to the creation of a contrast between apparently rational and irrational political action and discussion. Those who gathered inside the City Tavern or the Old London Coffeehouse sought to develop this contrast in ways that marginalized the claims and opinions of those who demonstrated outside. The collapse of the movement for price controls in the aftermath of the Fort Wilson incident in 1779 furnishes the most poignant example of this process.

In December 1778 "Mobility" told readers of the *Pennsylvania Packet* that "this country has been brought to the brink of ruin." As the price of basic foodstuffs rose on the back of inflation, farmers and merchants withheld supplies of flour and other staples in search of the best possible price. By February 1779 so little grain was coming into the city that there was a scarcity of bread.[81] In May 1779 radical laborers, joined by some of the middling traders and merchants who had led the coalition that brought independence to the city and helped secure the adoption of a radical state constitution, formed a Committee of Trade. This body reminded merchants that "want of flour has in all countries produced the most fatal resentments" and warned that "discontents, far beyond our power to remedy," might arise if they continued to forestall the market. At the same time the committee told impoverished workingmen to "manage as best you can" and reminded them not to take the law into their own hands. The city's consumers would have to accept that merchants holding back "concealed hoards" possessed a "subtlety equal to their delinquency" and might well evade the punishment properly due unto them.[82] The city's merchants, led by Robert Morris and James Wilson, opposed price regulation with free trade arguments that, as Ronald Schultz has noted, elevated Adam Smith's invisible hand to the status of natural law.[83] Many laboring men, especially those serving in the militia, concluded that if merchants would not accept the moral justice of their case, price regulation would have to be imposed upon them by force. In September 1779, reluctant to sanction the direct assault on the rights of property implicit in radical demands, the Committee of Trade disbanded.

Rank-and-file militiamen, acting through a reconstituted Committee of Privates, now assumed leadership of the price control movement. The militiamen convened two mass meetings—one outside the Center House tavern, the other at the Bryne's tavern in Tenth Street—at which they planned direct action against engrossers and forestallers. The protesters invited a number of middle-class radicals—including Charles Willson Peale and James Hutchinson—to attend. None was prepared to address a mass meeting of armed militiamen held in the vicinity of a tavern. On October 4, 1779, protesting militiamen and laborers mustered at Byrne's. They sent out parties to "capture" four men—John Drinker, Matthew Johns, Buckridge Sims, and Thomas Story—whom they deemed to possess a particularly offensive history of Toryism and sharp trading practice. These captives were brought back to the tavern. Reassembling, the demonstrators marched down Arch Street, parading their captives and playing the "Rogue's March." When General Thomas Mifflin attempted to stop them, a fellow in the ranks jostled him with the butt end of a musket. The demonstrators made a point of marching by the Old London Coffeehouse and they paused outside the City Tavern to give three cheers. The crowd then marched on to the house of James Wilson. Wilson and a handful of other gentlemen fearful that they might be forcibly deported to British-held New York barricaded themselves inside the house and awaited the arrival of militia loyal to the state government. After an exchange of musket fire the protesters were dispersed by a cavalry charge led by former tribune of the people Timothy "Timmy Gaff" Matlack. At least six people were killed and seventeen wounded before the day's end.[84]

While these events reflected the influence on Philadelphia's laboring men of a small-producer ideology whose roots can be traced back to the English civil war, the content both of the demonstration and of reaction to it was shaped by the changing context of political discussion in the city.[85] The demonstration was planned and orchestrated in a tavern favored by laborers and militiamen; the protesters quite deliberately made targets of two public houses patronized by merchants and legislators. The City Tavern had associations with Loyalism; the Old London Coffeehouse, with that "swarm" of overbearing merchants, monopolizers, and speculators who were oppressing the workingman.[86] The demonstrators knew that patrons of the City Tavern and Bradford's coffeehouse believed that their view of the world and their threnodies on its state were more rational, less passionate, and better informed than the rough chatter of a crowd gathered for a mass meeting at Byrne's. The demonstrators sensed that they stood on one side of a discursive divide likely to marginalize their views in the eyes of both opponents and erstwhile allies. For these reasons, the centerpiece of the day's events—the ritual humiliation of four Tories conducted to the beat of the "Rogue's March"—was designed to appeal as much to conscience as to reason. By humiliating Tories the demonstrators reidentified themselves as patriots in the hope of legitimating their intervention. Their ritualized action sent two messages to the watching world. The first, which the demonstrators hoped witnesses would accept, was that regardless of where they originated, and however crudely or even improperly they were phrased, the demonstrators' demands were synonymous with the views of patriots and therefore had a claim on the public's attention. But interwoven with this theme was the barely veiled hint that men who operated behind closed doors to deprive the virtuous and patriotic laboring man of basic commodities were as deserving of punishment as avowed Tories such as Drinker, Johns, Sims, and Story. This second theme determined the content of reaction to the demonstration.

Patrician conservatives dismissed the content or substance of the militiamen's position largely because the context in which it originated was alien and threatening. Just as laborers seldom entered the City Tavern, merchants seldom drank in workingmen's taverns. Alienated laborers and radical militiamen knew that when politicians threw a banquet at the City Tavern, or when militia officers staged a barbecue on the banks of the Schuylkill, the invariable result was a drunken excess that belied their celebrants' claim to gentility. However, wealthy merchants and state legislators took an equally dim view of the drunkenness which accompanied militia musters or mass meetings at sites like Byrne's tavern. When, as in the movement for price controls, plebeian Philadelphians alleged that the policies of state were being determined by clandestine cabals meeting in exclusive public houses, patricians pointed out that taverns frequented by truculent workers did not—as Erkuries Beatty found out—extend a particular warm welcome to genteel interlopers. Just as laborers believed that nests of conspirators operated in taverns they seldom visited, so patricians believed that incendiary demagogues whipped up the masses in sites like Byrne's tavern. The significance of the Fort Wilson incident is that for the first time small traders and middling merchants who had previously provided working-class radicals with support and leadership publicly expressed their dissatisfaction with the milieu in which plebeian radicalism was fomented and expressed.

As Eric Foner has argued, we need not interpret the likes of Charles Willson Peale's refusal to address a mass meeting of militiamen as a manifestation of social conservatism. Some radical leaders disavowed crowd actions and riots because they wanted to get laboring men off the streets and into committee rooms.[87] In the fall of 1779 radical leaders were fighting to defend Pennsylvania's state constitution from conservatives bent on its fundamental revision. Considerations of higher political strategy led some radical leaders to turn their back on the mass protests in favor of price controls. On the other hand, by 1779 it was clear that some former radicals, notably Benjamin Rush and Timothy Matlack, had concluded that the masses, as ignorant as they were passionate, had no function to perform in the machinery of government other than as voters in a carefully controlled electoral system. Matlack's actions during the Fort Wilson incident support Ronald Schultz's conclusion that in its aftermath "the loud and vulgar voice of the journeyman and sailor was disallowed; the rough, coarse behavior of the crowd was judged improper."[88]

While well-to-do Philadelphians regarded crowd actions fomented in mass meetings staged at plebeian taverns as improper, they did not press charges of sedition or treason against the Fort Wilson demonstrators. The same state government that had sent out the cavalry to suppress the demonstration later issued a general pardon to its plebeian participants. Joseph Reed, then president of Pennsylvania, blamed the day's events on "some licentious and unworthy characters" who, "taking advantage of the unhappy tumult artfully kindled by themselves, have led many innocent and otherwise well-disposed persons into outrages and insults, which, it is hoped, on cool reflection they will condemn."[89] While on the surface Reed's pardon suggested a recognition of the laboring man's right to participate in political debate, it distinguished that "cool reflection" upon which participation in political debate depended from the milieu of the laborer's tavern and the rough music of mass protest. The events surrounding a protest by mutinous Continental soldiers in Philadelphia in the summer of 1783 suggest that at least some plebeians were prepared to accept this distinction as the price of their continuing participation in the political process.

On June 12, 1783, troops of the Pennsylvania line garrisoned in Philadelphia mutinied. Their protest was prompted by a plan to offer Pennsylvania's soldiers, most of whom were owed substantial amounts of back pay, a furlough in lieu of full settlement of their claims. Other elements of the regiment marched from Lancaster to join their colleagues in Philadelphia. On June 21 the troops surrounded the Pennsylvania statehouse, with the intent of coercing Pennsylvania's government into negotiations with a committee appointed from among the mutineers.[90] At the statehouse, two sergeants went inside to visit with the president of Pennsylvania, John Dickinson. Dickinson attempted to deal with the situation in time-honored manner, treating the sergeants to a bottle of rum. When he uncorked a second bottle the sergeants told him, "we didn't come to get groggy," and demanded that he sign their request to allow the troops to elect a negotiating committee. Talks dragged on.[91] Meanwhile, the day was warm, there was a tavern close at hand, and the soldiers outside, joined by some citizens, milled around the statehouse drinking and grumbling. The Pennsylvania assembly was not actually in session that day, but the Confederation Congress was. The crowd outside the statehouse could see many congressmen still inside the building. Some of the soldiers pointed their muskets at the windows of the statehouse, while others aimed offensive language at the congressmen inside.[92]

At around three o'clock, the remaining congressmen, fearing "hasty excesses" might be brewing, began to leave the statehouse. As they filed out, some citizens in the tavern pointed out the president of Confederation Congress, Elias Boudinot, to Private Andrew Wright and two other soldiers, suggesting they should not let him escape. The soldiers surrounded and detained Boudinot, while the crowd around the tavern exhorted the soldiers to "Stand for your rights!" Boudinot lived to tell the tale; the mutineers later went out of their way to apologize for the affront, and Madison dismissed the incident as a "mock" obstruction. The soldiers were dispersed and soothed by "indifferent" persons, and that night, at a meeting at the Three Tuns, Captain Carberry persuaded the soldiers that their interests would be served best if they refrained from any further mass actions. Nevertheless, the day's events were instrumental in Congress's decision to retire to Princeton.[93]

As in the aftermath of the Fort Wilson incident, congressional and military authorities dealt with the mutiny in terms that presumed there was a difference between passionate, and therefore pernicious, protest and reasoned, and therefore acceptable, remonstrance. When men of the Third Pennsylvania Regiment marched off to join the mutiny, their commanding officer pleaded with them to return, arguing; "In warmth men are sometimes led beyond the bounds of interest and propriety both to themselves and their best friends, and attempts to reason while the mind is agitated often rather tends to inflame than calm the passions or opinions whatever they may be."[94] Government and mutineers alike identified the tavern as a wellspring of warmth and "inflammation" that ought to have played no part in the soldiers' protest. The depositions and affidavits describing the demonstration at the courthouse picture an innocent, almost naive soldiery being menaced by a licentious citizenry. James Madison, for example, thought that there had been no danger of premeditated violence but that excesses became a possibility when "spirituous drink . . . began to be liberally served out to the soldiers."[95]

The claim that Private Wright would neither have recognized President Boudinot nor detained him had he not been put up to it by civilians hanging around the tavern was generally accepted. Benjamin Rush, who saw more menace in the mutiny than most observers, believed that the soldiers had been suborned by incendiaries the night before the demonstration.[96] A court-martial conducted by Major General Robert Howe, an authoritarian with a good deal of experience in the suppression of mutinies, concluded that "capital fomenters" Captain Carberry and Lieutenant Sullivan had egged on the soldiers' representatives at a meeting in the upstairs room of the Doctor Franklin tavern.[97] For their part, the mutineers disavowed previous links between protest, drink, and taverns. Their leaders had declined to strike a deal within the territory circumscribed by the "friendly glass," resisting Dickinson's attempts to deflect them from their purpose with treats of rum. Although swayed by the crowd drinking outside the statehouse, the soldiers did not assault Elias Boudinot and, indeed, they later apologized for confronting him. In the aftermath of the demonstration a soldier wrote to the *Freeman's Journal*, the city's most radical newspaper, urging his colleagues to leave the resolution of their grievances to the proper authorities and to refrain from taking matters into their own hands.[98]

As Edmund Morgan has pointed out, it was precisely because contemporaries recognized that "ordinary people" gathered in various public settings espoused and contested all manner of opinion and prejudice that they marveled that government could find any acceptable place for public opinion within a system of checks and balances. Morgan's remarks take their inspiration from a passage in David Hume's *First Principles of Government*: "Nothing is more surprising to those, who consider human affairs with a philosophical eye, than to see the easiness with which the many are governed by the few; and to observe the implicit submission with which men resign their own sentiments and passions to those of their rulers. When we enquire by what means this wonder is brought about, we shall find, that as Force is always on the side of the governed, the governors have nothing to support them but opinion."[99]

Where did the people form and express their opinions? How could freedom of expression and conscience be safeguarded from what Jefferson termed the tyranny of the majority? How could government act upon incompatible expressions of popular will? Ought government to take steps to inform and control that opinion upon which it depended for survival? These questions engaged Hume, Madison, and delegates of the Constitutional Convention because even in the 1780s, and especially in the city of Philadelphia, it did not seem certain that men would easily resign their own sentiments and passions to those of their rulers. Public speech and behavior, along with political texts and newspaper reportage, formed the basis upon which Americans generated a range of political opinion that government could neither control nor easily incorporate within its decision-making processes. Philadelphians, like other Americans, chose to believe that speech and action in public, especially in taverns, possessed a potentially deceptive significance that transcended its ostensible origins in sites of leisure or in chance encounter. What they saw, heard, and did in taverns and other public sites mattered intensely to them. Most Americans believed that government should represent, and act upon, public opinion. They disagreed as to whether tavern conversation was, or could ever be, an accurate, valid, or useful representation of public opinion. This issue was particularly vexed in the city of Philadelphia because evolving patterns of taverngoing created a dramatic change in the context of public political discussion precisely at the moment when Pennsylvanians adopted a state constitution that sought to ensure that the raw, unmediated views of the public, as actually expressed in sites like taverns, would inform and judge the conduct of legislative politics.

The American Revolution was a divisive issue in tavern discussion, but tavern talk was a divisive issue in the American Revolution. Changing patterns of taverngoing produced a distinction of context in political discussion, no less powerful for being more apparent than real, which informed Philadelphians' reaction to the Coercive Acts, the first state constitution, the collapse of the movement for price controls, and outbreaks of popular protest. By the close of the Revolutionary War, laborer and merchant alike were coming to accept as normative definitions of political debate in which literary forms were emphasized over oratorical performances, reasoned argument was deemed superior to passionate outburst, and voting was the preferred mode of confronting one's leaders. The more Philadelphians valued election manifestos, newspaper essays, and debate in formal governmental chambers, the more they undermined what had been one of the raisons d'être of the colonial tavern; its claim to be the preeminent site for the production and transmission of public opinion via careful and persistent observation, and comment on, speech and behavior encountered in company.

I believe that something important was lost in this transition. I would accept that a just and viable polity cannot entertain the claim that drunken citizens and armed militiamen have the right to confront and jostle the president of Congress, or to detain elected officials, until they accede to demands made with menace. However, a polity in which the ruled feel that their rulers are accessible, even to the point of entertaining personal encounters on terrain suggestive of the discourses of the many rather than the few, differs in quality from one in which exchanges between rulers and ruled are structured, filtered, and ultimately controlled by voting and partisan activism.

As we have seen, colonial Philadelphians had demanded that political discussion and decision-making be governed by notions of accessibility that were defined and articulated through the experience of drinking in mixed assemblies. Rich and poor disagreed as to whether the Quaker establishment was corrupt, and over the merits of paper currency, a militia, or royal government. But emboldened by the robustly undeferential climate that prevailed within the taverns in which they argued over these issues, laboring Philadelphians successfully asserted their right to pronounce upon them. Ordinary Philadelphians seized the opportunity to confront or support their erstwhile leaders and betters in direct, face-to-face encounters in taverns and other public spaces. But in the 1760s and 1770s, while Philadelphians continued to discuss and debate politics in taverns, they did so increasingly in the company of their own kind. This encouraged taverngoers to conjure distinctions between, for example, the passionate and therefore pernicious chatter of a workingman's alehouse and the rational and therefore wholesome discussion conducted by sober merchants in a coffeehouse. Of course some Philadelphians stood the value judgments implicit in this distinction on their head. But as they toyed with the meaning of the apparent discursive distinction their changing patterns of taverngoing had created, most Philadelphians came to conclusions that served to marginalize plebeian opinion.

In a recent examination of the political songs, toasts, iconography, and demonstrations of the 1790s, Simon Newman has shown how ordinary Americans in the young republic created a national political culture from the bottom up. Tavern companies played a part in the construction of this culture. Newman argues that through their partisan gatherings and crowd actions, "Americans pulled politics out of the corridors of power and onto the streets of the new republic."[100] In the 1790s Federalists and Democratic Republicans staged events and fomented partisan allegiances in Philadelphia's taverns and on its streets. But, in Philadelphia at least, the process which Newman summarizes as the "regularization of popular political culture"[101] stifled the robustly undeferential and fiercely independent tavern culture of the colonial city. It gave rise instead to a political culture, less accessible than that which dominated the colonial era, within which "politics" was more closely associated with the committee room or the stage-managed event than with face-to-face discussion conducted in and around taverns by men who demanded, and at least temporarily received, an equality of esteem from their betters.

Epilogue

"All the Apparatus of Eastern Fable"

On July 15, 1782, the chevalier de la Luzerne, France's minister to America, staged a grand fete at his Philadelphia residence. The event celebrated the dauphin's birthday and, more generally, Franco-American friendship on the eve of peace. The minister invited eleven hundred guests. Since no public house could accommodate such a crush, the chevalier transformed his official residence to entertain the invited dignitaries. He built a temporary roofed dancing area, forty by sixty feet square, on the embassy's grounds. Benjamin Rush noted that "the garden contiguous to this shed was cut into beautiful walks, and divided with cedar and pine branches into artificial groves." As the conversion continued, the fete dominated conversation in the city. On the day, the city's "idle and curious," numbering ten thousand in Rush's estimate, gathered outside the house to catch a glimpse of the revels. Rush, who confessed to feeling some puzzlement that a Protestant republican should rejoice in the birth of a prince "whose religion he had always been taught to consider as unfriendly to humanity," was nonetheless carried to "enchantment" by the "world in miniature" assembled by candlelight inside the grounds. He spotted gentlemen and tradesmen, lawyers and doctors, painters and poets mingling with political leaders and diplomats. "In a word," Rush wrote, "the assembly was truly republican. The company was mixed, it is true, but the mixture formed the harmony of the evening."[1] Whigs and Tories suspended their differences, acting toward one another as though they were "members of the same family."

The peculiarly harmonious atmosphere that prevailed throughout the evening prompted Rush to speculation:

Human nature in this instance seems to be turned inside outwards. The picture is still agreeable, inasmuch as it shows in the clearest point of view that there are no prejudices so strong, no opinions so sacred, and no contradictions so palpable, that will not yield to the lover of liberty. . . . Here were to be seen heroes and patriots in close conversation with one another. Washington and Dickinson held several dialogues with each together. Here were to be seen men conversing with each other who had appeared in all the different stages of the American war. Dickinson and Morris frequently reclined together against the same pillar. Here were to be seen statesmen and warriors, from opposite ends of the continent, talking of the history of the war in their respective states. . . . Here were to be seen men who had opposed each other in the councils and parties of their country, forgetting all former resentments and exchanging civilities with each other. Mifflin and Reed accosted each other with all the kindness of former friends. . . . An Indian chief in his savage habits, and the count Rochambeau in his splendid and expensive uniform, talked with each other as if they had been the subjects of the same government, generals in the same army, and partakers of the same blessings of civilized life.[2]

He noted that some guests declined the opportunity to attach themselves to convivial conversational clusters: "Here and there, too, appeared a solitary character walking among the artificial bowers of the garden. The celebrated author of 'Common Sense' retired frequently from the company to analyze his thoughts and to enjoy the repast of his own original ideas."[3] However, Rush and his fellow guests forswore the temptation to make such behavior the subject of critical and divisive comment.

When, led in by the ladies, the company sat down to dine, "a decent and respectful silence pervaded the whole company." Such solemnity was in marked contrast to the raucous atmosphere that normally prevailed at a civic banquet, even one held in a public house with the pretentions of the City Tavern. Rush commented on the difference: "Intemperance did not show its head; levity composed its countenance, and even humor itself forgot for a few moments its usual haunts; and the simple jest no less than the loud laugh, were unheard at any of the tables."[4] But Rush found this silence unsettling. He noted that "the company looked and behaved more as if they were worshipping than eating."[5]

Rush considered but rejected the idea that the guests' willingness to suspend their political differences and forego intemperance and levity was due to "good breeding." It must have been tempting for the guests, aware of the presence of a crowd of "idle and curious" onlookers on the other side of a wooden palisade, to conclude that they were drawn from an elite uniquely capable of conducting themselves with restraint, decorum, and harmony. (The chevalier had intended to distribute two pipes of Madeira and $600 of small change to the crowd assembled outside. He was dissuaded "from this act of generosity by some gentlemen of the city, who were afraid that it might prove the occasion of a riot or some troublesome proceedings.")[6] Yet, as Rush stressed, the company was mixed. Rush could not quite bring himself to attribute good breeding to Thomas Paine, or to "an Indian chief" in "savage habit." Moreover, he knew that similar events hosted by American statesmen were more declamatory and partisan than the chevalier's fete. Seeking to avoid the conclusion that republican society lacked refinement or decorum, Rush wondered whether breeding alone accounted for the guests' restrained behavior.

Rush therefore developed a second explanation for the evening's tone. His account suggests that the guests were fully conscious of both the potentially troublesome crowd of impoverished spectators outside the chevalier's residence and of the luxurious splendor of their surroundings. The ironies inherent in republican leaders' celebrating the birthday of a Catholic prince in an age of inflation and shortage, combined with the chevalier's minute concern for the proper staging of the event, seem to have cowed or overawed the assembled multitude. Although he doubted whether a meal eaten in virtual silence was a manifestation of true taste and understanding, Rush believed that the occasion and, more particularly, its design and conduct had determined the guests' behavior.

Although Rush appreciated the harmony produced by the chevalier's careful planning, he felt manipulated. The tone of the evening's events was slightly oppressive:

Notwithstanding all the agreeable circumstances that have been mentioned, many of the company complained of the want of something else to render the entertainment complete. Everybody felt pleasure, but it was of too tranquil a nature. Many people felt sentiments, but they were produced by themselves, and did not arise from any of the enjoyments of the evening. . . . An ode on the birth of the Dauphin, sung or repeated, would have answered the expectations and corresponded with the feelings of everybody. The understanding and taste of the company would have shared with the senses in the pleasures of the evening.[7]

In the last quarter of the eighteenth century, many establishments opened for business in Philadelphia whose design mirrored the key assumption of events such as the French ambassador's party: that particular values, especially those associated with respectability, could be inculcated in a diverse clientele via the provision and manipulation of carefully designed amenities without parallel in the city's existing stock of public houses. Yet many of the Philadelphians who used pleasure gardens, hotels, and refurbished taverns shared Rush's reaction to the chevalier de la Luzerne's fete, believing that public sociability ought to offer a means of self-expression. Although Philadelphians expressed increasing impatience with the conflict produced by a general discussion of social and political ideas in companies of mixed class and outlook, the city's public spaces continued to appeal as sites in which a man might publicly signify his agreement with the values of those of a like-mind. Hence Philadelphians continued to use taverns, pleasure gardens, and hotels to display and assess social values which had political connotations. The values they were most interested in affirming and ascribing changed in ways which offered a further stimulus to the provision of new amenities and attractions. But despite licensees' attempts to anticipate and exploit changing mores by providing a wider variety of public space in which to display and observe, taverngoers remained frustrated and dissatisfied. By the close of the eighteenth century many Philadelphians had abandoned as hopeless the search for a public space where they could express a sociability which was republican and yet restrained, consensual and yet declaratory, and which afforded a measure of privacy even in heterogeneous company. This development ushered in the age of the saloon and hotel.

*   *   *

The idea that a man's mood and behavior could be altered or determined by his surroundings had a peculiar resonance among Philadelphians. The city's grid of streets and squares was laid out in the belief that it would promote health and sobriety among the city's population. The notion that a carefully designed environment could effect behavioral change would be made manifest most strikingly early in the nineteenth century in the panoptical architecture of Philadelphia's Eastern State Penitentiary. But, as early as the 1780s, many establishments founded in Philadelphia sought to accommodate a growing preference for consensual public sociability by providing facilities whose novelty, splendor, and refinement would induce patrons to abandon the disputatious mores previously associated with taverngoing.

In the final quarter of the eighteenth century the collapse of controls on the maximum retail price of goods and services sold in public houses allowed publicans to court a core constituency in the expectation that, if their judgment proved sound, they could make a profit while serving only a portion of the community. In July 1789, for example, George and Robert Gray announced that they had acquired two ferryboats and a steel-sprung carriage for the use of ladies and gentlemen who wished to cross to the west bank of the Schuylkill and travel a short distance to their recently opened pleasure gardens.[8] Magistrates had for some time licensed a tavern on the west bank of the Schuylkill, close to the present-day campus of the University of Pennsylvania, for the use of travelers approaching Philadelphia from the south and west. In 1785 Jacob Hiltzheimer attended a Tammany feast at "David Beveridge's place over the Schuylkill, late Reese Meredith's." Judging from Hiltzheimer's description of that event, the tavern was already of a substantial size.[9] However, at some point in the 1780s the merchant Samuel Vaughan advised the licensee to purchase and landscape the land adjoining the inn, "assuring him he would soon reimburse his expences and accumulate a large estate from the company he would draw from Philadelphia." Vaughan undertook to plan the pleasure garden and an English gardener was brought in to complete the works.[10] Aided by George and Robert Gray's investment in improved transportation links, the crowds who flocked to the gardens and tavern fulfilled Samuel Vaughan's confident prediction.

Both the design and operation of the Grays' gardens speak to an attempt to inculcate consensual sociability by manipulating architecture and facilities. As Manasseh Cutler noted, the gardens were large, but artfully divided into numerous areas of differing size that offered various prodigies of art and nature. "As we were walking on the northern side of the garden," he recalled,

We found ourselves on the borders of a grove of wood and upon the brow of a steep hill. Below us was a deep, shady valley, in the midst of which was a purling stream of water, meandering among the rocks in its way down to the river. At a distance we could see three very high arched bridges, one beyond the other. They were built in the Chinese style; the rails on the side open work of various figures, and beautifully painted. We saw them through the grove, the branches of the trees partly concealing them, which produced the more romantic and delightful effect . . . though we saw that it was the work of art, yet it was a most happy imitation of nature.[11]

Continuing his perambulation, Cutler discovered a "federal temple" and an "antique hermitage" which, on closer inspection, proved to be a bathing house. Closer to the Schuylkill, Cutler came upon grottoes and a summerhouse in the Chinese style. "During the whole of this romantic, rural scene," Cutler wrote, "I fancied myself on enchanted ground, and could hardly help looking out for flying dragons, magic castles, little Fairies, Knights-errant, distressed ladies, and all the apparatus of eastern fable. I found my mind really fatigued with so long a scene of pleasure."[12] Cutler took his tour soon after breakfast and apparently met no other visitors. However, the gardens were designed to cater to crowds. Customers were offered bowers, arbors, and shelters within whose comparative privacy the visitor might conjure in his mind's eye a sense of enchantment comparable to that Cutler experienced on his solitary tour.

The tavern buildings also emphasized privacy. The tavern was divided in half. One section was "appropriated to a greenhouse . . . finished in the completest manner for the purpose of arranging trees and plants in the most beautiful order." Visitors could sit in a gallery to gaze upon the plants. The gallery connected with several "handsomely furnished" rooms in the other half of the house. As Cutler noted, these rooms, of varying size, could accommodate simultaneously "several large companies, who would not wish to have intercourse."[13] The proprietors staged a weekly concert to guide and stimulate romantic reflections. At seven o'clock patrons were invited to view the waterfall, illuminated for the occasion, to accompaniment of music from a band concealed in the gardens' federal temple. After a short break the band moved down to the riverside, drawing the spectator's eye over the artful illumination of the gardens.[14]

The colonial tavern had provided the man of discernment with the opportunity to observe the character of neighbors and newcomers through a minute examination of their speech and behavior. This had produced tensions and conflicts within tavern sociability because by insisting that every man had the right to form his own judgments, taverngoers tested the viability of the deferential social relationships that the continued existence of both a social hierarchy and an oligarchic political system seemingly demanded and presumed. In contrast, the visitor to the Grays' gardens was encouraged to observe not man but nature. The gardens' design militated against the conflation of the small politics of everyday sociability with the larger politics of the state that made encounters between men of different backgrounds and opinions in traditional public houses so uneasy. A man's opinion on a purling stream or a collection of flowers and vegetables in a greenhouse was a less obvious signifier of his social and political beliefs than his behavior in a tavern encounter with a merchant prince or idle pauper. Moreover, the gardens and tavern were designed in such a way that visitors stood a fair chance of avoiding unsolicited discussion of the attractions on offer.

The Gray brothers had to compete for customers with entrepreneurs offering equally novel entertainment, as well as with publicans offering genteel and elevated facilities in centrally located public houses. On the eve of independence David Ricketts opened America's first permanent circus, an event commemorated to this day by a small plaque in downtown Philadelphia. Although the circus changed sites, it continued to operate in Philadelphia after the Revolution. Overcoming religious and ideological opposition, entrepreneurial thespians like Lewis Hallam managed to reestablish regular theater performances in federal Philadelphia.[15] Following the lead

Ricketts's Circus and Oeller's Hotel. 1797. Library Company of Philadelphia. Newer forms of public space, such as Ricketts's Circus, transformed the urban landscape of Philadelphia towards the close of the eighteenth century. Oeller's Hotel, a portion of whose frontage is shown on the right hand side of the circus, opened for business in 1791. It immediately established itself as the largest and most luxurious hotel in the city. Oeller's was the site of a grand feast in honor of Citizen Génet, as well as events staged by the Society of Cincinnati and Philadelphia's Dancing Assembly. In December 1799 Ricketts's Circus and Oeller's Hotel were destroyed in a fire.

of John White, householders and businessmen in the city and its outskirts opened spas, establishments that offered bathing, drinking, and quack cures.[16] A more macabre form of entertainment was offered at the museum housed on the third floor of the College of Physicians. Its collection of skeletons and anatomies included the remains of a young woman executed in London for beating a servant girl to death. Manasseh Cutler, noting that the skeleton possessed a fine set of teeth, concluded that she must have been a young woman of distinction.[17]

As the range of attractions on offer outside licensed premises increased, the landlords of traditionally appointed public houses redoubled their efforts to draw in crowds. In 1790, for example, William Geisse announced that on the recommendation of the governor of North Carolina, he had booked a noted waxworks for display at the Bunch of Grapes. Attractions included likenesses of George Washington, the British royal family, the bishop of New York, the duchess of Orleans, and Moll, "a mad woman who shows her ill-nature by attempting to strike those who approach her."[18] This curious assortment of figurines was presumably calculated to appeal to a broad spectrum of potential visitors. It was with a distinct air of resignation that the landlord of the White Horse and Fountain announced that he had secured the exclusive rights to stage the gymnastic performances of William Powers, a lad lately arrived from London. Powers could dance the hornpipe with both feet on the crown of his head, perform an imitation of porpoises in the sea, and carry off "other feats too tedious to mention." The landlord concluded this rather halfhearted encomium with the offer to refund dissatisfied customers' admission fees.[19]

Meanwhile, as Philadelphians demonstrated an ever stronger demand for rational, sober, and harmonious sociability, the number of houses attempting to provide a refined service uncommon in the city's existing stock of inns and taverns increased. In 1780 Vincent Pelosi took on both the Old London Coffeehouse and the City Tavern by opening the Pennsylvania Coffeehouse on Front and Market Streets. Pelosi undertook to supply food, wines, and coffee "always fresh even by the single cup." He announced his intention to establish a directory of traders in the coffeehouse and also to maintain there a directory of ship's news.[20] Pelosi was unable break the hold the City Tavern and the Old London Coffeehouse had on Philadelphia's mercantile community. He crossed the Delaware to open the first coffeehouse in Camden, New Jersey.[21] But the Pennsylvania Coffeehouse continued to trade under the management of Albert Warnick. In 1789 Warnick announced: "The old Pennsylvania Coffeehouse is not yet annihilated, but open for the reception and accommodation of farmers, mechanics, millers, captains of vessels and others, as well as merchants, where almost all the public prints, magazines, etc. of America, and those of Europe as often as they come to hand are regularly filed for their perusal, information and entertainment—and that as usual, good and constant attendance will be given."[22] Warnick was gambling that farmers, mechanics, and millers now craved the rational and self-consciously respectable sociability that had led the city's wealthiest merchants to found a tavern and a coffeehouse of their own.

Demand for their services was spread among a broad cross section of the community and was strong enough to keep both the Old London and the Pennsylvania Coffeehouses in business. Keepers of the City Tavern were less successfully able to compete with a new establishment opened by James Oeller. Oeller's Hotel, which opened for business in 1791, was the first public house in Philadelphia formally styled as a hotel. It stood on the south side of Chestnut Street, close to the Pennsylvania statehouse and next door to Ricketts's Circus. It was conducted in substantial premises originally built to house the Episcopalian Academy. With a frontage on of 190 feet on Chestnut Street, Oeller's Hotel was the largest building yet used as a public house. Twice the size of the City Tavern, Oeller's soon eclipsed its rival in fame. In 1794 the English traveler Henry Wansey happened upon Oeller's during a tour of the city on a summer's day. Ordering a glass of punch to quench his thirst, Wansey was delighted to find it served with a large chunk of ice, thanks to Oeller's investment in an ice house. Wansey was staying at the City Tavern, where he had been tormented by bedbugs and poor service. He immediately moved to Oeller's. Rather than spend another night at the City Tavern, he accepted a bed in the hotel's assembly room, alongside a number of other travelers, until a bedroom became free. The assembly room delighted Wansey. "It is," he wrote, "a most elegant room, sixty feet square, with a handsome music gallery at one end." It was "papered after the French taste, with Pantheon figures in compartments . . . festoons, pillars, and groups of antique drawings, in the same style as lately introduced in London."[23] When not housing visitors, this room was used by the city's Dancing Assembly and as a site for formal banquets.[24] Wansey was delighted with his new billet. He described Oeller's as the "most agreeable lodgings in Philadelphia." Moreau de St Méry agreed; the hotel was, he averred, "the most beautiful and comfortable inn in the United States."[25]

There is a barely concealed subtext to the praise European visitors lavished on sites like the Grays' gardens or Oeller's Hotel. The refinement foreign travelers identified in these exceptional sites contrasted in their eyes with the crudeness, even vulgarity, that they perceived in tavern gatherings in the young republic. But new public attractions such as the Grays' gardens, or amenities such as Oeller's Hotel, vied with waxwork exhibits or displays of gymnastic feats staged in tavern yards for the patronage of an increasingly choosy public. The keepers of established houses did not give up their attempts to draw in crowds, and the willingness of the landlord of the White Horse and Fountain to go so far as to offer a money-back guarantee to those members of the public who attended William Powers's gymnastic display testifies to a belief that crowds could be induced to visit a traditionally appointed tavern. Although more exclusive than the typical tavern, Oeller's Hotel depended for its survival on the custom of locals as well as strangers. Philadelphians, and most American visitors to the city, frequented both traditional taverns and newer sites like the Grays' gardens. As a result, the company a customer might encounter in Philadelphia's public houses continued to exhibit a social diversity that European visitors, unfamiliar with the heterogeneity of the colonial tavern, found symptomatic of an offensive egalitarianism.

Philadelphians retained a healthy appetite for public appearance and, in contrast to fastidious visitors, a marked capacity to tolerate public assemblies in which tradesmen and professionals, if not paupers and merchant princes, mixed on terms of implied equality. However, the very existence of sites like Oeller's Hotel or the Grays' gardens reflected, and further promoted, a gradual evolution in the assumptions Philadelphians brought to the conduct of sociability in public gatherings. Two factors produced this evolution. The first was a growing dissatisfaction with the behavioral forms through which fellowship and consensus were expressed. The second was the continuing influence of a partisan understanding of the significance of speech and behavior in public.

Dissatisfaction with toasting and dancing, ritual behaviors through which Philadelphians had been accustomed to express fellowship, grew from the frequency with which they were employed rather than from a perception that they were irrelevant. Although by the close of the Revolution both rich and poor Philadelphians were beginning to conclude that the tavern milieu was a site inimical to rational discussion of the details of state policy, they continued to believe that speech and deportment in public places could hold political significance. Benjamin Rush was among the first to denounce the quasi-constitutional role afforded to tavern companies by Pennsylvania's state constitution. Yet at the French minister's fete, Rush fretted lest the company should demonstrate through its behavior values that were less than satisfactorily republican and Protestant. Standing amidst the bowers and groves erected in the chevalier de la Luzerne's garden, Benjamin Rush had felt pleasure in the harmony that prevailed. Nevertheless, he felt that something—a song perhaps—was wanted. For Rush and many of his contemporaries it was not enough merely to feel as though one was a member of an extended republican family in a public gathering. In the context of continuing partisanship and ever widening divisions of wealth, Philadelphians felt compelled to make explicit expressions of fellowship in sociable gatherings, lest in the absence of any such gesture implicit snubs or checks might fester into conflicts that would tear mixed companies apart.

In order to achieve harmonious yet meaningful sociability, Philadelphians placed renewed emphasis and weight on the behavioral forms by which they believed they could express or signify fellowship. Yet the manner in which respectable Philadelphians used toasting in an attempt to secure harmony occasioned a dissatisfaction and disgust that drove many of them to explore new forms of sociability and provided a market for sites such as pleasure gardens or spas. In December 1788, for example, 45 members of the St. Andrew's Society gathered for their annual banquet. They drank 38 bottles and 2 "bowls" of Madeira, 27 bottles of claret and 26 of porter, 2 bowls of punch, and eight bottles of port.[26] Such heavy drinking, by no means untypical of the period, cannot be attributed to a desire to stage an ostentatious demonstration of wealth.[27] On the contrary, members objected to the growing expense involved in staging dinners. In 1790 the society agreed that in the future the cost of a banquet should not exceed 10 s. per person—a decision that suggests that the Scotsmen were not an especially greedy bunch.[28] The size of the wine bill that accompanied even a comparatively modest gathering such as the St. Andrew's Society's annual dinner can be explained by a craving to express explicitly through copious toasts and healths the shared sense of fellowship that Rush had sought at the French ambassador's fete.

Visitors to Philadelphia in the 1780s and 1790s found the urgency with which locals toasted one another puzzling. When the marquis de Chastellux visited Philadelphia he found it "an absurd and truly barbarous practice, the first time you drink and at the beginning of dinner, to call out successively to each individual, to let him know you drink his health." The "actor in this ridiculous comedy," he wrote,

is sometimes ready to die with thirst, whilst he is obliged to inquire the names, or catch the eye of five or twenty or thirty persons, and the unhappy persons to whom he addresses himself [wait] with impatience; for it is certainly not possible for them to bestow a very great attention to what they are eating, and what is said to them, being incessantly called to the right or the left, or pulled by the sleeve by charitable neighbors who are so kind as to acquaint them of the politeness they are receiving . . . these . . . attacks terminate in downright duels. They call to you from one end of the table, "Sir, will you permit me to drink a glass of wine with you?" This proposal is always accepted, and does not admit the excuse . . . *"one does not drink without being acquainted."* The bottle is then passed to you, and you must look your enemy in the face . . . you wait [un]til he likewise has poured out his wine, and taken his glass; you then drink mournfully with him, as a recruit imitates the corporal in his exercises.[29]

Mathew Carey described the "savage and barbarous custom . . . worthy of Creeks and Cherokees" of "bumper toasts." Every man had to fill his glass and drain it for a bumper. "If he attempted to flinch," then, Carey recalled, "However weak his head might be and however unable to bear much wine, his delinquency was pointed out and a clamor raised to force him to finish the glass. Sometimes the doors of the dining room were locked to prevent the escape of the guests."[30]

In 1744 Dr. Alexander Hamilton had been able to express what he took to be a gentlemanly reserve by deflecting conversational initiatives from the company he found gathered around the Three Tuns's "great oblong table." Such an expression of detachment was denied the guests at dinner parties in federal Philadelphia. The substance of Chastellux's complaint was that he was forced to drink with strangers. Moreau de St. Méry, a critical observer of American manners, conceded that in this respect they were superior to French etiquette. He was slightly puzzled to receive lengthy introductions to the guests he met at a dinner in Philadelphia but reflected that this was "prudent" and that in French houses a guest "frequently" makes "offensive remarks about someone who is there but whom he does not know."[31]

However, the frequency with which even Philadelphians who already knew one another asked the question "Will you permit me to drink a glass of wine with you?" promoted a heavy consumption of alcohol which many found irksome. Moreau de St. Méry reported that when the ladies retired at the dessert stage of an American dinner, the male guests invariably made a rush to the corner of the room to search for night tables and vases in which to relieve themselves in order to make room for more liquor.[32] The expense, excess and, possibly, vulgarity associated with toasting and health drinking as means of achieving consensual sociability go a long way toward explaining the appeal a site like the Grays' gardens held for well-to-do Philadelphians. At the Grays' a man and his intimates might sup in privacy, free

Glass Decanter, with replica stopper. English. C. 1760. Philadelphia Musuem of
Art: Bequest of Mr. George Burford Lorimer. (*Facing page*) Silver Cann.
Richard Humphreys. 1775. Philadelphia Museum of Art. The Richardson Fund.
Drinking vessels of this sort were commissioned by men eager to establish their
drinking mores as respectable. The decanter would have been used in a genteel
home. It was designed to hold punch that had been prepared in advance, thus
depriving a company of the opportunity to comment on the ingredients of the

drink they were to consume. The decanter allowed a host to control the strength of the punch he served to his guests, making it a vessel more suitable than a punch bowl for use at gatherings attended by ladies. The cann's owner would not have supped from a communal vessel and, by demanding that he drink only from a vessel bearing his initials, would have been able to exert some control over the pace of his consumption.

from that "intercourse" with other companies that might lead to the challenge, "a glass of wine with you sir?"

Dancing was another activity through which well-to-do Philadelphians believed they could express a willingness to forego dispute in the interests of promoting a consensual sociability. Refusing to dance, or dancing out
of turn, was as serious a social offense as refusing to drink a toast. Designed
to force guests to dance, the addition of commemorative ascriptions such as
"Burgoyne's defeat" to individual dances by the managers of Philadelphia's
Dancing Assembly actually encouraged some subscribers to stand aside. As
in the case of toasting, the punctilio that accompanied the arrangement of a
dance had by 1790 become so onerous that some potentially eligible dancers
declined to attend. In 1791, in an attempt to boost attendance, the assembly
abandoned the long gallery of the City Tavern in favor of the more fashionable rooms available at Oeller's Hotel.[33] Henry Wansey, who was impressed
by the decor of Oeller's assembly room, was puzzled by the rules that governed the dances held there. Dances were to begin at seven o'clock and end
at midnight. Their conduct was the sole responsibility of a board of managers elected from among the assembly's subscribers. The managers placed
women guests within a number of sets. (A "set" denoted the number of men
and women required to perform a country or square dance.) They retained
the right to place brides or distinguished strangers at the head of a dance,
but in all cases precedence within a set was determined by lot. Precedence
was a matter of moment, since dances were called in rotation by the head of
each set on the floor. A cotillion could be danced only after each set had
chosen a country dance. Ladies could not quit a dance, alter its figure, or
dance outside their set without the managers' permission. Gentlemen, who
would not be admitted in boots, colored stocking, or undress, were required
to comply with managers' decisions on pain of being black balled. Nobody
but the managers could instruct the musicians and no member was permitted to block the view of the dancers.[34]

Such stringent regulation was necessary because Philadelphians read a
great deal of meaning into matters of precedence, dress, and deportment,
even, or perhaps especially, at a social event such as a ball. The chevalier de la
Luzerne had avoided dispute at his fete by assigning each of his guests a
partner in one of two sets. Even so, the presence of "several Quaker ladies,"
presumably members of established Philadelphia families, taxed the chevalier's command of etiquette. These ladies arrived in plain dress, signifying an
intention to uphold Quaker values and suggesting that it was unlikely they
would take their place in either of the two sets of dancers. To avoid offend-

ing either the ladies or the partners they might snub, these guests were accommodated in a private room from which they could view the dancing and be seen by the dancers through "a gauze curtain."[35] Benjamin Rush recorded, with a degree of surprise, that this arrangement succeeded in preventing dispute. But regularly scheduled balls and assemblies were accompanied by squabbles over status. Moreau de St. Méry recorded gleefully, as an example of the hypocrisy of republican values, the fisticuffs that broke out at a ball as a result of a dispute over precedence between the wife of a jeweler and the wife of a hairdresser.[36] Given the existence of these tensions, one of the attractions of the Grays' gardens (or even a large converted tavern) was that in a number of private rooms, each containing a small company, issues of precedence and ranking were less likely to arise.

Although the popularity of sites like the Grays' gardens reflects the influence among Philadelphians of a dissatisfaction with the mores that governed sociability in public spaces, the manner in which George and Robert Gray staged a grand Fourth of July event in 1790 suggests something of the positive appeal of the city's new public attractions. Ticket holders were invited to travel out to the Grays' tavern in the late afternoon. The newly completed floating bridge across the Schuylkill was flagged with the colors of the thirteen states and garlanded with flowers to mark the occasion. On arrival at the Grays', visitors were confronted with the "Federal ship *Union*" that had formed the centerpiece of the "great Federal procession" held in Philadelphia to celebrate the ratification of the Constitution. Thirteen lads dressed as shepherds and thirteen lasses in the garb of shepherdesses sang a specially composed ode to liberty in the federal temple. As dusk fell, customers were treated to a fireworks display, as well as the illumination of a transparent portrait of George Washington and statues representing the "heathen deities." Food and drink could be obtained from three bars and several tables, groaning under the weight of elaborate cold collations, which were dotted around the grounds.

There was some risk involved in using the gardens to stage a Fourth of July spectacular. In advertisements for their event, the Grays asserted rather nervously: "We cannot but acknowledge the obligations we are under to all persons for their general good conduct, and have not the least doubt but on this day, designed to celebrate the most remarkable revolution in the annals of mankind, the same order will be observed."[37] The proprietors were well aware that many Philadelphians were accustomed to celebrating the Fourth with a rowdiness ill suited to the tone these festivities sought to establish. In 1777 George Bryan viewed the approach of the first anniversary of American independence with some alarm. Despite the fact that two hundred soldiers had been detailed to join the city's watchmen on the streets and that word had gone out that all illuminations and bonfires were to be extinguished by eleven, Bryan was still concerned that "some disorder may happen." John Adams, who had been invited to a banquet at the City Tavern and would not, therefore, have to swill rum at a street-corner bonfire, argued that the celebration would strike "the utmost terror into the hearts of every lurking Tory."[38] However the implicit contrast between plebeian celebrations of the Fourth—heavily policed street-corner bonfires—and the banquets with which patricians marked the day produced each year a tense atmosphere that held the potential for disorder to be visited on well-to-do citizens rather than "lurking Tories." Bourgeois dissatisfaction with existing celebrations of the Fourth produced a market for the Grays' carefully managed spectacle, but nonetheless such an event could have been the occasion of a riot.

Many factors explain why the Fourth of July celebration at Grays' gardens passed off without disorder. The cost of admission, drinks, and travel across the Schuylkill deterred the "curious and idle" who gawked at the French minister's fete from attending. The brothers could make the potentially inflammatory announcement that they sought the custom of the "respectable public" secure in the knowledge that only comparatively well-to-do Philadelphians could afford to attend. Then again there was the potentially overwhelming scale of the day's events. The Grays' patrons were offered a full evening of comparatively novel entertainment. Of course, men and women who paid for admission to the city's theater were also offered novelty and spectacle, yet far from being subdued by the theatricality of the entertainment on offer, theater-goers were notorious for interrupting the players, calling for songs, demanding the reprise of popular soliloquies, booing unpopular actors, and even fighting in their seats. That the Philadelphians who attended the Grays' Fourth of July celebration did not interrupt the federal shepherds and shepherdesses, call on the band to strike up more stirring tunes, interfere with the illumination of Washington's portrait, or barge in on small groups enjoying the event in private booths and shelters was ultimately due to the implicit message of the events staged in the gardens.

The attractions the Grays offered the respectable public who paid to attend their Fourth of July spectacular eschewed partisan comment but nevertheless made a subtle political point. The American Revolution, the most remarkable political event in the history of mankind, was concluded.

Respectable citizens might disagree as to the proper conduct of future republican governments, but their shared consciousness of the awesome achievements of the Revolution ought to impart a sense of proportion to their disputes. These were comfortable nostrums. Members of the Grays' audience would have felt little need to contest the values being enacted before them. Moreover, by remaining passive and suspending partisanship, ticket holders enacted and garnered a respectability many of them were denied in more time-honored entertainments. To demonstrate this respectability, the public had to do nothing more than mind its own business and enjoy the show. The event passed off without disorder because those who attended felt they had more to gain by refraining from criticizing some or all of its political assumptions than they had from scoring a narrow political point by interrupting an ode to liberty or jeering the appearance of the federal ship *Union*.

Yet the Grays did not repeat their experiment and competitors did not emulate it. Perhaps the paying public at Fourth of July spectacular preferred, like Benjamin Rush at the French ambassador's fete, events staged in ways that allowed some means of making an active statement of values. Certainly, however popular or profitable the Grays' Fourth of July celebration might have been, throughout the 1790s Philadelphians also staged events through which they could publicly express partisan political allegiances rather than a politically passive "respectability."

In 1793 Oeller's Hotel was the scene of a grand dinner in honor of Citizen Gênet. This event drove William Cobbett to distraction, and Cobbett's fulminations ensured that it achieved a kind of fame. James Oeller was a Francophile. He kept a French staff at his hotel and, as mentioned above, the hotel's assembly room was furnished in the French style. It is hardly surprising that the hotel became the headquarters of the city's Democratic Republican community. Two hundred of the city's Democratic Republicans gathered to honor Citizen Gênet in May 1793. The guests, marshaled by Charles Biddle and the governor of Pennsylvania, Thomas Mifflin, enjoyed a lavish meal. A liberty cap was paraded on a liberty pole and then placed ceremoniously on the head of each diner in turn. These tokens of liberty were then presented to a deputation of sailors from the frigate *L'Ambuscade*, who accepted them with a promise to defend American liberties to the death. Then diners sang the "Ça Ira," "Marseillaise," and an ode specially composed to Franco-American fraternity. Outside the hotel a battery of artillery fired salutes to mark the toasts drunk within. These included "The guillotine to all tryants, plunderers and *funding* speculators" and "The persecuted Citizen Gênet: may his country reward his honest zeal, and the shafts of *calumny* levelled against him, recoil upon the *Archers*."[39]

As details of Gênet's illegal activities and the depredations of French privateers began to circulate within Philadelphia's maritime community, this feast recoiled upon its sponsors. William Cobbett and other opponents of republican excess whipped up the frenzy of denunciation.[40] "Respectable" citizens, a group defined in large measure by their willingness to observe the rules governing balls staged by the Dancing Assembly or to refrain from disorder at a Fourth of July celebration at the Grays' gardens, formed a natural constituency for such attacks on partisan frenzy. Conservative critics denounced not only the occasional use of public houses to stage political events but also the continuing use of traditionally appointed taverns as sites in which parties were organized and marshaled. Jeremiads on the link between taverns and politics had been written through the eighteenth century. As we saw in Chapter 5, the cumulative effect of repeated attacks both on the legitimacy of political discussion in taverns and on the corruption presumed to originate in the use of taverns for electioneering was that by the 1770s and 1780s Philadelphians had begun to devalue the significance of political discussion and action in the tavern milieu. This trend continued in the 1790s as Federalist polemics against tavern demagogues widened their focus to argue that any involvement with the tavern trade disqualified a man from involvement in the political process.

In 1797, for example, Israel Israel, keeper of the Cross Keys on Chestnut Street (the house formerly one as the One Tun and kept in the 1770s by Joseph Ogden), stood as a candidate for election to the Pennsylvania assembly. Israel had built a following in Philadelphia largely on the strength of his efforts on behalf of victims of the city's yellow fever epidemics. Nonetheless, "Civis," writing in the Federalist interest, was appalled that a tavernkeeper should have the temerity to present himself for election. "I object to no man as a legislator who has the character and talents for the situation," he wrote. "However," he continued,

I would not . . . select a man for Senator, because he was a merchant, mechanic or publican, or because he had in either of these characters performed an office of humanity. Will anyone who values the privilege of an elector, chuse a man to legislate . . . merely because he risked his life in nursing the sick, or because he made a fortune by keeping a public house? . . . Israel Israel is objected to not simply for being a publican; but being a publican, and his friends not pretending that he possesses the requisite qualifications for a legislator, the circumstance of his being a publican renders his being chosen totally improper.[41]

Creamware Punch Bowl, transfer printed. English. C. 1800. Philadelphia Museum of Art: Bequest of R. Wistar Harvey. The exterior of the bowl presents pastoral images. The interior is inscribed "The Fœderal Union." This artifact is suggestive of the values which accompanied that process which Simon Newman has described as the "regularization of popular political culture" in the 1790s. Americans continued to symbolize political allegiances through feasts and toasts. But their willingness to buy and use relatively crude ceremonial wares from English potteries testifies to the extent to which political discussion in the 1790s had become detached from the passionate world of debate in mixed tavern companies typical of the colonial era.

Israel was elected to the assembly in the fall of 1797 but stripped of his seat in Februray 1798 for alleged electoral irregularities. By arguing that publicans could not show a disinterested public spirit, Civis was, in effect, suggesting that Israel had bribed his supporters with treats of liquor.

But as important as the ever more heated rhetoric with which Federalist and Democratic Republican denounced one another's demagoguery and corruption was the evolution of a new sensibility within which Philadelphians viewed political discourse. In election campaigns in the 1720s, 1742, and 1764, Philadelphians had found it almost impossible to express political neutrality in conversational exchanges conducted in public houses. In contrast, while the 1790s witnessed an unprecedented partisan frenzy, increasing numbers of Philadelphians stood aloof. Whereas previous generations of Philadelphians had read a wealth of meaning into speech and action in public places, by the close of the century, self-consciously "respectable" and "philosophically inclined" citizens refrained from pouncing on the significance of scenes and events witnessed during the course of public life. Ezekiel Forman demonstrated the values of the new sensibility when, in March 1794, he paid to view two automatons displayed by "Mess. L'Egalité" at Mr. Poor's Academy for Young Ladies. Forman wrote to his friend John Rockhill that,

One of these figures is inte[nded] to represent an *Aristocrat* and the other a *Sans Culotte*. The former cons[istent]ly refuses to dance the tune of the "Ça Ira" or the "Carmagnole" which as you know are Republican airs. In short they so nearly resemble human nature in looks, gesture, in attitude and action that as a person wittily observed they only want to be animated with some of the fire Prometheus stole from heaven to make them perfect men in every respect. To a Philosophic or reflecting mind I consider these artificial men as one of the greatest curiosities ever exhibited in this Country as they are a remarkable and striking proof to what an amazing extent the powers of Philosophical mechanism may be carried.[42]

Earlier generations of Philadelphian taverngoers would have had no need of an automaton to suggest and mimic the political values of human behavior. Earlier generations read political significance into dancing, singing, or silence as observed in the behavior of strangers and locals in intimate and spontaneous encounters in taverns. Reflecting minds in colonial Philadelphia were obsessed with decoding the meaning and significance of speech and action in public places. In the federal city, in sites like the Grays' gardens, Philadelphians were offered inanimate scenes and objects as proper studies for thought and contemplation. Some Philadelphians continued to read meaning into speech and behavior observed in boozy encounters even

as others participated in the tranquil pleasures of a morning spent peram-
bulating in a pleasure garden or an evening spent in the strictly controlled
environment of the assembly room at Oeller's Hotel. All agreed that an
event such as the feast in honor of Citizen Gênet held political significance.
However, by the 1790s most "respectable" citizens had abandoned the notion that speech and behavior overheard and observed casually in traditionally appointed taverns offered unique or even important insights into
the social and political issues of the day.

In 1791 Benjamin Rush wrote a widely reprinted treatise on the harmful
effects of rum and other spirituous liquors. From midcentury, pamphlets on
the medical dangers of drinking, some of them written by Rush himself, had
contributed to the creation of a climate in which Philadelphians viewed
heavy drinking as harmful. (Of course well-to-do Philadelphians' willingness to accept this message can also be attributed to the fact that the assumptions they brought to sociability led them into heavy drinking sessions.)
Rush's *The Drunkard's Emblem* is significant, not for its novelty but for the
precision with which its arguments demolished any lingering attraction
sociability in mixed tavern company might hold for a respectable citizen.
Rush asked how a man could identify whether he or his companions were
drunk. The symptoms of drunkenness included unusual garrulity and unusual silence. A drunk displayed a disposition to quarrel and also an uncommon good humor. Observers could spot drunkenness in its victim's propensity to disclose his, or other people's, secrets. The drunkard confessed his own
faults and passed comment on the failings of the company in which he found
himself.[43] For Rush, very nearly all forms of behavior in sites where liquor
was consumed, especially behavior liable to be observed in taverns, indicated
drunkenness. There was, then, nothing to be gained from close observation
of speech and behavior in such sites; indeed, any such interest might indicate
morbid fascination with liquor characteristic of the drunkard.

In this book I have attempted to explain why taverngoing was so
popular with residents of Philadelphia in the first hundred years of its
history. I have argued that Philadelphians believed they could garner from
speech and behavior observed in mixed, competitive, and often drunken
tavern encounters insights and information about themselves and the world
around them of a quality unattainable in any other site. Colonial Philadelphians kept returning to the tavern, despite the conflicts and contests
taverngoing produced, because they believed that speech and behavior in
public houses provided vitally important, even if potentially deceptive, indicators of a man's character and opinions. In *The Drunkard's Emblem* Ben-

jamin Rush encapsulated a set of values that demoted taverngoing to the status of aberrant social behavior. If speech and behavior in public houses said nothing more about a man's character than that he was a drunkard, what possible claim could a tavern have on the time and interest of a respectable and philosophical citizen? If such a citizen needed to demonstrate his respectability in public, he should do so in a coffeehouse booth or an arbor at the Grays' gardens. Some Philadelphians disdained Rush's arguments, but increasing numbers of respectable citizens followed his advice.[44] In the nineteenth century, only saloongoing laborers maintained the traditionalist assumptions that had once drawn colonial Philadelphians of all ranks, religions, and ethnicities to drink side by side in the shared and cramped space of the tavern.

Abbreviations

APS	American Philosophical Society
Assembly	"Votes of the Pennsylvania House of Assembly," in Gertrude McKinney et al., eds., *Pennsylvania Archives*, 8th. ser., 9 vols. (Harrisburg, Pa.: The State Printer, 1931–1939).
Chronicle	*Pennsylvania Chronicle*
Common Council	*Minutes of the Common Council of the City of Philadelphia, 1704 to 1776*. Philadelphia: Crissy and Markley, 1847.
Court 1685–1686	Philadelphia Court Records Taken by Patrick Robinson, 1685–1686, MSS HSP.
Court 1695	Philadelphia County Court of Quarter Sessions Docket, 1695, MSS HSP.
CPA	City of Philadelphia Archives
Franklin Papers	*The Papers of Benjamin Franklin*, ed. Leonard W. Labaree, William B. Willcox, Claude-Anne Lopez, Barbara B. Oberg, et al. 32 vols. to date. New Haven, Conn.: Yale University Press, 1959– .
Gazette	*Pennsylvania Gazette*
HSP	Historical Society of Pennsylvania
LCP	Library Company of Philadelphia
Mercury	*American Weekly Mercury*
Packet	*Pennsylvania Packet*
PCC	*The Papers of Continental Congress*. Microfilm ed. National Archives.
PCMCP	Philadelphia County, Miscellaneous Court Papers, 5 vols. MSS HSP. These volumes which are not numbered are identified in notes by reference to their title within the HSP's catalogue. The date of material cited from this collection will not always match the dates assigned to an individual volume within the series.

PCS	Philadelphia Contributionship Insurance Company. Loose Surveys. Microfilm. HSP.
PGM	*Pennsylvania Genealogical Magazine*
PMHB	*Pennsylvania Magazine of History and Biography*
Provincial Council	"Minutes of the Provincial Council of Pennsylvania: From the Organization to the Termination of Proprietary Government," in Samuel Hazard, ed., *Colonial Records of Pennsylvania*, 16 vols. Harrisburg, Pa.: Joseph Severns, 1852–1853.
Wallace	Wallace Collection of Ancient Records of Philadelphia. MSS HSP.
WMQ	*William and Mary Quarterly*

Notes

Quotations in the text, except citations from songs, toasts, and poems, have been altered to conform to modern conventions regarding spelling, punctuation, and capitalization. Dates in the text and endnotes are given in their modern version. Citations to rare pamphlets are accompanied by their catalogue number in Charles Evans's *American Bibliography*, 14 vols. (Chicago 1903–1959).

Introduction

1. See David E. Shi, *The Simple Life: Plain Living and High Thinking in American Culture* (New York: Oxford University Press, 1985), 28–37; Frederick B. Tolles, *Meeting House and Counting House: The Quaker Merchants of Colonial Philadelphia, 1682–1763* (New York: W. W. Norton, 1963), 64; Mark Edward Lender and James Kirby Martin, *Drinking in America: A History*, rev. ed. (New York: The Free Press, 1987), 1–40; Bruce C. Daniels, *Puritans at Play: Leisure and Recreation in Colonial New England* (London: Macmillan, 1995), 19.

2. "The Drinker's Dictionary," *Gazette*, Jan. 13, 1737.

3. Cited in Joseph J. Kelley, Jr., *Life and Times in Colonial Philadelphia* (Harrisburg, Pa.: Stackpole Press, 1973), 163.

4. Shi, *The Simple Life*, 35. In a letter written to the Free Society of Traders in 1683, Penn extolled the quality of Pennsylvania's great red, muscatel, and black grapes. Cited in Jean R. Soderlund, ed., *William Penn and the Founding of Pennsylvania, 1680–1684: A Documentary History* (Philadelphia: University of Pennsylvania Press, 1983), 311.

5. "The Antediluvians Were All Very Sober," in J. A. Leo Lemay, ed., *Benjamin Franklin: Writings* (New York: Library of America, 1987), 303–304.

6. Ibid. See also 1226–1228; *Franklin Papers*, 8:5–8.

7. For expressions of concern over heavy drinking, see *Gazette*, Dec. 7, 1732; *Mercury*, Jan. 22, 1734; "Boy, Bring a Bowl of China Here," cited in *Franklin Papers*, 2:168.

8. Aquila Rose, Pennsylvania's first poet, associated drinking with "laughter" and "noble living." See "Pennsylvania Poets of the Provincial Period," *PMHB* 17 (1893): 7–8.

9. In seventeenth-century Rotterdam, a city renowned for hard drinking, there was one tavern for every two hundred inhabitants; Simon Schama, *The Embarrassment of Riches: An Interpretation of Dutch Culture in the Golden Age* (Berkeley: University of California Press, 1988), 190–193. The ratio was similar in Paris in the

1700s; Thomas Brennan, *Public Drinking and Popular Culture in Eighteenth-Century Paris* (Princeton, N.J.: Princeton University Press, 1988), 76. See also Table 1.

10. See Chapter 1.

11. Cited in [William C. Reichel], *A Red Rose from the Olden Time: Or, A Ramble through the Annals of the Rose Inn and the Barony of Nazareth, in the Days of the Province, 1752–1772*, ed. John W. Jordan (Bethlehem, Pa., 1883), 35.

12. For powerful statements of this argument, see Michael Zuckerman, "The Fabrication of Identity in Early America," *WMQ*, 3d ser., 34 (1977): 183–214; and Zuckerman, "Identity in British America: Unease in Eden," in *Colonial Identity in the Atlantic World*, ed. Nicholas Canny and Anthony Pagden (Princeton, N.J.: Princeton University Press, 1987), 115–159.

13. "Some Account of the Province of Pennsylvania," in Soderlund, ed., *William Penn and the Founding of Pennsylvania*, 65.

14. William Penn, "A Further Account of Pennsylvania," *PMHB*, 9 (1885), 67.

15. Cited in Gary B. Nash, *Quakers and Politics: Pennsylvania, 1681–1726*, rev. ed. (Boston: Northeastern University Press, 1993), 10.

16. See Tolles, *Meeting House and Counting House*, 13.

17. Cited in Nash, *Quakers and Politics*, 47. See Nash for a discussion of the evolution of Penn's thoughts on government.

18. Roger Chartier, *The Cultural Origins of the French Revolution*, ed. Lydia G. Cochrane (Durham, N.C.: Duke University Press, 1991), 195.

19. For overviews of the nature and breadth of Penn's plans for Philadelphia, see Soderlund, ed., *William Penn and the Founding of Pennsylvania*; Richard S. Dunn and Mary M. Dunn, eds., *The World of William Penn* (Philadelphia: University of Pennsylvania Press, 1986).

20. "Laws and Orders for the Keepers and Frequenters of Ordinaries" (c. 1683), in Soderlund, ed., *William Penn and the Founding of Pennsylvania*, 206–207.

21. "Some Indictments by the Grand Jury of Philadelphia," *PMHB*, 22 (1898), 497. Franklin's argument is discussed in greater detail in Chapter 1.

22. David S. Shields has charted the emergence of belles lettres from Philadelphia's taverns and coffeehouses; see *Civil Tongues and Polite Letters in British America* (Chapel Hill: University of North Carolina Press, 1997), esp. 55- 98.

23. Benjamin Boggs and Mary Boggs, "Inns and Taverns of Old Philadelphia," MSS, Boggs Collection, HSP; Alice Morse Earle, *Stage-Coach and Tavern Days* (1900; rpt., Detroit: Singing Tree Press, 1968); Edward Field, *The Colonial Tavern: A Glimpse of New England Town Life in the Seventeenth and Eighteenth Centuries* (1897; rpt., Ann Arbor, Mich.: n.p., 1979).

24. Roy Rosenzweig, *Eight Hours for What We Will: Workers and Leisure in an Industrial City, 1870–1920* (Cambridge: Cambridge University Press, 1987), esp. 35–64. See also Perry Duis, *The Saloon: Public Drinking in Chicago and Boston, 1880–1920* (Urbana and Chicago: University of Illinois Press, 1983).

25. David Weir Conroy, "The Culture and Politics of Drink in Colonial and Revolutionary Massachusetts, 1681- 1790" (Ph.D. diss., University of Connecticut, 1987), 4–9; Conroy, *In Public Houses: Drink and the Revolution of Authority in Colonial Massachusetts* (Chapel Hill: University of North Carolina Press, 1995).

26. Conroy, *In Public Houses*, 6–7, 83.

27. Ibid., 11.

28. For a valuable survey of this literature and a critique of some of its past practices, see Tim Harris, "Problematising Popular Culture," in *Popular Culture in England c. 1500–1800*, ed. Tim Harris (London: Macmillan, 1995), 1–27.

29. For a superb evocation of this theme, see Sam Bass Warner, Jr., *The Private City: Philadelphia in Three Periods of its Growth*, 2d ed. (Philadelphia: University of Pennsylvania Press, 1987), 3–21.

30. This theme has been developed ably by Richard Bushman. See "American High-Style and Vernacular Cultures," in *Colonial British America: Essays in the New History of the Early Modern Era*, ed. Jack P. Greene and J. R. Pole (Baltimore: Johns Hopkins University Press, 1984), 345–383; and *The Refinement of America: Persons, Houses, Cities* (New York: Knopf, 1992).

31. For a brief and lucid description of events in Massachusetts, see Elisha P. Douglass, *Rebels and Democrats: The Struggle for Equal Political Rights and Majority Rule During the American Revolution* (New York: Quadrangle/The New York Times, 1965), 137–213. For accounts emphasizing the radicalism of Pennsylvania's revolution, see Eric Foner, *Tom Paine and Revolutionary America* (New York: Oxford University Press, 1976); Steven Rosswurm, *Arms, Country, and Class. The Philadelphia Militia and the "Lower Sort" During the American Revolution, 1775–1783* (New Brunswick, N.J.: Rutgers University Press, 1987); Ronald Schultz, *The Republic of Labor: Philadelphia Artisans and the Politics of Class, 1720–1830* (New York: Oxford University Press, 1993).

32. Brennan, *Public Drinking and Popular Culture in Eighteenth-Century Paris*, 6.

33. Ibid., 7.

34. This definition is informed by the work of Georges Duby. See *A History of Private Life: Revelations of the Modern World* (Cambridge: Harvard University Press, 1988), 3–33. My interest in public space was first aroused by Richard Sennett, *The Fall of Public Man: On the Social Psychology of Capitalism* (New York: Vintage Books, 1978).

35. In this sense my approach to the mores of taverngoing is similar to Rhys Isaac's "dramaturgical" treatment of ritualized displays of power and resistance in Tidewater Virginia; *The Transformation of Virginia, 1740–1790* (Chapel Hill: University of North Carolina Press, 1982), esp. 5–10, 94–98, 323–357.

36. Jürgen Habermas, *The Structural Transformation of the Public Sphere: An Inquiry into a Category of Bourgeois Society*, trans. Thomas Burger (Cambridge: MIT Press, 1989).

37. Keith Michael Baker, "Defining the Public Sphere in Eighteenth-Century France: Variations on a Theme by Habermas," in *Habermas and the Public Sphere*, ed. Craig Calhoun (Cambridge: MIT Press, 1992), 183.

38. Alan Tully, *Forming American Politics: Ideals, Interests, and Institutions in Colonial New York and Pennsylvania* (Baltimore: Johns Hopkins University Press, 1994).

Chapter 1. "For Strangers and Workmen"

1. This citation from Proverbs introduced Penn's "Laws and Orders for Keepers and Frequenters of Ordinaries," in Soderlund, ed., *William Penn and the Founding of Pennsylvania*, 206.

2. "The Fundamental Constitutions of Pennsylvania . . ." (1681), Article 21, in Richard S. Dunn and Mary M. Dunn, eds., *The Papers of William Penn*, 5 vols. (Philadelphia: University of Pennsylvania Press, 1981–1987), 2:151; "Laws and Orders for Keepers and Frequenters of Ordinaries," in Soderlund, ed., *William Penn and the Founding of Pennsylvania*, 206.

3. Boggs and Boggs, "Inns and Taverns," 407–410; Hannah Benner Roach, "The Planting of Philadelphia: A Seventeenth-Century Real Estate Development," *PMHB*, 92 (1968), 146–147.

4. Roach, "The Planting of Philadelphia," 146, 182; Roach, "A Philadelphia Business Directory for 1690," *PGM*, 23 (1963–1964), 126; Thomas Allen Glenn, "The Blue Anchor Tavern," *PMHB*, 20 (1896), 429–432; "Presentments of the Grand Inquest of Philadelphia County, 1683," *PMHB*, 23 (1899), 403–405. For a summary of Jones's relations with Penn, see *Lawmaking and Legislators in Pennsylvania: A Biographical Dictionary*, ed. Craig Horle and Marianne Wokeck, 2 vols. (Philadelphia: University of Pennsylvania Press, 1991–1997), 1:469–478.

5. See William Penn to Provincial Council, 1686, in "Letters of William Penn," *PMHB*, 33 (1909), 307. In 1686 cavedweller Hannah Gooding became one of the first publicans charged with keeping a disorderly house; Court 1685–1686, Mar. 3, 1686. Gooding's near neighbor on the bank, Benjamin Chambers, a future president of the Free Society of Traders, also established a tavern in a cave; "Minutes of the Board of Property of the Province of Pennsylvania," in John B. Linn and William H. Egle, eds., *Pennsylvania Archives*, 2d ser., 19 vols. (Harrisburg, Pa.: Lane S. Hart, 1879–1890), 19:3–4; Petition of Benjamin Chambers to the Commissioners Impowered to Inspect the Caves, Penn Manuscripts, Philadelphia Land Grants, HSP, 7:11; Gary B. Nash, "The Free Society of Traders and the Early Politics of Pennsylvania," *PMHB*, 89 (1965), 147–173; Benjamin Chambers, Quit Rent Minute Book, HSP, 99.

6. See *Provincial Council*, Mar. 29, 1683, 1:69; "Presentments of the Grand Inquest," 405; Soderlund, ed., *William Penn and the Founding of Pennsylvania*, 196 n. 2.

7. See Roach, "A Philadelphia Business Directory," 126–127; Dunn and Dunn, eds., *Papers of William Penn*, 2:559 n. 1; Wayland Fuller Dunaway, "The English Settlers in Colonial Pennsylvania," *PMHB*, 52 (1928), 321; Roach, "The Planting of Philadelphia," 168–169.

8. Frampton, a resident and freeman of New York, had been trading in the Delaware Valley area for some years. Frampton brought the first cargo of slaves to Philadelphia. See Gary B. Nash, *Forging Freedom: The Formation of Philadelphia's Black Community* (Cambridge: Harvard University Press, 1988), 8. In the winter of 1684–1685 Penn granted Frampton a lot on the southwest corner of Front and Walnut Streets. In February 1685 Frampton petitioned the provincial council asking

that the caves in front of his lot be vacated in order that he might build a wharf (*Provincial Council*, Feb. 1, 1685, 1:167). Later that year, Robert Turner noted that "William Frampton has built a good brick house by his brewhouse and bakehouse and let the other for an ordinary"; Turner to William Penn, Aug. 3, 1685, cited in Josiah Granville Leach, "Colonial Mayors of Philadelphia," *PMHB*, 18 (1894), 420. See also Roach, "The Planting of Philadelphia," 148–149 n. 10, 172–173; Roach, "A Philadelphia Business Directory," passim; *Provincial Council*, Jan. 16, 1686, 1:167; Horle and Wokeck, eds., *Lawmaking and Legislators in Pennsylvania*, 1:359–360.

　9. Dunn and Dunn, eds., *Papers of William Penn*, 2:558–559. Among the signatories were William Frampton, John Test, Samuel Carpenter, Robert Turner, and Thomas Wynne. A subsequent attempt to establish an excise on rum was also repulsed; Markham to Holme, May 2, 1688, reprinted in Gary B. Nash, "The First Decade in Pennsylvania: Letters of William Markham and Thomas Holme to William Penn," *PMHB*, 90 (1966), 508–509.

　10. "A Planter," cited in Zuckerman, "Identity in British America," 133.

　11. Lemay, ed., *Franklin: Writings*, 303.

　12. Penn, "A Further Account of Pennsylvania," 66. He also told emigrants that a brewery had been established in Philadelphia, ibid., 73. In a similar vein the provincial council linked the number of taverns in the city to its location on "the road, where sailors and others frequently pass and repass between Virginia and New England." Cited in Frances May Manges, "Women Shopkeepers, Tavernkeepers and Artisans in Colonial Philadelphia" (Ph.D. diss., University of Pennsylvania, 1958), 74.

　13. Nicholas More to William Penn, December 1684, in Nash, "The First Decade in Pennsylvania," 326 n. 41. In 1683, one Timothy Metcalf became the first Philadelphian to be prosecuted for being "disordered in drink"; *Provincial Council*, Mar. 28, 1683, 1:68. For early cases of illicit tavernkeeping, see "Presentments of the Grand Inquest," 403–405; Court 1685–1686.

　14. *Provincial Council*, Feb. 9, 1698, 1:527. On this occasion, the council resolved to "suppress" some public houses, to consider not issuing any further licenses, and to collect bonds ensuring good behavior from all publicans; *Provincial Council*, Feb. 10, 1698, 1:528.

　15. *Provincial Council*, Jan. 9–10, 1686, 1:166–167; Court 1685–1686, fol. 17v.

　16. The figure of twelve houses in 1693 represents the total number of taverns for which any documentary evidence establishing location, owner, or date of operation exists. See Boggs and Boggs, "Inns and Taverns"; Robert Earle Graham, "Philadelphia Inns and Taverns," MSS, Graham Collection, APS; Walter C. Brenner, "Taverns and Inns in Philadelphia, 1680–1850," MSS, HSP; Roach, "A Philadelphia Business Directory," 96–105; Roach, "The Planting of Philadelphia," 3–47, 143–194; "Notes and Queries," *PMHB*, 44 (1920), 358; John E. Pomfret, "The First Purchasers of Pennsylvania," *PMHB*, 80 (1956), 137–163; William Brook Rawle, "The First Tax List for Philadelphia County, A.D. 1693," *PMHB*, 8 (1884), 82–105. My estimate of the number of unlicensed houses is based on the frequency of prosecutions against tippling houses between 1683 and 1704. See Court 1685–1686; Court 1695; Wallace; "Presentments of the Grand Inquest," 403–405; "Some Indictments by the Grand Jury," 497.

17. *Provincial Council*, Aug. 7, 1704, 2:163. For subsequent reaffirmations of the principle, see *Provincial Council*, Jan. 12, 1705, 2:239; Dec. 21, 1706, 2:293.

18. The extant portion of the constables' returns can be found in PCMCP 1697–1732. Some publicans named by the constables appear in no other document. This, and the fact that the surviving fragment of their enumeration lists so many persons as dramshopkeepers, suggests that the constables listed all houses in operation. The constables found nine taverns and seven dramshops in operation in Middle Ward in 1721. In 1756, 17 percent of the city's public houses were located in Middle Ward. Assuming the same distribution in 1721, one arrives at a total of ninety-four licensed and unlicensed houses in operation. A passing comment made by James Logan in 1719 suggests that even central authorities had little idea how many licensed taverns were in operation: "The Governor has no certain profits, besides the grants of [the] assembly, except the fees for licenses to public houses; amounting to £60 or £70, or perhaps somewhat better, per annum." James Logan to S. Clement, May 13, 1719, cited in Linn and Egle, eds., *Pennsylvania Archives*, 2d ser., 7:65–66.

19. *Assembly*, 2:1356.

20. "Some Indictments by the Grand Jury," 497.

21. Richard Peters, Cash Book, 1755–1759, Moore Collection, HSP; Hannah Benner Roach, comp. "Taxables in the City of Philadelphia, 1756," *PGM*, 22 (1961), 3–41. Only seventy-one members of this group appear on the 1756 tax list under "tavernkeeper" or its synonyms. A further thirty licensees appear on the tax list under other occupations. I assume that the ten "missing" licensees, five of whom were women, were not actually keeping licensed taverns in the city of Philadelphia that year.

22. See Philadelphia County Tax List, Provincial, 1767, MSS, Rare Books Collection, Van Pelt Library, University of Pennsylvania (hereafter 1767 Tax List); Philadelphia County Tax List, Proprietary, 1769, microfilm, HSP (hereafter 1769 Tax List). Annual lists of licensees recommended can be found in Mayor's Court Docket, 1767–1771, HSP. These lists of recommendees were carefully kept. "Pd" seems to indicate payment of the annual fee. The lists also include approximate addresses—for example, "Front Street." A few of those appearing on this list kept house just outside the city boundaries in Southwark and Northern Liberties. For numerous reasons, including death, removal, and inability to pay the fee, some of the individuals recommended did not actually take up a license.

23. Mayor's Court Docket, 1767–1771. In 1767 twenty-five persons were specifically not recommended for a license; in 1769, twenty-eight. In most cases the proscribed individual had not paid the previous year's license fee and so had kept house without a license. All licensees charged with keeping a disorderly house were specifically rejected at the next annual session.

24. Roach, "The Planting of Philadelphia," 176–177.

25. Penn made his offer to Samuel Carpenter in 1684, on the eve of his return to England. Carpenter responded by giving Penn £300 to ease his financial situation. See "Minutes of the Board of Property of the Province of Pennsylvania," in Linn and Egle, eds., *Pennsylvania Archives*, 2d ser., 19:5–10; Roach, "The Planting of Philadelphia," 181. Joshua Carpenter was made a justice of the peace in 1686. He was

elected to the provincial assembly in 1697 but barred from taking his seat. In 1702 James Logan reported that Joshua Carpenter was refusing to pay tax and had "secured" anything that might be distrained in lieu of payment, going so far as to eat from earthenware bowls rather than use his silver. Logan to Penn, Aug. 9, 1702, in Edward Armstrong, ed., *Correspondence Between William Penn and James Logan*, 2 vols. (1870; rpt., New York: AMS Press, 1970) 1:120–121, (hereafter cited as *Penn-Logan Correspondence*); Judith Diamondstone, "The Philadelphia Corporation, 1701–1776" (Ph.D. diss., University of Pennsylvania, 1969), 138; Roach, "A Philadelphia Business Directory," 103; Horle and Wokeck, eds., *Lawmaking and Legislators in Pennsylvania*, 1:254–257.

26. Joshua Carpenter may have briefly conducted the Tun personally in the earliest months of its existence; thereafter, the house was rented. Roach, "A Philadelphia Business Directory," 103; Boggs and Boggs, "Inns and Taverns," 424.

27. For the Globe, see Boggs and Boggs, "Inns and Taverns," 422–424. The career of one of the Globe's earliest keepers, Grimstone Boude, is discussed later in this chapter. For Carpenter's Coffeehouse, see Boggs and Boggs, "Inns and Taverns," 180–181, 423–424; Shields, *Civil Tongues and Polite Letters*, 60–63.

28. The 1693 tax list showed West located there and rated his estate at £100; Rawle, "First Tax List"; Hannah Benner Roach, "Benjamin Franklin Slept Here," *PMHB*, 84 (1960), 122–123; James West and Gregory Marlow, Account Book, MSS, HSP. I am grateful to Professor Richard S. Dunn for bringing this record to my attention.

29. West and Marlow, Account Book, HSP. Access to liquor, as much as the expectation of wages, was regarded by working Philadelphians an absolute prerequisite of any labor. Even Penn, when faced with a shortage of rum to dole out to the workers on his Pennsbury mansion, fired off a series of urgent letters to James Logan demanding more rum rather than attempt to exhort his workers to labor without liquor. Penn to Logan, Oct. 14, 1700, in Armstrong, ed., *Penn-Logan Correspondence*, 1:16.

30. West and Marlow, Account Book. For legislation limiting credit, see *Provincial Council*, Mar. 21, 1683, 1:65. Among "Fifty Laws Relating to Morals" enacted in 1705 was an "Act for Mariners Not to Be Trusted"; *Provincial Council*, Jan. 12, 1705, 2:239–240.

31. West and Marlow, Account Book. The widow Jane Dryver, presented by a grand jury in March 1686 for selling liquor without license, contested the charge on the grounds that whatever drink she had sold was only that she had received in payment from her debtors; Court 1685–1686.

32. Rawle, "First Tax List"; Boggs and Boggs, "Inns and Taverns," 201–202. Hannah Penn asked James Logan to visit Emlen to purchase Madeira for Pennsbury; Hannah Penn to James Logan, 1701, in Armstrong, ed., *Penn-Logan Correspondence*, 1:43; Will Book C, #191, 235, microfilm, HSP. An inventory of Emlen's estate is transcribed in Philadelphia Wills and Inventories, #90, Collections of the Genealogical Society of Pennsylvania, HSP.

33. Logan to Penn, Dec. 5, 1703, in Armstrong, ed., *Penn-Logan Correspondence*, 1:256–257. For a description of Samuel Carpenter's estate, see *Penn-Logan Correspondence*, 1:332 n. 2; also, Boggs and Boggs, "Inns and Taverns," 180–181.

34. Wallace, Nov. 4, 1702, fol. 26; Oct. 30, 1722, fol. 44.

35. Judith M. Bennett, "The Village Ale-wife: Women and Brewing in Four-teenth-Century England," in *Women and Work in Pre-Industrial Europe*, ed. Barbara A. Hanawalt (Bloomington: Indiana University Press, 1986), 20–36; Maryanne Kowalesk, "Women's Work in a Market-Town: Exeter in the late Fourteenth-Century," in Hanawalt, ed., *Women and Work in Pre-Industrial Europe*, 145–166; Keith Wrightson, "Alehouses, Order and Reformation in Rural England, 1590–1660," in *Popular Culture and Class Conflict, 1590–1914: Explorations in the History of Labour and Leisure*, ed. Eileen Yeo and Stephen Yeo (Atlantic Highlands, N.J.: Harvester Press, 1981), 2–27, esp. 3–5; Peter Clark, *The English Alehouse: A Social History, 1200–1830* (New York: Longmans, 1983).

36. For George Guest's warrant to make bricks, see Roach "The Planting of Philadelphia," 163 n. 39. See also *Provincial Council*, Jan. 16, 1686, 1:167; Boggs and Boggs, "Inns and Taverns," 406, 413–414; Rawle, "First Tax List"; Wallace, Feb. 7, 1706, fol. 34. Guest left a bequest to the monthly meeting and her "great bible" to her son George; Will Book C, #6, 7, microfilm, HSP.

37. Wallace, Mar. 1, 1704, fol. 31, Nov 2, 1703, fol 20. Boude was presented for selling liquor without a license in September 1702. He "submitted" to the charge and was fined £5; Wallace, Sept. 26, 1702, fol. 3. See also Boggs and Boggs, "Inns and Taverns," 432; Will Book D #60, 48, microfilm, HSP.

38. *Common Council*, July 1, 1745, 446–447.

39. In 1695 a court of quarter sessions court gave Daniel Jones a month to dispose of his stock of wines and spirits; Court 1695, 31. Examples of promises to desist can be found in Court 1685–1686, Court 1695, and Wallace. Between 1739 and 1752, the Common Council of Philadelphia considered 17 petitions for clemency submitted by men and women who had been convicted of keeping an unlicensed tavern and fined £5. The petitioners argued for the remission of the fine on the grounds that they were too poor to pay it. Eleven petitions of this type were submitted by women. We can be sure of the outcome of eight of these eleven petitions, and in only one instance was a women denied clemency. Six petitions were lodged by men. The council waived fines in four cases and upheld fines in one case. The outcome of one petition is unknown. All petitions reprinted in *Common Council*.

40. In 1703 five shopkeepers were prosecuted in a single session for allowing rum drinking in their shops; Wallace, Nov. 3, 1703, fol. 22. As early as 1686 the provincial council ordered all storekeepers to take out a tavern license if they wished to permit people to drink liquor on their premises; *Provincial Council*, Jan. 9, 1686, 1:165.

41. Court 1685–1686; Court 1695; Wallace, Sept. 26, 1702 to Nov. 3, 1703, fols. 1–22; Philadelphia Court Cases, Sept. 2, 1701, Autograph Collection, HSP.

42. Court 1685–1686, fol. 17v. Russell was found guilty and fined £5. For identi-fication of Holleman as a tavernkeeper, see William Markham to Penn, Aug. 22, 1686, in Nash "The First Decade in Pennsylvania," 331; *Provincial Council*, Jan. 16, 1686, 1:167.

43. Wallace, Nov. 2, 1703, fol. 20. Faullonberg pleaded guilty but was presented on the same charges at the next session (fol. 25). See also "Some Indictments by the Grand Jury," 497.

44. See Court 1685–1686; Court 1695; Wallace.

45. For an overview of English licensing policy, see Sidney Webb and Beatrice Webb, *The History of Liquor Licensing: Principally from 1700 to 1830* (rpt. Hamden, Conn.: Archon Books, 1963), 19–42. For Shrewsbury, see Angus McInnes, "The Emergence of a Leisure Town: Shrewsbury 1660–1760," *Past and Present*, 120 (1988), 86. For Preston, see Peter Borsay, "The English Urban Renaissance; the Development of a Provincial Urban Culture, c. 1680–c. 1760," *Social History*, 5 (1977), 585.

46. John W. Barber, ed., *Historical Collections of the State of New Jersey* (Newark: New Jersey State Printing Office, 1857); Glenn, "The Blue Anchor Tavern," 428; Paton Yoder, "Tavern Regulation in Virginia: Rationale and Reality," *Virginia Magazine of History and Biography*, 87 (1979), 274.

47. Boston was allowed six wine taverns, ten innholders, and eight retailers of wine and liquor. Salem was permitted two wine taverns, four inns, and four retailers. See Richard P. Gildrie, *The Profane, the Civil, and the Godly: The Reformation of Manners in Orthodox New England, 1679–1749* (University Park: Pennsylvania State University Press, 1994), 65, 63–83; Conroy, *In Public Houses*, 12–98.

48. See Conroy, "The Culture and Politics of Drink in Colonial and Revolutionary Massachusetts," 85.

49. *Assembly*, 1:355–356, 363.

50. *Provincial Council*, Feb. 9, 1697, 1:527; Dunn and Dunn, eds., *Papers of William Penn*, 4:104–109.

51. *Provincial Council*, Sept. 7, 1704, 2:163; Oct. 3, 1704, 2:164–165; Dec. 23, 1706, 2:299; Feb. 24, 1707, 2:355–356; Mar. 4, 1707, 2:363.

52. "Reply to the Remonstrance of the Mayor of Philadelphia," Oct. 3, 1704, in George Edward Reed, ed., *Pennsylvania Archives*, 4th ser., 12 vols. (Harrisburg, Pa.: State Printer, 1900–1902), 1:196; *Provincial Council*, Mar. 4, 1707, 2:363.

53. *Provincial Council*, Feb. 1707, 2:316.

54. Evans, in the course of a remarkable speech to the assembly, argued that a system in which tavernkeepers received their license directly from the governor could "easily" be managed in Pennsylvania (ibid., 2:316). His concern was to ensure that the proprietary interest promptly received the revenue due from license fees. The system that developed led lieutenant governors to charge their provincial secretaries with keeping a close eye on the number of licenses issued, in order that they might recoup from the courts the revenue raised. See, for example, Peters, Cash Book, 1755–1759. In 1762 Joseph Shippen took over from Richard Peters as secretary to the lieutenant governor. He made strict inquiry of outlying districts as to the number of licenses granted. George Stevenson of York County sent a witty response to Shippen: "By the bearer hereof Mr. Peter Shugart, our late sheriff, I send you £77 for forty-three tavern licenses and £10 for marriage licenses dispensed since Jan. 1st. 1762. . . . Be pleased to send me [by the] same bearer a quarter of a hundred marriage licenses. I expect cold weather will incline the people to creep together, if it does not effect that, it will certainly freeze the Susquehanna and stop our communication, so that I can get no licenses and it is better to have ten too many than two too few." Stevenson to Shippen, Oct. 2, 1762, in Linn and Egle, eds., *Pennsylvania. Archives*, 2d. ser., 4:102. See also ibid., 4:132.

55. Cited in Soderlund, ed., *William Penn and the Founding of Pennsylvania*, 64.

56. Cited in Bernard Bailyn, *The Origins of American Politics* (New York: Vintage Books, 1970), 87. As Bailyn points out, this principle was also used to justify a restricted franchise.

57. Petitions for licenses can be found in Petitions for Tavern Licenses, Society Miscellaneous Collections, Folder 2, Box 4-a, HSP; Wallace; PCMCP.

58. PCMCP 1697–1732, Oct. 27, 1730.

59. PCMCP 1729–1821, n.d.

60. PCMCP 1732–1744, n.d.

61. Wallace, Mar. 1, 1704, fol. 29; Peter J. Parker, "Rich and Poor in Philadelphia, 1709," *PMHB*, 99 (1975): 3–19.

62. Wilkinson had submitted to a charge of selling "strong liquors" without a license in 1701; Philadelphia Court Cases, Sept. 1701. For his petition protesting against the magistrates refusal to grant him a license, see James Logan Papers, HSP, 3:125.

63. Wallace, Mar. 1, 1704, fol. 27.

64. Ibid., Nov. 2, 1703, fol. 20.

65. PCMCP 1732–1744, n.d. See also petitions dated 1740, 1741. On Jan. 1, 1740, Carrol was brought to court charged with keeping a tippling house. The case was discharged; PCMCP Indictments, 1715–1790.

66. Antwerp: PCMCP 1732–1744, 1740; Perkins: PCMCP 1729–1821, 1760; Hamper: PCMCP 1732–1744, n.d.

67. PCMCP 1732–1744, 1740.

68. This calculation is based on analysis of cases contained in PCMCP; Wallace; Petitions for Tavern Licenses.

69. In 1728 John Newberry was granted a license to keep a public house. When he died in 1735, he specified his wife Elizabeth as executrix. The following year, Elizabeth petitioned successfully for a license on the grounds that she had followed that "imploy" for several years; Petitions for Tavern Licenses; Will Book K, #378, 299, microfilm, HSP; PCMCP 1732–1744. Elizabeth Newberry had previously served as the executrix of the estate of George Forrington, vintner: Will Book C, #72, 69, microfilm, HSP.

70. Mayoral Court Docket, 1759–1764, CPA. Similar rates appear in lists compiled between 1767 and 1771, Mayor's Court Docket, 1767–1771.

71. Between 1767 and 1771, 243 individuals were recommended for a tavern license before at least one of the annual licensing sessions held by the mayor's court. The names and approximate addresses of those recommended were listed in the court docket. Annotations such as "dead" or "gone away" suggest that the docket was amended with some care. Some 40 percent of the 171 men included in this sample were recommended at four or more annual meetings. The same percentage of repeat recommendations can be found among the far smaller group of 72 women who appeared before the licensing magistrates at least once in this period. (These calculations reflect the imperfect legibility of the docket. They take into account annotations in the margin whose meaning seems clear. It should be noted that it did not always follow from the fact that a person was recommended that he or she took up a license and actually kept tavern.) See Mayor's Court Docket, 1767–1771.

72. In 1756 the median value of 101 licensees' estates was £20. The 16 women licensees who appear on that year's tax list had estates whose median value was £14, whereas the 85 male licensees had estates whose median value was £17; Roach, comp., "Taxables in the City of Philadelphia," 3–41.

73. *Provincial Council*, Jan. 16, 1686, 1:167. Of 111 licenses issued in Philadelphia in 1756, 21 were issued to women; see Peters, Cash Book, 1755–1759. Between 1759 and 1761, 32 licenses, from a total of 134, were issued to women; Mayoral Court Docket, 1759–1764. In 1769, 45 licenses from a total of 172 were issued to women; Mayor's Court Docket, 1767–1771. When an independent woman householder had to work to support a family, she generally chose either tavernkeeping or shopkeeping. See Patricia Cleary and Peter Thompson, "Commerce and Gender: Women Shopkeepers and Tavernkeepers in Colonial Philadelphia," unpublished paper; Patricia Cleary, " 'She Will Be in the Shop': Women's Sphere of Trade in Eighteenth-Century New York and Philadelphia," *PMHB*, 119 (1995), 181–205; Carole Shammas, "The Female Social Structure of Philadelphia in 1775," *PMHB*, 107 (1983), esp. 73–75.

74. "Some Indictments by the Grand Jury," 497. The question of whether or not there was a Helltown or red-light district in Philadelphia is difficult to answer from the available records. I argue that Franklin's rhetoric may have got the better of his analysis.

75. Franklin included in the report an impolitic comparison between Philadelphia's magistrates and the notoriously rapacious magistrates of Middlesex who were being held responsible for London's "gin binge." This angered the magistrates; ibid. 497–498. See also Webb and Webb, *The History of Liquor Licensing*, esp. 20 n.1, 27–26, 85. A report on London's gin binge written by the Middlesex magistrates was reprinted in *Gazette*, July 22, 1736.

76. Johnston: PCMCP 1732–1744, 1740; Hawkins and Devonshire: PCMCP 1732–1744, n.d.

77. PCMCP 1729–1821, circa 1759.

78. PCMCP 1732–1744. In contrast, when Isaac Milner informed the court that he had taken over the Delaware Ferry, and argued that it was "necessary" for the convenience of passengers that he should be granted a license, the magistrates issued a license to be held as long as he kept the ferry; PCMCP 1732–1744, circa 1739. See also the petition of ferryman Peter Brown; ibid., 1741.

79. Baker: PCMCP 1729–1821, 1760; Donner: PCMCP 1732–1744, n.d.

80. "The Autobiography of Benjamin Franklin," in Lemay, ed., *Franklin: Writings*, 1399; Benjamin Rush, *Thoughts Upon Female Education, Accommodated to the Present State of Society . . .* (Philadelphia, 1787) [Evans #20691].

81. In 1760 Hannah Levy's petition for a license, making the case that she was a widow with a child to support, was signed by eight men. Levy signed "her mark"; PCMCP 1729–1821.

82. Court 1695.

83. Court 1685–1686, May 3, 1686.

84. PCMCP Indictments, 1741. In 1760 one Margaret Cook was fined £5 for keeping a disorderly house and "entertaining whores"; PCMCP 1697–1732.

85. Cases gathered from Philadelphia Court Cases, 1701; Wallace; "Some Indictments by the Grand Jury"; PCMCP; Mayoral Court Docket, 1759–1764; Mayor's Court Docket, 1767–1771; *Common Council*.

86. Cases gathered from Philadelphia Court Cases, 1701; Wallace; "Some Indictments by the Grand Jury"; PCMCP; Mayoral Court Docket, 1759–1764; Mayor's Court Docket, 1767–1771; *Common Council*.

87. In most cases it is impossible to check the names of those persons charged with keeping a bawdy house against lists of persons recommended to keep tavern. However, although some keepers of bawdy houses were, or had once been, licensees, it is my impression, based on an imperfect record, that most were completely detached from involvement in the licensed trade.

88. See Constables' Returns, PCMCP 1697–1732. (This calculation assumes that the distribution of taverns by ward in 1721 was the same as in 1756.)

89. "List of Public Housekeepers Recommended," Mayor's Court Docket, 1767–1771.

90. Ibid.; 1767 Tax List; 1769 Tax List; Peter Thompson, "A Social History of Philadelphia's Taverns, 1683- 1800" (Ph.D. diss., University of Pennsylvania, 1989), 399–409.

91. Wallace, Feb. 4, 1702, fols. 9–11, 15. For another case of Boxing Day masking, see Steven J. Rosswurm, "Arms, Culture and Class: The Philadelphia Militia and the 'Lower Orders' in the American Revolution" (Ph.D. diss., Northern Illinois University, 1979), 52. On Saltell, see Wallace, Feb. 3, 1703, fol. 8; Presentment of Anne Simes, Wallace, Feb. 4, 1704, fol. 25. Simes's previous employment may have been as a shipwright in James West's yard, see West and Marlow, Account Book.

92. Between April 1767 and October 1769, the mayor's court prosecuted twenty such cases. By comparison, over the same period the court heard fifty-two individual cases of felony and thirty-three cases of assault and battery; Mayor's Court Docket, 1767–1771. No other category of presentment rivaled these three. See also Diamondstone, "The Philadelphia Corporation," 170–176.

93. The Connollys' career can be followed in Mayoral Court Records, 1759–1764; "Minutes of the Mayor's Court," PCMCP 1729–1821; PCMCP Indictments. For their appeal for relief from bonds imposed on them, see *Common Council*, Mar. 30, 1764, 698; May 28, 1764, 700; May 27, 1765, 706.

94. Samuel Foulke recalled that this petition was "solemnly considered" and found its most zealous supporter in Joseph Galloway. See "The Pennsylvania Assembly in 1761–1762," *PMHB*, 8 (1884), 413.

95. *Chronicle*, Jan. 4, 1768.

96. Lists of licensees drawn up at annual licensing sessions on the eve of the Revolution show obvious signs of care and attention. Those drawn up between 1767 and 1771, for example, include marginalia describing the fate of licensees, such as "dead," "left off," "gone away," or "harbors negroes"; "List of Public Housekeepers," Mayor's Court Docket, 1767–1771. Similar lists covering 1759–1761 include plus and minus signs in the margins, indicating approval or rejection; "List of Public Housekeepers," Mayoral Court Docket, 1759–1764.

97. Fanny Saltar recalled that in the 1750s "Philadelphia was so small . . . that

my grandfather used to say he not only knew every gentleman in town, but every gentleman's black servant and dog." See "Fanny Saltar's Reminiscences of Colonial Days in Philadelphia," *PMHB*, 40 (1916), 187.

98. The petition, and the assembly's deliberation on it, can be found in *Assembly*, 2:1356. It is not known what proportion of the city's licensees signed this petition. The assembly responded to the publicans' remonstrance by strengthening the terms of the licensing system. Sales to slaves, servants and Indians were once more prohibited. So too were sales to minors—although the age at which an adolescent could buy a drink in a tavern remains unclear. Publicans were not to sell liquor on credit beyond 10 s., and they were required to furnish a £100 bond for their good behavior; *Assembly*, 2:1368. See also Manges, "Women Shopkeepers, Tavernkeepers and Artisans," 77.

99. PCMCP 1697–1732.

100. That Pennsylvania's authorities were divided as to how, or whether, to suppress dramshops can be demonstrated by the debate over a proposal made in 1734 by the assembly that, in addition to the license fee, retailers of spirits should be liable to a further "excise fee" of £3. Lieutenant governor Patrick Gordon questioned the assembly's motives and claimed that the scheme would encourage "those who take permits, to use all means in their power to promote . . . consumption that they may not pay any part of that three pounds for nothing." There were already, he claimed, grog shops in the city conducted in cellars and other clandestine sites. He reasoned that far from encouraging retailers to combat drunkenness, the scheme would encourage illicit sales; *Provincial Council*, Jan. 4., 1734, 3:534–535.

Chapter 2. "Contrived for Entertainment"

1. *Provincial Council*, Aug. 7, 1704, 2:163.

2. In a series of draft tavern regulations Penn recommended that publicans should be allowed to charge no more than sixpence for a meal of "flesh" meat and small beer, and that strong beer was to be no more than twopence a Winchester quart; "Laws and Orders for the Keepers and Frequenters of Ordinaries," in Soderlund, ed., *William Penn and the Founding*, 216–217. In 1718 the provincial council addressed a bill requiring justices to settle the prices charged in taverns, *Provincial Council*, May 23, 1718, 3:43. The assembly's reaffirmation of this law is cited in Boggs and Boggs, "Inns and Taverns," 9. In 1731 the justices set a wide range of maximum prices. No more than two shillings could be charged for a quart of wine; a quart of punch made from double refined sugar should cost no more than fourpence, arrack punch eightpence and best hay eightpence per night; Quarter Court, July 1731, in Wallace, fol. 50. See also *Evening Post*, Sept. 11, 1778; "Some Indictments by the Grand Jury," 496.

3. Susan E. Klepp and Billy G. Smith, eds., *The Infortunate: The Life and Adventures of William Moraley, an Indentured Servant* (University Park: Pennsylvania State University Press, 1992), 63–105.

4. Moreover, as we saw in Chapter 1, licensing magistrates denied petitions for tavern licenses submitted by men and women who, like Gabriel Wilkinson, Ann Donner, or Richard West, sought to serve only a narrow section of the public.

5. [James Boswell], *Life of Johnson*, ed. R. W. Chapman (Oxford: Oxford University Press, 1980), 697.

6. Peter Clark, *The English Alehouse*, passim. See also Conroy, *In Public Houses*, 12–56.

7. After praising England's felicity in its taverns and inns, Johnson contrasted public and private houses. He suggested facetiously to Boswell that a man received more attentive service as a customer in a public house than he did as a guest in a private home: "The master of the [private] house is anxious to entertain his guests; the guests are anxious to be agreeable to him; and no man, but a very impudent dog indeed, can as freely command what is in another man's house as if it were his own. Whereas, at a tavern, there is a general freedom from anxiety. You are sure you are welcome: and the more noise you make, the more trouble you give, the more good things you call for, the welcomer you are. No servants will attend you with the alacrity which servants do, who are incited by the prospect of an immediate reward in proportion as they please" (*Life of Johnson*, 697).

8. *Provincial Council*, Oct. 28, 1756, 7:340. For a description of this quartering crisis and the rancor it generated, see John S. Zimmerman, "Governor Denny and the Quartering Act of 1756," *PMHB*, 91 (1967), 266–281. See also "Memoir of Colonel William Denny," *PMHB*, 44 (1920), 112–115.

9. Attempting to comply with Loudon's request, Governor Denny demanded a list of all persons recommended and licensed in the city wards; *Provincial Council*, Dec. 5, 1756, 7:346; Dec. 8, 1756, 7:349. A list of licensees compiled by the provincial secretary suggests that only 111 licenses had been issued; Peters, Cash Book, 1755–1759. Only 101 of the individuals on Peters's list appear on the 1756 tax list; Roach, comp., "Taxables in the City of Philadelphia."

10. It was common for genteel travelers to double up in the same bed and so perhaps only the most senior officers were given the luxury of a personal bed. Colonel William Denny spoke of sixty-two beds being needed for 124 of his men who were sleeping on straw, but it may be overly charitable to assume that only two private soldiers were placed in the same bed; "Memoir of Colonel William Denny," 113.

11. "Petition of the Mayor and Aldermen to the Pennsylvania Assembly," cited in *Provincial Council*, Dec. 20, 1756, 7:366–367.

12. *Provincial Council*, Dec. 23, 1756, 7:371–372.

13. "Return of Beds, Dec. 24, 1756," cited in Samuel Hazard, ed., *Pennsylvania Archives*, 1st ser., 11 vols. (Philadelphia: Joseph Severns, 1852–1855), 3:85; *Provincial Council*, Dec. 24, 1756, 7:376. Among the houses Tulliken visited were establishments kept by Mary O'Hara, Robert May, and Michael Edge. O'Hara, May, and Edge appear in no other licensing, tax, or tavern records, which suggests that they kept illegal, although quite substantial, taverns or dramshops. See Peters, Cash Book, 1755–1759: Roach, comp., "Taxables in the City of Philadelphia."

14. "Return of Beds," in Hazard, ed., *Pennsylvania Archives*, 1st ser., 3:85; *PCS*, Survey #229, Jan. 25, 1754. (I am very grateful to Professor Sharon Salinger for bringing this source to my attention.) In a letter written in December 1774 Dr.

Solomon Drowne drew attention to the dimensions of Philadelphia's stock of buildings. "There are few elegant dwelling houses here," he wrote. "Many appear old and shabby and they are very irregular as to their height; some of them are three or four stories high, and about fifteen front. . . . As we were walking one day, we saw a brick house building, and had the curiosity to go measure it. Believe me this famous edifice was near fifteen feet square. . . . I say give me a wooden one, that I may swing a cat around in it." Cited in Harrold E. Gillingham, "Dr. Solomon Drowne," *PMHB*, 48 (1924), 367.

15. "Return of Beds," in Hazard, ed., *Pennsylvania Archives*, 1st ser., 3:85. Captain Tulliken found that thirty-five publicans were either offering no accommodation or providing substandard beds. Twenty-eight of the keepers of these houses appear on the 1756 tax list and their average estate was valued at £28, substantially greater than the average estate for tavernkeepers as a whole, which was £20. See also, Roach, comp., "Taxables in the City of Philadelphia."

16. "Return of the Officers' Quarters of the 17th Regiment of Foot," in Hazard, ed., *Pennsylvania Archives*, 1st ser., 3:559; *Gazette*, July 17, 1742; *PCS*, Survey #344, July 6, 1756. This survey valued the Indian King tavern, its stables, and its two-story kitchen at £500.

17. The house alone was insured for £380. See *PCS*, Survey #1346, n.d.; Boggs and Boggs, "Inns and Taverns," 68. Presumably the garret rooms held servants belonging to the Indian Queen as well as servants attending the tavern's guests. Aside from the Indian King and the Indian Queen, the Hendricks, King of the Mohawks, the Three Crowns, the George, the White Oak, the Wagon, the King's Arms, and the Fountain were used by Forbes' officers. "Return of the Officers' Quarters," in Hazard, ed., *Pennsylvania Archives*, 1st ser., 3:559.

18. Alexander Graydon recalled a number of tense encounters between officers and locals over the dinner table at his mother's boardinghouse; *Memoirs of a Life, Chiefly Passed in Pennsylvania, Within the Last Sixty Years* (1811; rpt., Edinburgh: George Ramsay, 1822), 69.

19. "Return of the Officers' Quarters," in Hazard, ed., *Pennsylvania Archives*, 1st ser., 3:559.

20. R. Alonzo Brock, ed., "Extracts From the Journal of Daniel Fisher, 1755," *PMHB*, 17 (1893), 264.

21. Alexander Graydon made this point with regard to boardinghouses. His mother kept such a house and "had the honor, if so it might be called, of entertaining strangers of the first rank who visited the city." But Graydon felt it necessary to point out that her success owed as much to her character as it did to the appointments of her house and that character did not depend on wealth, see Graydon, *Memoirs*, 57–58.

22. See, for example, the advertisements of Owen Owen of the Indian King (*Gazette*, Feb. 10, 1729), Joseph Gray of the Conestoga Wagon (*Gazette*, Jan. 24, 1749), and William Whitebread of the King's Arms (*Mercury*, July 8, 1742).

23. Humphreys: *Mercury*, Mar. 26, 1724; Knowles: *Gazette*, Oct. 13, 1739. Phillip Halbeart, keeper of the Boatswain and Call, "took up" a brand new yawl he found abandoned on the Delaware and kept it for whomsoever could describe it to reclaim; *Mercury*, Apr. 17, 1740. Tavernkeepers typically levied charges for keeping

stray horses. See, for example, George Shoemaker of the Red Lion (*Gazette*, Dec. 30, 1730), William Hawkins of the Three Jolly Sailors (*Gazette*, Dec. 18, 1744), David Lewis of the Plough and Harrow (*Gazette*, Jan. 3, 1749). Although keepers hoped and intended to profit by their actions, they also hoped to establish themselves as "reputable" characters.

24. Most information on servants in taverns comes from newspaper advertisements describing runaways. It is possible that the presence of cash and alcohol made tavern servants especially prone to run away. In September 1734, for example, Richard Ashton ran away from his master, Thomas Dunning, keeper of the George. An advertisement Dunning placed seeking Ashton's apprehension informed the public that Ashton had made off with a half moidore, five "pistoles," and a large sum of English silver coin, all filched, presumably, from the George's till; *Mercury*, Sept. 19, 1734. On slaveowning among tavernkeepers, see Gary B. Nash and Jean R. Soderlund, *Freedom by Degrees: Emancipation in Pennsylvania and Its Aftermath* (New York: Oxford University Press, 1991), 19–22.

25. Boggs and Boggs, "Inns and Taverns," 42. Nicholas Scull, one of the earliest tenants of the George, handled a sideline in lime, "merchantable and well-burn'd." The next tenants, the Dunnings, had an interest in weaving. Thomas Dunning sold his family's engine loom in the George's yard; *Mercury*, Apr. 25, 1723, Aug. 2, 1733. John Clifton announced his intention to give good entertainment and proper attendance at the George while at the same time keeping a general store; see *Gazette*, July 23, 1747, Oct. 22, 1747, Jan. 26, 1748, Sept.1, 1748.

26. Roach, comp., "Taxables in the City of Philadelphia"; Peters, Cash Book, 1755–1759. The most common occupational ascriptions in this group were "shopkeeper" and "widow," each with four cases. The range of outside interests undertaken by tavernkeepers was even broader than the tax list might suggest. Richard Pitts, keeper of the small Ship-A-Ground, sold leather chairs, wool cards, and "good pickled cod fish" by the barrel; *Mercury*, Feb. 12, 1740. See also Pitts's sale of sugar by the hundred-weight or smaller quantity; *Mercury*, Nov. 13, 1740. Edward Bridges was keeper of the Scales, located on the waterfront near Carpenter's Wharf. Bridges sold, from the Scales, diverse West Indian and European goods, such as silks, woolens, and double flint wine glasses. He also sold the indentures of "likely servants." For Bridges's interests, see *Mercury*, Nov. 20, 1740, Dec. 25, 1740. Andrew Hook, who took over Shewbart's tavern near Hanover Square, had a sideline selling engravings of, among other things, the battle of Quebec, the Saint Lawrence River, and General Wolfe; *Gazette*, Mar. 26, 1761. In the Society Hill area, Abraham Carpenter offered the public "good entertainment" at his Duke of Cumberland tavern and reminded readers of the *Gazette* that he still made and sold truss hoops, cringles, hoe-hefts, ladle, and skimmer handles for the West Indies; *Gazette*, June 7, 1750.

27. The society was founded "in imitation of a useful society in London . . . [which] is encouraged there by persons of the first rank; their late Royal Highnesses the Prince and Princess of Wales contributing largely to its support and reputation" (*Gazette*, Feb. 25, 1729). Three plumed feathers are the insignia of the Prince of Wales. The events at Owen Owen's Indian King are described in *Mercury*, Mar. 7, 1732.

28. *Gazette*, Feb. 25, 1729; Boggs and Boggs, "Inns and Taverns," 420–421.

29. *Mercury*, Feb. 19, 1730.

30. For Penn's dinner, see *Mercury*, Sept. 7, 1732.

31. *Mercury*, Feb. 11, 1735. The English Society held its annual celebrations on St. George's Day, April 21. What seems to have been the society's inaugural event was held at the Tun tavern; see, *Mercury*, Apr. 10, 1729. Subsequent meetings were held at the Crown; *Mercury*, Apr. 20, 1732, Mar. 28, 1734, Apr. 10, 1735.

32. Shewbart's wife, Mary, was formerly married to Richard Hockley, a merchant from Hull, Yorkshire, had been Thomas Penn's trading partner. Penn took an interest in Mary and her children by Hockley and helped John Shewbart by reserving, through Richard Peters, a number of lots around Hanover Square on which Shewbart eventually built a brickyard. See Hubertis Cummings, *Richard Peters: Provincial Secretary and Cleric, 1704–1776* (Philadelphia, 1944), 108–110. For John Penn's dinner, see *Mercury*, Sept. 11, 1735. When Thomas Lawrence stepped down as mayor of Philadelphia he held the customary retirement banquet at Shewbart's, see *Mercury*, Oct. 2, 1735.

33. See *Franklin Papers*, 1:177, 2:235, 2:274. (The editors' reference to the Sun Tavern is a misprint or error.) See also, Julius Frederick Sachse, "Roster of the Lodge of Free and Accepted Masons which met at the Tun Tavern, Philadelphia," *PMHB*, 20 (1896), 116–121.

34. See *Mercury*, June 9, 1737. Pratt was appointed riding postmaster for all stages between Philadelphia and Newport, Virginia, by Franklin; *Gazette*, Oct. 27, 1737. He eventually became director of the Library Company and served as coroner of Philadelphia from 1741 to 1748; *Franklin Papers*, 2:233, n.6. The St. John's Lodge also met at the Tun (2:274). For an account of a grand Masonic procession, see "Extracts from the Journal of Daniel Fisher," 273.

35. Joseph Taylor, Ledger, HSP. This document is not paginated nor is it as detailed as the description "ledger" would imply. Taylor rented and eventually purchased the brewery from a cooper, Nehemiah Allen. See also Nehemiah Allen, Account Book, 1698–1736, HSP.

36. In all calculations of profit from the sale of beer that follow, I assume that a barrel contained 36 gallons. It should be noted that American units of capacity were already diverging from British imperial standards and that the capacity of a barrel varied according to whether it contained wine, beer, rum, or whisky. See William L. Downard, *Dictionary of the History of the American Brewing and Distilling Industries* (Westport, Conn.: Greenwood Press, 1980), 16. Nonetheless, by assuming that a barrel of Taylor's beer contained 36 gallons, one also assumes that it contained 144 quarts. Given that publicans sold beer by the quart, a barrel's capacity ought to have possessed a round, and familiar, number of quarts.

37. See Taylor, Ledger; [Eight Partners'] Brewery Account Book, 1732–1737, HSP; Reuben Haines and Godfrey Twells Account Book, 1767–1771, APS.

38. West and Marlow, Account Book, HSP.

39. Taylor, Ledger.

40. Hubbard repaid Taylor £31 in a mixture of cash and credits at her daughter's store during this nine-month period. The location or nature of her daughter's store is not known; Taylor, Ledger.

41. Peter Lloyd to Isaac Norris, Jr., Mar. 24, 1734, Norris Collection, Family Papers, HSP, 1:19.

42. [Eight Partners'] Brewery Account Book, 1732–1737.

43. Davis's advertisement, *Mercury*, Feb. 20, 1722. See also *Mercury*, Dec. 21, 1725, Oct. 16, 1729, Dec. 9, 1731, June 8, 1732.

44. [Eight Partners'] Brewery Account Book, 1732–1737.

45. Taylor, Ledger; Haines and Twells, Account Book, 1767–1771.

46. Haines and Twells may have sold their beer at unusually high prices, but they did not lack customers. They charged less per gallon for beer purchased in bulk—in a butt or hogshead—than they did for beer purchased by the barrel. Individual publicans purchased varying combinations of barrels, hogsheads, and butts. For this reason the general margin of profit on the sale of their beer cannot be determined precisely.

47. Mayor's Court Docket, 1767–1771; 1769 Tax List; Haines and Twells, Account Book, 1767–1771. In calculating the profit made by the sale of Haines and Twells's beer in public houses I have assumed that publicans sold beer at 3d. a quart and that a barrel contained 36 gallons, a hogshead 72 gallons, and a butt 104 gallons.

48. Mayor's Court Docket, 1767–1771. The tax assessors did not ascribe an occupation to Moore and rated his estate at £4; 1769 Tax List.

49. *Gazette*, Apr. 13, 1769, Jan. 4, 1770.

50. Haines and Twells, Account Book, 1767–1771.

51. Between December 1767 and December 1768 Terry and a lone servant sold 20 barrels and 21 hogsheads of Haines and Twells's beer out of the Crooked Billet. Terry's profit on this would have amounted to £19; Haines and Twells, Account Book, 1767–1771. In 1769 Terry's taxable estate was valued at £5; 1769 Tax List.

52. The 1769 tax list shows that Elizabeth Clampfer owned a house on the west side of Second Street between Mulberry and Vine Streets valued at £50. She was recommended for a license in 1768 and each subsequent year until 1771. She presumably kept tavern in the house on Second Street. Clampfer also owned a slave. In 1769 the tax assessors rated Clampfer's estate at a value of £47—substantially above the mean value of licensees' estates in Mulberry ward. In her first year in operation as a publican, Clampfer purchased 22 barrels, 42 hogsheads, and 1 butt of beer from Haines and Twells. These purchases cost £163 10s. Clampfer would have made a profit of £33 on beer sales that year. See 1769 Tax List; Haines and Twells, Account Book, 1767–1771.

53. Joseph Ogden, Innkeeper's Account Book, 1769–1771, HSP; Boggs and Boggs, "Inns and Taverns," 206–209.

54. On Ogden's other interests, see Joseph Ogden, Shopkeeper's Account Book, HSP; Ogden, Innkeeper's Account Book 1767–1771; Mayor's Court Docket, 1767–1771; 1767 Tax List; 1769 Tax List. On mean wealth for tavernkeepers and shopkeepers, see Thompson, "A Social History of Philadelphia's Taverns," 399.

55. Thompson, "A Social History of Philadelphia's Taverns," 225–240.

56. *Gazette*, Mar. 5, 1772. At that time the house was known as the Cross Keys.

57. The ledger is not paginated or indexed. Like many eighteenth-century documents, it contains what might be variant spellings of individual surnames, for example, John Crowford, John Crawford, and John Crauford. The record appears to have been kept haphazardly. In order to analyze the ledger, I had to reorganize its entries by date rather than by the customer's name. Although the ledger covers the

period 1769–1771, the fullest entries are for the winter months of 1770. It may be that the tavern did a slower trade in the summer months, or that 1770 was a banner year for the One Tun. More likely, Ogden's willingness to advance credit, and hence employ the ledger, varied according to the tavern's profitability. The difference between the number of entries made in the ledger for 1771 and 1770 probably is accounted for by a decision on Ogden's part to restrict credit rather than by a cataclysmic decline in the number of customers visiting the tavern. Ogden, Innkeeper's Account Book, 1769–1771.

58. Ogden's prices were in keeping with those charged by an unknown publican in Delaware County who in 1752 entertained the judges of the Supreme Provincial Court. See Henry Graham Ashmead, *The History of Delaware County* (rpt. Concord, Pa.: Concord Township, 1968), 189. The keeper of the Red Rose in Gnadenstadt, Pennsylvania, charged the same price for dinner and lodgings as Ogden. See [Reichel], *A Red Rose from the Olden Time*, 29–30.

59. Customers who stabled their horse at Ogden's paid handsomely for the privilege but nevertheless the stable's stalls were often full. The account book rarely discloses the weight of hay and oats provided to horses. It is also unclear how expensive these items were on the open market. Newspapers regularly printed lists of "prices current" in Philadelphia. Unfortunately oats did not feature in these lists. However, in June 1770 a bushel of oats fetched 3 s. in Barbados; *Gazette*, June 26, 1770. We might expect this to be a high price. An inventory of the stock of the Rose Inn, Gnadenstadt, taken in 1764 described oats as costing 2s. per bushel; [Reichel], *A Red Rose from the Olden Time*, 29. Assume for the moment that a bushel of oats cost 2s. 6d. in Philadelphia in 1770. On October 20, 1770, James Marshall left five horses with Ogden. These animals consumed forty-five quarts of oats. There were thirty-two quarts in a bushel and eight quarts made a peck. So Marshall's horses ate nearly a bushel and a half, for which Ogden charged Marshall 7s. 6d. If we assume a price per bushel of 2s. 6d., Ogden was marking up the price of oats within his charges for stabling. Ogden's fussy measurements (in Marshall's case, one bushel and thirteen quarts, rather than a bushel and two pecks) confirm this impression. Ogden, Innkeeper's Account Book, 1767–1771.

60. For a discussion of the ingredients of sling, toddy, clubb, punch, etc., see Israel Acrelius, *A History of New Sweden; or, The Settlements on the River Delaware*, trans. M. Reynolds, HSP *Publications*, vol. 11 (Philadelphia, 1874), 160–163. See also Peter Thompson, "'The Friendly Glass': Drink and Gentility in Colonial Philadelphia," *PMHB*, 113 (1989), 549–573.

61. For example, a note in the front of the account book for January 1771 reminded Ogden that he owed Samuel Horlick £14 for cloth sold on Horlick's account; Ogden, Innkeeper's Account Book, 1769–1770.

62. Ibid., Nov. 2, 1770. A note made on Nov. 3, 1770, lists goods that Ogden delivered to Elisha Winters on Horlicks's account.

63. Ibid., Feb. 18, 1771.

64. Ibid., April 1770.

65. Ibid.

66. While he was keeping the One Tun, he rented out his store on Chestnut Street for £33 per quarter, ibid.

67. *Gazette*, Mar. 5, 1772.

68. In the five months in 1770 studied, Ogden's mean monthly income from all sources was £49 10s. (In addition to the figures cited in Tables 2 and 3, this includes a mean monthly income from miscellaneous sources of £12 8s. The total does not include monies owed Ogden.) If profit margin amounted to a uniform 20 percent, then Ogden would have made, on average, a little less than £10 a month; Ogden, Innkeeper's Account Book, 1767–1771. Billy Smith has calculated that around this time a minimum household competency would have been £60 per annum; *The "Lower Sort": Philadelphia's Laboring People, 1750–1800* (Ithaca, N.Y.: Cornell University Press, 1990), 107.

69. Taylor, Ledger; Haines and Twells, Account Book, 1767–1771.

Chapter 3. *"Company Divided into Committees"*

1. See grand jury presentment against "divers infants, bond servants," and "unruly negroes" for disturbances "after darkish," Wallace, April 1717, fol. 43; presentment against "servants, apprentices, wild boys, and numbers of negroes" alleging excellence in "all lewdness and obscenity," PCMCP 1732–1744, 1741; instructions to magistrates regarding gatherings of "negroes and others" around the courthouse, *Common Council*, Aug. 17, 1741, 405. In 1731 Franklin drew up a petition denouncing drunken revelry at the city's annual fair; *Franklin Papers*, 1:211–212. The "merrymaking and tumult" associated with fishing parties on the banks of the Schuylkill was discussed in *Provincial Council*, Feb. 16, 1736, 4:24–25.

2. See "Laws and Orders for the Keepers and Frequenters of Ordinaries," in Soderlund, ed., *William Penn and the Founding of Philadelphia*, 206–207; *Provincial Council*, July 11, 1693, 1:380–381; "Fifty Laws Relating to Morals," *Provincial Council*, Jan. 12, 1705, 2:239–240. Games and sports and their tendency to lead to riots were addressed in the "Laws Agreed Upon in England," Article 37, cited in *Provincial Council*, Dec. 13, 1705, 2:216. Drinking by sailors ashore was discussed in the assembly following the election riot of 1742; *Assembly*, Oct. 14, 1742, 4:2800–2819. See also "Some Indictments by the Grand Jury," 497.

3. Warner Jr., *The Private City*, 3–45.

4. Thomas Penn to Richard Hockley, Sept. 18, 1746, in "Letters of Thomas Penn to Richard Hockley," *PMHB*, 40 (1916), 225. For an example of an eighteenth-century pub crawl, see Jacob Cox Parsons, ed., *Extracts from the Diary of Jacob Hiltzheimer of Philadelphia. 1765–1798* (Philadelphia: William F. Fell, 1893), Dec. 28, 1772, 25.

5. Warner, Jr., *The Private City*, esp. 3–45. Warner's account places great emphasis on the cultural influence of residential patterns in which rich and poor lived side by side within sub-divided city blocks. Some contemporaries believed that this gave the city a peculiar intimacy. See "Fanny Saltar's Reminiscences of Colonial Days in Philadelphia," 187. For an evocation of this Philadelphia, and its impact on the prosecution of the American Revolution, see Michael Zuckerman, "The Irrelevant Revolution: 1776 and Since," *American Quarterly*, 30 (1978), 224–242, esp. 231–233.

6. See especially Gary B. Nash, *The Urban Crucible: Social Change, Political Consciousness, and the Origins of the American Revolution* (Cambridge: Harvard University Press, 1979).

7. Shields, *Civil Tongues and Polite Letters*, xx.

8. West and Marlow, Account Book; Ogden, Innkeeper's Account Book, 1769–1771.

9. West and Marlow, Account Book; Ogden, Innkeeper's Account Book, 1769–1771.

10. *Mercury*, Mar. 31, 1737.

11. *Gazette*, May 22, 1740; *Gazette*, June 1, 1749. The curious were also invited to the Indian King to see that "beautiful, but surprising fierce" creature, the leopard; *Gazette*, Oct. 18, 1744.

12. *Mercury*, Feb. 22, 1738. This mechanism returned to the Coach and Horses seven years later; *Gazette*, July 18, 1745. See also an advertisement in the *Gazette*, Jan. 4, 1743, for a "merry dialogue between Punch and Judy" to be enjoyed at the Coach and Horses.

13. *Gazette*, Nov. 8, 1744. Men and women were charged sixpence, children threepence, to view the mechanism.

14. Blackwell displayed, at John Butler's Death of the Fox, the tragedy of Bateman—a love-lorn young man who hanged himself. Blackwell also offered representations of several species of birds in their natural settings and wax figures demonstrating every aspect of labor in a carpenter's yard; *Gazette*, Aug. 5, 1756.

15. *Chronicle*, Mar. 16, 1767.

16. For example, passengers and crew for the snow *Beginning* were directed to the Ship-A-Ground (*Mercury*, Mar. 30, 1732). The ship *Robert* and the snow *Joseph and Ann* could be contacted through Edward Bridges's (*Mercury*, Nov. 13, 1740, Dec. 21, 1742). Crew, passengers, and freight for the *George* were directed to the Boatswain and Call, (*Mercury*, July 30, 1741); for the *John*, to the Pineapple, (*Gazette*, Jan. 6, 1747); for the *Hawk*, to the Crown, (*Gazette*, Apr. 5, 1749); for the *Fox*, to the Tun, (*Gazette*, Sept. 21, 1749); for the *Royal Ranger*, to the Crown, (*Gazette*, Oct. 12, 1749). The privateers *Wilmington, Pandour, Warren, Dreadnought*, and *Le Trembleur* informed potential crewmen to report to the Boatswain and Call (*Gazette*, Mar. 5, 1745, Apr. 18, 1745, June 13, 1745, Aug. 22, 1745, July 23, 1747). The *George* asked crewmen to report to the Crooked Billet (*Mercury*, Sept. 20, 1739) and the Boatswain and Call (*Mercury*, July 16, 1741). The *Marlborough* asked volunteers to call at the Pewter Platter (*Gazette*, Jan. 1, 1745); the frigate *Pennsylvania* at the Michael McIntire's tavern (*Gazette*, Aug. 4, 1757).

17. Passengers and merchandise for the ship *Dove* were handled through Roberts's Coffeehouse; *Mercury*, June 13, 1727. Passengers and crew for the *Myrtilla* were advised to sign aboard at Bradford's coffeehouse; *Gazette*, Aug. 18, 1757.

18. Some vendues disposed of goods of very little value. For example, in 1761 a "black cow," a "rake and pitchfork," a pair of "old" blankets, and one "homespun tablecloth" were among lots disposed of at auction; "Notes and Queries," *PMHB*, 14 (1890), 216. Slaves were sold at the Scales (*Mercury*, July 13, 1732), at the King George (*Mercury*, Oct. 18, 1733), at the Indian King (*Gazette*, July 5, 1744), at James's coffeehouse (*Gazette*, Mar. 14, 1749) and at the Jolly Sailors (*Gazette*, Aug. 24, 1749).

Auctions of indentured servant labor were held at the Star and Garter (*Mercury*, Jan. 11, 1732), the Tun (*Mercury*, June 8, 1732), and at the Scales (*Mercury*, Dec. 25, 1740). Two prizes captured by privateers, the *Victory* and the *Lewis Joseph* were sold by vendue at James's coffeehouse (*Mercury*, May 21, 1741, Feb. 12, 1745). The ships *Marlborough, George, Pandour, Deborah*, and *Warren* were sold by vendue at James's (*Gazette*, May 22, 1746, July 2, 1747, Aug. 13, 1747, Aug. 20, 1747, Nov. 2, 1747). Gentlemen who wished to purchase a plantation on the east side of the Schuylkill were invited to Thomas Shute's Red Lion in Strawberry Alley (*Mercury*, May 14, 1741). An ironworks was sold by vendue at James's coffeehouse (*Mercury*, Oct. 11, 1739); a windmill at the Boatswain and Call (*Gazette*, Apr. 27, 1749).

19. See, for example, vendues and sheriffs' sales held at the Hen and Chickens (*Gazette*, Nov. 20, 1746), at the Rose and Crown (*Gazette*, May 29, 1746), at the Queen of Hungary (*Gazette*, Apr. 20, 1749), at the Blue Anchor (*Gazette*, July 1, 1756), at the Turk's Head (*Gazette*, Mar. 17, 1757), at the Amsterdam (*Gazette*, Apr. 7, 1757), at Peter Robeson's White Horse, (*Gazette*, Jan. 1, 1761) and at the Horse and Groom (*Gazette*, Mar. 12, 1761).

20. *Mercury*, Apr. 7, 1743, Nov. 29, 1722, June 27, 1723, Sept. 12, 1734.

21. *Gazette*, Mar. 10, 1747, June 3, 1756. See also, for example, a sale of spit dogs at Clark's Coach and Horses (*Gazette*, July 18, 1745). On interest in horses, and particularly racing, see Parsons, ed., *Diary of Jacob Hiltzheimer* Sept. 4, 1767, 13, Sept. 19, 1772, 24; Graydon, *Memoirs*, 36–37.

22. *Gazette*, Jan. 1, 1746. The advertisement was placed three weeks before his stay at the Three Tuns.

23. *Gazette*, July 5, 1750.

24. *Gazette*, Nov. 6, 1746.

25. *Gazette*, Feb. 26, 1756.

26. *Mercury*, Oct. 26, 1727.

27. *Mercury*, Apr. 3, 1735. John Atkins, proprietor of a fulling mill near Darby, took in cloth weekly at John Warner's Horse and Groom (*Gazette*, June 21, 1744).

28. *Gazette*, Aug. 11, 1757.

29. *Gazette*, Dec. 29, 1757, Jan. 12, 1758. (For confirmation that George Batholomew kept the Hendricks, King of the Mohawks, see "Return of the Officers' Quarters of the 17th Regiment of Foot," in Hazard, ed., *Pennsylvania Archives*, 1st ser., 3:559.

30. *Gazette*, Mar. 8, 1748.

31. *Gazette*, Dec. 5, 1749.

32. Carl Bridenbaugh, ed., *"Gentleman's Progress": The Itinerarium of Dr. Alexander Hamilton, 1744* (1948; rpt., Pittsburgh: University of Pittsburgh Press, 1992), 20.

33. Ibid., 18.

34. For details of this incident, and the text of Franklin's statement, see *Franklin Papers*, 1:199–202.

35. On the Mt. Regale Fishing Company, see John F. Watson, *Annals of Philadelphia, and of Pennsylvania in Olden Times*, ed. Willis P. Hazard, 3 vols. (Philadelphia: Lippincott, 1881), 3:291, 299–300. For the Schuylkill Fishing Club, see *The History of the Schuylkill Fishing Club* (Philadelphia, 1882). The city's Welshmen could join the Society of Ancient Britons; see *Gazette*, Feb. 25, 1729. English-

men formed the St. George's Society, see *Gazette*, Apr. 20, 1732. On the history of the St. Andrew's Society, see Edgar S. Gardner, *The St. Andrew's Society of Philadelphia* (Philadelphia: St. Andrews Society, 1947). For Irish associations, see Francis Von Cabeen, "The Society of the Sons of St. Tammany of Philadelphia," *PMHB*, 25 (1901), 433–451; *PMHB*, 26 (1902); 7–24, 207–223, 347–355, 443–463. For a general account of the explosive growth of clubs in the city, see Daniel R. Gilbert, "Patterns of Organization and Membership in Colonial Philadelphia Club Life, 1725–1755" (Ph.D. diss., University of Pennsylvania, 1952); Shields, *Civil Tongues and Polite Letters*, 17–19, 175–208, 324–326. For Charles Thomson's "young junto," see J. Edwin Hendricks, *Charles Thomson and the Making of a New Nation, 1789–1824* (Cranbury, N.J.: Fairleigh Dickinson University Press, 1979), 31–38. On the philosophical society, see Peter Stephen DuPonceau, *An Historical Account of the Origin and Formation of the American Philosophical Society* (Philadelphia, 1914). There were two Masonic lodges in colonial Philadelphia; the Grand, or Tun Tavern Lodge, and the St. Johns. See Sachse, "Roster of the Lodge of Free and Accepted Masons," 116–121; Sachse, *Benjamin Franklin as a Free Mason* (Philadelphia, 1906). On the Governor's club, see Bridenbaugh, ed., *"Gentleman's Progress,"* 21, 26, 189–190.

36. For an example of Christmas revelry in taverns, see Wallace, Feb. 4, 1702, fols. 9–11, 15. On the firing of guns on New Year's Eve see *Gazette*, Jan. 4, 1770. On the association to bring street-lighting to Philadelphia see, *Gazette*, Dec. 19, 1749. See also Joseph Ogden, Innkeeper's Account Book, 1767–1771.

37. R. Alonzo Brock, ed., "The Journal of William Black," *PMHB*, 1 (1878), 117–132, 232–249, 404–419; *PMHB*, 2 (1879), 40–49.

38. Ibid., June 13, 1744, 2:46; Bridenbaugh, ed., *"Gentleman's Progress,"* 26–27.

39. Bridenbaugh, ed., *"Gentleman's Progress,"* 21, 26, 29.

40. Ibid., 189–190. Hamilton found that some clubmen spoke in an extravagant and "absurd" manner, taking and maintaining perverse positions that checked rational conversation and strained civility. Hamilton attributed this to the "certain odd pleasure" some clubmen took in "talking nonsense without being contradicted." "This disposition," he concluded, "may arise from the natural perverseness of human nature, which is always most absurd and unreasonable when free from curb or restraint" (ibid., 174).

41. Black wrote, "I staid till after 11, and parted, [his friend] making me promise to be no stranger while I staid in town, of which there was no great fear, as he kept a glass of good wine, and was as free of it as an Apple-Tree of its fruit on a windy day in the month of July: I groped my way to where I lived, after having butted against some posts on the sides of the pavement" (Brock, ed., "The Journal of William Black," May 30, 1744, 1:249).

42. The impropriety of gentlemanly clubs using private homes for their drinking was the subject of an exchange of letters between "Amy Prudent" and "Amicus Curiae" (*Mercury*, July 3, July 17, 1729). These letters were probably journalistic inventions, but the attitudes they expressed were widely held. Amy Prudent complained on behalf of the wives of a set of men styling themselves the Meridional Club. At noon each day, Prudent claimed, the men of this club supped punch in one another's houses under the pretense of whetting their appetites. They inconvenienced wives and disturbed dining rooms set out in decent order. Prudent described

the practice as "vile." Amicus Curiae defended the club, arguing that its purpose was "to preserve an agreeable unity . . . a professional correspondence in regard to business and a happy decorum in mixt affairs, such as characters, controversies etc."

43. Brock, ed., "The Journal of William Black," June 2, 1744, 1:406.

44. Ibid., June 9, 1744, 2: 44. The Tun tavern was used by many civic groups.

45. "To the Philharmonical Merchants, and Others, Nov. 21, 1769," Broadside, LCP.

46. *Gazette*, Mar. 12, 1772.

47. A visitor to the George had an English hunting saddle stolen from his horse as it was tethered outside the front door of the tavern (*Gazette*, Dec. 23, 1729). See also, for example, William Gardiner's description of a horse that strayed or was stolen from his Horse and Groom tavern on Fourth Street (*Gazette*, June 24, 1756) and a similar incident at the Indian King (*Gazette*, Jan. 12, 1758). Isaac Webster had a superfine drab greatcoat with glazed linen sleeves taken from him while he stayed at the Indian King (*Gazette*, Jan. 12, 1758). A commercial traveler who stayed at Owen Humphreys's White Horse on Third Street had his stock of twenty-eight yards of satin pilfered and another unfortunate traveler lost his purse in Joseph Coburn's One Tun *(Mercury*, Jan. 14, 1729; *Gazette*, Oct. 10, 1748). See also a theft of clothes from Michael Israel's Blue Lion on Society Hill (*Gazette*, Mar. 13, 1750). Some thefts were attributed to organized gangs; see Edward Burd to Sarah Burd, Jan. 14, 1767, in *The Burd Papers. Selections from Letters Written by Edward Burd, 1763–1828*, ed. Lewis Burd Walker, (Pottsville, Pa.: 1899), 12–13; *Gazette*, Jan. 1, 1761; ibid., Oct. 3, 1734; ibid., Feb. 12, 1756.

48. *Gazette*, Mar. 5, 1761.

49. *Gazette*, Dec. 19, 1732, Jan. 11, 1733, reprinted in Lemay, ed., *Benjamin Franklin: Writings*, 203–205. Franklin took a keen interest in this case since it touched partially on printing. He pointed out the errors in the counterfeit's design and paper. Reports in the *Gazette* refer to the Indian Prince but the reference to Brockden suggests that the tavern was in fact the Indian King.

50. Thomas England, for example, was a victim of a theft perpetrated at Robert Davis' Queen's Head tavern on Water Street, Philadelphia. England's roommate, an Irishman named Hugh Bradford, stole 114 milled dollars while England slept. England broadcast a fairly detailed description of Bradford, but entrusted payment of the reward for Bradford's capture not to his host, Robert Davis, but instead to a nearby tallow chandler, Joseph O'Born. This suggests that England thought Davis complicit (*Gazette*, Jan. 19, 1749; for identification of O'Born, see *Gazette*, Aug. 4, 1748). This impression was strengthened when Bradford took out an advertisement to inform the public that he was not the man who robbed England (*Gazette*, Apr. 16, 1749). An advertisement for a runaway servant establishes one Robert Davies as keeper of the Queen's Head in Water Street (*Gazette*, Sept. 21, 1733; see also *Mercury*, Feb. 19, 1730).

51. See Karin A. Wulf and Susan E. Klepp, eds., *The Diary of Hannah Callender Sansom* (Philadelphia: University of Pennsylvania Press, forthcoming), Feb. 6, 1759.

52. "The Journal of Charlotte Brown, Matron of the General Hospital with the English forces in America, 1754–1756," in *Colonial Captivities, Marches and*

Journeys, ed. Isabel M. Calder (New York: Macmillan, 1935), 188, 190–192. I grateful to Professor Susan Klepp for bringing this source to my attention.

53. Elizabeth Coates Paschall, Recipe Book, 19A, College of Physicians, Philadelphia. I am again grateful to Professor Susan Klepp for bringing this citation to my attention.

54. Clark, *The English Alehouse*, 13–14; Shields, *Civil Tongues and Polite Letters*, 57–61.

55. For Carpenter's London Coffeehouse, see Boggs and Boggs, "Inns and Taverns," 180–181. For the widow Roberts's coffeehouse, see 183–184; Watson, *Annals of Philadelphia*, 339. For the widow James's coffeehouse, Boggs and Boggs, "Inns and Taverns," 184–186. For John Shewbart's London coffeehouse and tavern, see *Mercury*, Sept. 11, 1735, Oct. 2, 1735; John Shewbart, Ledger, HSP.

56. See Boggs and Boggs, "Inns and Taverns," 422–424, 181; *Common Council*, 5–6; Shields, *Civil Tongues and Polite Letters*, 59–63.

57. Logan to Penn, Mar. 3, 1703, in Armstrong, ed., *Penn-Logan Correspondence*, 1:174.

58. Cited in Cummings, *Richard Peters*, 86.

59. See Frederick B. Tolles, *James Logan and the Culture of Provincial America* (Boston: Little, Brown, 1957), 42; Howard Jenkins, *The Family of William Penn* (Philadelphia, 1899), 109–113.

60. Watson, *Annals of Philadelphia*, 260.

61. Cited in Carl Bridenbaugh and Jessica Bridenbaugh, *Rebels and Gentlemen: Philadelphia in the Age of Franklin* (New York, 1942), 182.

62. Graydon, *Memoirs*, 76, 48–49, 91.

63. See, for example, the use of taverns as the site of meetings of insurers, "The Fellowship Fire Company of Philadelphia," *PMHB*, 27 (1903), 480; Parsons, ed., *Diary of Jacob Hiltzheimer*, Mar. 10, 1770, 20. Hiltzheimer attended a meeting in tavern rooms to discuss relocating Philadelphia's Market (Oct. 25, 1784, 69) and met the street commissioners and the Philadelphia magistrates in the Indian Queen (Jan. 14, 1786, 77, Feb. 16, 1786, 79). See also Ogden, Innkeeper's Account Book, 1767–1771. As late as 1781 George Nelson served on a jury that met at Hess's tavern, George Nelson, Diary, MSS. HSP, Feb. 28, 1781.

64. Graydon, *Memoirs*, 91.

65. Parsons, ed., *Diary of Jacob Hiltzheimer*, Feb. 8, Feb. 10, Feb. 12, 1774, 28–29.

66. Ibid., Nov. 23, 1772, 25.

67. Ibid., Feb. 8, Feb. 14, 1767, 13. Jones did not keep a prominent house. In 1766 he married another publican, the widow Gray. Hiltzheimer was no stranger to her establishment; see ibid., July 31, 1766, 12; Dec. 16, 1766, 12.

68. Ibid., Nov. 7, 1795, 221.

69. See Foner, *Tom Paine and Revolutionary America*, 36–38.

70. See Franklin's description of Watts's printinghouse in London; "Autobiography" in Lemay, ed., *Franklin: Writings*, 1348–1349.

71. For the treating of shipyard workers, see Harrold E. Gillingham, "Some Colonial Ships Built in Philadelphia," *PMHB*, 56 (1932), 156–186. John Dickinson gave the men who built his house an entire hogshead of rum. John Cadwalader

treated the workers who remodeled his home to rum; Nicholas B. Wainwright, *Colonial Grandeur in Philadelphia: The House and Furniture of General John Cadwalader* (Philadelphia: HSP, 1964), 35. The workmen who built the Pennsylvania statehouse received treats of liquor with each floor they completed; Harold Donaldson Eberlein and Cortlandt Van Dyke Hubbard, *Diary of Independence Hall* (Philadelphia: Lippincott, 1948), 38–39. The workers who built President George Washington's official residence in Philadelphia were similarly treated, see Parsons, ed., *Diary of Jacob Hiltzheimer*, July 7, 1792, 179; Sept. 7, 1792, 182.

72. Cited in Foner, *Tom Paine and Revolutionary America*, 36.

73. Theodore G. Tappert and John Doberstein, eds., *The Journals of the Rev. Henry Melchior Muhlenberg*, 3 vols. (Evansville, Ind.: Lutheran Historical Society, 1982), 1:390, 526.

74. Ibid., 1:320. See also Graydon on songs and music; *Memoirs,* passim.

75. Daniel B. Shea, ed., "Some Account of the Fore Part of the Life of Elizabeth Ashbridge," in *Journeys in New Worlds: Early American Narratives*, ed. William L. Andrews (Madison: University of Wisconsin Press, 1990), 162.

76. "Laws and Orders for the Keepers and Frequenters of Ordinaries," in Soderlund, ed., *William Penn and the Founding of Pennsylvania*, 206.

77. See for example, George Alexander Stevens, *Songs, Comic, Satyrical, and Sentimental* (Philadelphia, 1777) [Evans #15603]; *The Charmer. Being a Select Collection of English, Scots and American Songs, Including the Modern: With a Selection of Favorite Toasts and Sentiments* (Philadelphia, 1790) [Evans #22400]; Arthur M. Schlesinger, Jr., "A Note on Songs as Patriot Propaganda," *WMQ*, 3d ser., 11 (1954): 78–89. In 1779 John Blakely passed on to a friend the fashionable toasts of the Philadelphia season; "Letters of John Blakely to Jesse Sharpless," *PMHB*, 44 (1920), 192. For an account of the popularity and significance of toasting, see Thompson, " 'The Friendly Glass,' " 549–573.

78. Logan to Penn, 1702, Armstrong, ed., *Penn-Logan Correspondence*, 1:174.

79. See Tolles, *James Logan and the Culture of Provincial America*, 31–37.

80. *Mercury*, Feb. 3, 1736. Foner, *Tom Paine and Revolutionary America*, 48–51.

81. Steven Rosswurm and Stephanie G. Wolf, "Leisure Time in Colonial Philadelphia," unpublished paper, presented at the Bicentennial Summer Institute, Philadelphia, 1976.

82. Foner, *Tom Paine and Revolutionary America*, 110–111; Rosswurm and Wolf, "Leisure Time," 20. On Timothy Matlack's political career, see Richard Alan Ryerson, *The Revolution Is Now Begun: The Radical Committees of Philadelphia, 1765–1776* (Philadelphia: University of Pennsylvania Press, 1978), esp. 210–218.

83. Gary Nash argues that Evans had done nothing "but play the gentleman since reaching adulthood"; *Quakers and Politics*, 256–257. The younger Penn had a reputation for revelry which went before him. See Frederick B. Tolles, *James Logan and the Culture of Provincial America*, 40–43; Jenkins, *The Family of William Penn*, 109–113. Penn worried James Logan with a succession of letters regarding his son's character and care. One of these charged Logan not to let Penn stay out in taverns after hours. The proprietor had hoped that Logan would immediately take young Penn away to Pennsbury to "watch him, outwit him, and honestly overreach him for his own good." Logan also received a letter from Penn Jr. that assured Logan that he

was never "anything" to excess, and that though he liked to dress in a "genteel" style, he did not and would not wear a "poking iron" or sword; Jenkins, *The Family of William Penn*, 110–111; Armstrong, ed., *Penn-Logan Correspondence*, 1:315–319.

84. Jenkins, *The Family of William Penn*, 115–116. Story's tavern was a favored haunt of raffish young gentlemen who, like John Evans and William Penn, Jr., were reluctant to defer to the city's Quaker elders. David Shields has reconstructed brilliantly the tone of Story's tavern and the background to the great fight there. See *Civil Tongues and Polite Letters*, 63–64.

85. *Provincial Council*, Nov. 2, 1704, 2:175–176.

86. Graydon, *Memoirs*, 44–45.

87. Ibid., 45–46.

88. See Boggs and Boggs, "Inns and Taverns," 277–283; Parsons, ed., *Diary of Jacob Hiltzheimer*, Sept. 4, 1767, 13; Dec. 12, 1767, 14. Records of the [Philadelphia] Jockey Club, Alfred Stoddard Papers, Dreer Collection, HSP. On highwaymen see *Chronicle*, Jan. 4, 1768; *Gazette*, Jan. 14, 1768.

89. Hannah Penn to Logan, 1701, in Armstrong, ed., *Penn-Logan Correspondence*, 1:43.

90. In 1737 Roger Ellicott, keeper of the Center House, reminded "gentlemen who would divert themselves at bowls" that his tavern's bowling green was open for their reception; *Mercury*, May 12, 1737. On his visit to Philadelphia in 1744, William Black diverted himself with bowls and billiards at the Center House; Brock, ed., "The Journal of William Black," May 31, 1744, 1: 404, June 9, 1744, 2:41.

91. Alexander Mackraby to Sir Philip Francis, Aug. 17, 1768, reprinted in "Philadelphia Society Before the Revolution: Extracts from Letters of Alexander Mackraby to Sir Philip Francis," *PMHB*, 11 (1887), 286; *Mercury*, Aug. 22, 1745; *Autobiography of Charles Biddle: Vice-President of the Supreme Executive Council of Pennsylvania, 1745–1821*, ed. Charles Biddle (Philadelphia: E. Claxton, 1883), 387.

92. Wulf and Klepp, eds., *The Diary of Hannah Callender Sansom*, Aug. 27, 1760.

93. Arthur H. Cole, "The Tempo of Mercantile Life in Colonial America," *Business History Review*, 33 (1959): 277–300; Thomas M. Doerflinger, *A Vigorous Spirit of Enterprise: Merchants and Economic Development in Revolutionary Philadelphia* (Chapel Hill: University of North Carolina Press, 1986).

94. Boggs and Boggs, "Inns and Taverns," 186–190; John D. R. Platt, *The City Tavern* (Denver, Colo.: National Parks Service, 1973), 33.

95. Boggs and Boggs, "Inns and Taverns," 189; Watson, *Annals of Philadelphia*, 339.

96. Kelley, Jr., *Life and Times in Colonial Philadelphia*, 167. Bradford advertised for a "sprightly young man" to serve as "waiter" at the Coffeehouse; *Chronicle*, May 4, 1767.

97. "Letter of Edward Shippen of Lancaster, 1754," *PMHB*, 30 (1906), 89–90. For evidence that there were gentlemen in Philadelphia who lived the life Shippen warned his son to avoid, see Brock, ed., "Journal of William Black," June 12, 1744, 2:45.

98. Graydon, *Memoirs*, 48–49, 76, 91.

99. Doerflinger, *A Vigorous Spirit of Enterprise*, 70–134, 368; Elizabeth Grey

Kogan Spera, "Building for Business: The Impact of Commerce on the City Plan and Architecture of the City of Philadelphia, 1750–1800" (Ph.D. diss., University of Pennsylvania, 1980).

100. *Gazette*, May 11, 1774.

101. *Chronicle*, Oct. 28, 1771; *Gazette*, Feb. 3, 1763.

102. Spera, "Building for Business," passim.

103. *Chronicle*, May 23, 1768; Boggs and Boggs, "Inns and Taverns," 64.

Chapter 4. "Of Great Presumption"

1. Cited in *Provincial Council*, 1:316.

2. "Minutes of the Provincial Council and Assembly of Pennsylvania, 10 March–4 April 1683," in Soderlund, ed., *William Penn and the Founding of Pennsylvania*, 232.

3. Roach, "The Planting of Philadelphia," 168–169; Petty Jury, June 2, 1686, Court 1685–1686, fols. 25r, fol 32.

4. Thomas Long, *A Sermon Against Murmuring: Preached in the Cathedral Church of St. Peter [Exeter] 29th. May 1680* (London, 1680) [microfilm, Early English Books, Wing L2982, Reel 1335], 8.

5. Ibid., 27.

6. Tim Harris, *London Crowds in the Reign of Charles II: Propaganda and Politics from the Restoration Until the Exclusion Crisis* (Cambridge: Cambridge University Press, 1990).

7. Ibid., 28.

8. "An Additional Proclamation Concerning Coffee-Houses . . ." (London, c. 1676) [microfilm, Early English Books, Wing C2888, Reel 863], 22.

9. "Certain Conditions or Concessions agreed upon by William Penn . . ." (1681), in Soderlund, ed., *William Penn and the Founding of Pennsylvania*, 71–75, 74. The thirtieth article of the "Laws Agreed Upon in England . . ." stated that "all scandalous and malicious reporters, backbiters, defamers, and spreaders of false news, whether against magistrates or private persons, shall . . . be severely punished, as enemies to the peace and concord of this province" (131). See also "Laws and Orders for the Keepers and Frequenters of Ordinaries" (206).

10. Penn's use of the admonition from *Proverbs* "Righteousness exalts a nation but sin is the shame of any people" to introduce a slate of tavern regulations subtly echoed Thomas Long's warning that "Nothing doth more portend the displeasure of God against a nation, than when he permits popular clamors and tumults to invade the public authority." See Soderlund, ed., *William Penn and the Founding of Pennsylvania*, 206; Long, *A Sermon Against Murmuring*, 7. William Shewell, for example, argued that tattlers, "busiebodies," and "medlers with other men's matters" displayed by their behavior "infallible signs" of wanting the "inward adorning of a weak and quiet spirit." See *A Brief Testimony Against Tale-bearers, Whisperers, and Back-Biters, Shewing that where they are given ear unto amongst Friends Neighbours*

and Relations, or in any Christian Society, such can never live in Peace, Concord and Unity (Philadelphia, 1701) [Evans #1024], 16–17.

11. Shewell, *A Brief Testimony*, 16. Shewell's answer was that the victim of false reports should find and confront their authors.

12. Cited in Zuckerman, "Identity in British America," 138.

13. Nash, *Quakers and Politics*, 202–207.

14. On the size of Philadelphia's elite, and its forms of expression, see Gilbert, "Patterns of Organization and Membership in Colonial Philadelphia Club Life"; Stephen Brobeck, "Revolutionary Change in Colonial Philadelphia: The Brief Life of the Proprietary Gentry," *WMQ*, 3d ser., 33 (1976): 410–434. For a compelling treatment of the divisions within Philadelphia's elite, see Robert Gough, "Towards a Theory of Class and Social Conflict: A Social History of Wealthy Philadelphians, 1775–1800" (Ph.D. diss., University of Pennsylvania, 1977); Gottlieb Mittelberger, *Journey to Pennsylvania*, ed. Oscar Handlin and John Clive (Cambridge: Harvard University Press, 1960), 48; Duché cited in John K. Alexander, "Deference in Colonial Pennsylvania and That Man from New Jersey," *PMHB*, 102 (1978), 435.

15. These themes and problems can be identified in other historical settings. See Richard C. Trexler, *Public Life in Renaissance Florence* (Ithaca, N.Y.: Cornell University Press, 1991); Brennan, *Public Drinking and Popular Culture in Eighteenth-Century Paris*; Chartier, *The Cultural Origins of the French Revolution*. My discussion of the ways in which colonial Pennsylvania's political culture was shaped by the existence of an independent public realm is informed by the work of Jürgen Habermas (see *The Structural Transformation of the Public Sphere*, esp. 14–26). Note, however, that unlike Habermas, I do not identify this realm with a bourgeoisie nor do I link its existence to acceptance of a normative ideal of rational-critical debate.

16. Robert H. Wiebe, *The Segmented Society: An Introduction to the Meaning of America* (New York: Oxford University Press, 1975).

17. "Autobiography," in Lemay, ed., *Franklin: Writings*, 1363.

18. Ibid., 1366. Hugh Meredith's father had been unable to advance Franklin and Meredith all the money they needed to start up their business. Franklin and Meredith were being sued by creditors for £100. William Coleman and Robert Grace separately informed Franklin that they would loan him the money if he ditched Meredith. A potentially troublesome dilemma was resolved for Franklin when Meredith decided that he was not cut out to be a printer.

19. Ibid., 1332–1333.

20. Ibid., 1382.

21. Cited in Shi, *The Simple Life*, 35; see also 28–49.

22. Bridenbaugh, ed., *"Gentleman's Progress,"* 134. For a sustained statement of this sumptuary concern, see William Mentz, *The Miraculous Power of Clothes, and the Dignity of the Tailors: Being an Essay on the Words "Clothes Make Men"* (Philadelphia, 1772) [Evans #12466].

23. Such literature can be found in newspapers, for example, "The Art of Saying Much in Little," *Gazette*, June 17, 1736, as well as in frequently reprinted collections such as *The Friendly Instructor* (Philadelphia, 1745) [Evans # 5600]; and *The Polite Philosopher, Or, An Essay on that Art which Makes a Man Happy in Himself and Agreeable to Others* (Philadelphia, 1758) [Evans #8125].

24. "Autobiography," in Lemay, ed., *Franklin: Writings*, 1328–1329. William Moraley, an indentured servant, left a similarly detailed account of what he was wearing, and what others wore, on the day of his arrival in Philadelphia; Klepp and Smith, eds., *The Infortunate*, 54, 63–64, 70–71.

25. "Autobiography," in Lemay, ed., *Franklin: Writings*, 1328. That appearances could be deceptive was a stock theme of eighteenth-century literature. It recurs in Franklin's *Poor Richard* series. See, for example, "Distrust and Caution are the Parents of Security," "Full of Courtesy, Full of Craft," and "Don't Judge of Men's Wealth or Piety, by Men's Sunday Appearance," in Lemay, ed., *Franklin: Writings*, ibid., 1187, 1196, 1268.

26. See F. G. Bailey, "Gifts and Poison," in *Gifts and Poison* (New York: Oxford University Press, 1971), 1–25.

27. Bridenbaugh, ed., *"Gentleman's Progress,"* 28, 26. In 1775 another visitor to Philadelphia, Robert Honyman, dined on oysters at the Cross Keys and noted that he was detained "talking with company" until he was "excessively fatigued." Phillip Padelford, ed., *Colonial Panorama, 1775: Doctor Robert Honyman's Journal* (San Marino, Calif.: Huntington Library, 1939), 13.

28. Tappert and Doberstein, eds., *Journals of Henry Muhlenberg*, Nov. 30, 1742, 1:68.

29. Ibid., Aug. 3, 1752, 1:346–347. On board the ship that first brought him to America, Muhlenberg "had a yearning desire to express myself forcefully the next Sunday and to denounce all the sins of drinking, fighting, cursing, sport and buffoonery" (Aug. 13, 1742, 1:43).

30. Bridenbaugh, ed., *"Gentleman's Progress,"* 192.

31. See Robert Micklus's biographical sketch of Alexander Hamilton in, *The Tuesday Club. A Shorter Edition of* The History of the Ancient and Honorable Tuesday Club *by Dr. Alexander Hamilton* (Baltimore: Johns Hopkins University Press, 1995), xi–xxiii.

32. *Gazette*, Jan. 27, 1757, Jan. 1, 1749. For other examples in this vein, see warnings about David Hopkins, "supposed to be very troubled in mind" (*Mercury*, Sept. 6, 1733) and a runaway slave "slow of speech, but very subtle," (*Mercury*, Dec. 9, 1729).

33. For dissatisfaction with tavern talk see Bridenbaugh, ed., *"Gentleman's Progress,"* Brock, ed., "The Journal of William Black"; Tappert and Doberstein, eds., *Journals of Henry Muhlenberg*; Busybody #2, *Gazette*, Feb. 11, 1729; "On Pertinaceous Obstinacy in Opinion," *Gazette*, Mar. 27, 1735; "Rules for Making Oneself a Disagreeable Companion," *Gazette*, Nov. 15, 1750.

34. Klepp and Smith, eds., *The Infortunate*, 113, 96–97.

35. Petty Jury, June 2, 1686, Court 1685–1686, fol. 25r. Guest had been discussing an action in which he and Claypoole were involved, when somebody told him that Claypoole planned to paint Guest in court as "not a good liver" and a "person convicted of ill-fame." It was in this context that Guest called Claypoole a knave. The court dismissed Claypoole's case. In March 1695 Robeson was fined £5 for selling liquor without a license; Court 1695, Mar. 7, 1695. For studies of defamation in seventeenth-century speech, see Mary Beth Norton, "Gender and Defamation in

Seventeenth-Century Maryland," *WMQ*, 3d ser., 44 (1987): 3–39; Robert St. George, " 'Heated' Speech and Literacy in Seventeenth-Century New England," in *Seventeenth-Century New England,* ed. David D. Hall and David Grayson Allen, *Collections* vol. 43 (Boston: Colonial Society of Massachusetts, 1984), 275–322.

36. For the best guide to the Keithian controversy, see Nash, *Quakers and Politics,* 144–161. Nash has suggested that in Keith's case, the "pendulum of human emotions swung in an arc so wide as to suggest an unstable, if not disturbed, personality" (145).

37. Ibid., 148.

38. Ibid., 152–153.

39. Daniel Leeds, *News of a Strumpet Co-inhabiting in the Wilderness* (New York, 1701) [Evans # 982], 7.

40. Ibid., 4.

41. George Keith, *New England's Spirit of Persecution Transmitted to Pennsilvania* (New York, 1693) [Evans #642], 14, also 12–18.

42. Ibid., 12. See also George Keith, *An Appeal from the Twenty-Eight Judges to the Spirit of Truth of all Faithful Friends called Quakers that Met at this Yearly Meeting at Burlington, 7 mo. 1692* (New York, 1692) [Evans #598]. John McComb had worked as a tailor before gaining his tavern license. He was also a former Quaker, which may help explain why the court that stripped him of his tavern license cited his "contemptuous behavior." See Keith, *New England's Spirit of Persecution,* 12; Roach, "A Philadelphia Business Directory," 116.

43. Keith, *New England's Spirit of Persecution,* 15.

44. Nash, *Quakers and Politics,* 337.

45. Tully, *Forming American Politics,* 377. See also ibid., 365–381.

46. Sir William Keith championed the Pennsylvania assembly as a means of undermining the provincial council. This was duplicitous since his ultimate goal was to return Pennsylvania to royal rule by arguing that the assembly had assumed powers beyond its station. See Roy N. Lokken, *David Lloyd: Colonial Lawmaker* (Seattle, 1959), 208–235; Nash, *Quakers and Politics,* 330–336.

47. On David Lloyd's hostility to the proprietary interest, Sir William Keith's motives in siding with the assembly, and for background to the crisis of 1724–1726, see Nash, *Quakers and Politics,* 288–305, 332–336; Thomas Wendel, "The Keith-Lloyd Alliance: Factional and Constitutional Politics in Colonial Pennsylvania," *PMHB,* 92 (1968), 300.

48. Cited in Nash, *Quakers and Politics,* 333.

49. James Logan to John Wright, Jan. 21, 1726, in Linn and Egle, eds., *Pennsylvania Archives,* 2d ser., 7:86–88.

50. See Ronald Schultz, *The Republic of Labor,* 23–24; Nash, *Quakers and Politics,* 334.

51. Cited in Nash, *Quakers and Politics,* 334.

52. Norris cited in Gary B. Nash, "Artisans and Politics in Eighteenth-Century Philadelphia," in *The Origins of Anglo-American Radicalism,* ed. Margaret C. Jacob and James R. Jacob (Atlantic Highlands, N.J.: Humanities Press, 1991), 265.

53. *The Observator's Trip to America, in a Dialogue between the Observator and his Countryman Roger* (Philadelphia, 1726) [Evans #2794], 21–22.

54. *A Dialogue Shewing What's Therein to Be Found* . . . (Philadelphia, 1725) [Evans #2652], 30.

55. *Proclamation by the Hon. Patrick Gordon Oct. 4, 1726* (Philadelphia, 1726) [Evans #2801]; Lokken, *David Lloyd*, 234–235.

56. The best study of the riot is Norman S. Cohen, "The Philadelphia Election Riot of 1742," *PMHB*, 92 (1968), 306–319.

57. *Assembly*, 4:2957–2958. Some deponents construed the care with which Allen and Plumstead sought to avoid provoking a riot by precipitate action as a partisan act in favor of the proprietary interest (4:2829). For other views, see Cohen, "The Philadelphia Election Riot," 316–317; Richard Hockley to John Penn, Nov. 1, 1742, in "Letters from the Letter-books of Richard Hockley," *PMHB*, 28 (1904), 38; Cummings, *Richard Peters*, 77.

58. Cohen, "The Philadelphia Election Riot," 318; *Assembly*, 4:2967.

59. *Assembly*, 4:2959.

60. Ibid., 4:2975.

61. Ibid., 4:2967.

62. Ibid.

63. Ibid.; Cohen, "The Philadelphia Election Riot," 312.

64. Cohen, "The Philadelphia Election Riot," 314.

65. Ibid., 317.

66. Ibid., 314.

67. *Assembly*, 4:2978.

68. Ibid., 4:2992–2993.

69. Cited in Cummings, *Richard Peters*, 77–78.

70. Douglass, *Rebels and Democrats*, 229.

71. Cited in Benjamin H. Newcomb, *Franklin and Galloway: A Political Partnership* (New Haven, Conn.: Yale University Press, 1972), 96–97. See also *Franklin Papers*, 11:369.

72. Newcomb, *Franklin and Galloway*, 96.

73. Ibid., 86.

74. [Hugh Williamson], *An Answer to the Plot* (Philadelphia, 1764) [Evans #9581]. See also Newcomb, *Franklin and Galloway*, 93–98.

75. [Hugh Williamson], *What is Sauce for a Goose is also Sauce for a Gander* (Philadelphia, 1764) [Evans # 9879]. Newcomb, *Franklin and Galloway*, 93, passim.

76. Newcomb, *Franklin and Galloway*, 89. See also David L. Jacobson, "John Dickinson's Fight Against Royal Government, 1764," *WMQ*, 3d ser., 19 (1962): 71–77.

77. Newcomb, *Franklin and Galloway*, 97.

78. Henry Dawkins, *The Paxton Expedition. Inscribed to the Author of the Farce*, 1764.

79. Henry Dawkins, *The Election Medley*, 1764.

80. *Franklin Papers*, 11:139. Pennsylvania's governor received 6 s. for every license issued (11:521 n. 1). This brought him an appreciable revenue. In 1752, for example, James Hamilton issued 831 tavern licenses for the province as a whole, bringing £250 to the governor; James Hamilton, Cash Book, MSS. Book 1 #11, Hamilton Papers, HSP.

81. Thomson to Franklin, Dec. 18, 1764, *Franklin Papers*, 11:521–522.

82. [Henry Dawkins?], *A New Song Suitable to the Season, to the Tune of "Good English Beer"* (Philadelphia, 1765) [Evans #10093].

83. On the "politics of ingratiation," see James Hutson, *Pennsylvania Politics, 1746–1770: The Movement for Royal Government and Its Consequences* (Princeton, N.J.: Princeton University Press, 1972), esp. 200–210.

84. *Gazette*, May 16, 1766.

85. Samuel Wharton to Benjamin Franklin, Oct. 13, 1765, *Franklin Papers*, 11:315–316.

86. Joseph Galloway to William Franklin, Nov. 14, 1765, *Franklin Papers*, 11:373–374.

87. Cited in Foner, *Tom Paine and Revolutionary America*, 187.

Chapter 5. "Councils of State"

1. *Gazette*, June 14, 1764. John Butler, landlord of the Death of the Fox in Strawberry Alley, undertook to transport by wagon passengers bound for New York; *Gazette*, Nov. 6, 1756. At the George, Daniel and Sarah Mackennett advertised their "stage-waggon," suitable for any journey; *Gazette*, June 2, 1763.

2. See David John Jeremy, ed., *Henry Wansey and His American Journal: 1794* (Philadelphia: 1970), 116; Thompson, "A Social History of Philadelphia's Taverns," 478–480.

3. *Packet*, July 10, Aug. 8, 1789.

4. *Gazette*, Oct. 14, 1771; Boggs and Boggs, "Inn and Taverns," 203.

5. The magistrates of Philadelphia's court of quarter sessions published a schedule of maximum retail liquor prices in the *Evening Post*, Sept. 11, 1778. Thereafter Philadelphia's extra-legal price control committees attempted to fix the retail price of drinks. However, the court schedule of 1778 seems to have been the last measure of its kind aimed specifically at licensees. For discussions of Philadelphia's price control movement, see Foner, *Tom Paine and Revolutionary America*, 145–182; Schultz, *Republic of Labor*, 44–68.

6. Platt, *The City Tavern*, 30–31.

7. Earle, *Stage-Coach and Tavern Days*, 160; J. Thomas Scharf and Thompson Westcott, *History of Philadelphia, 1609–1884*, 3 vols. (Philadelphia: L. H. Evarts, 1884), 2:987. The precise location of this tavern and the date on which it adopted its name are unknown. Bruce Laurie has argued that the tavern, or a successor using its sign, traded in Philadelphia's Moyamensing district in the early nineteenth century; *Working People of Philadelphia, 1800–1850* (Philadelphia: Temple University Press, 1980), 55.

8. Cited in Foner, *Tom Paine and Revolutionary America*, 62.

9. Schultz, *Republic of Labor*, 32.

10. Boggs and Boggs, "Inns and Taverns," 446.

11. Tully, *Forming American Politics*, 377; see also 365–381.

12. Erkuries Beatty to Reading Beatty, May 20, 1783, cited in Joseph M. Beatty, "Letters of the Four Beatty Brothers of the Continental Army, 1774–1794," *PMHB*, 44 (1920), 234.

13. The other trustees were Edward Shippen, Samuel Powell, Samuel Mifflin, Lambert Cadwalader, John Penn, James Allen, Andrew Allen, and John Allen, George Clymer, John Wilcocks, Henry Hill, and Samuel Meredith; Platt, *City Tavern*, 10–23. John Cadwalader's influence on the project was such that the finished building bore a marked resemblance to his Philadelphia townhouse; see Wainwright, *Colonial Grandeur in Philadelphia*, 9–10. The trustees later drew up a document that set out subscribers' voting rights and procedures for decision making. It provided a means of dissolving the company and clearly stated that the trust's purpose was to run a tavern. After taxes, ground rent, mortgage principle, and repairs had been paid, net profits in excess of £100 were to be invested; City Tavern Declaration of Trust, Feb. 9, 1776, MSS. APS.

14. Platt, *City Tavern*, 29–31, esp. nn. 54, 55, 56.

15. *Pennsylvania Journal*, Aug. 11, 1773. The lease offered Smith has not survived. John Platt believes that it was probably identical in its provisions to that granted to Smith's successor, Gifford Dalley. Dalley's lease contained a number of provisions designed to protect the tavern's tone and reputation. Platt, *City Tavern*, 57 n. 101.

16. Cited in Boggs and Boggs, "Inns and Taverns," 82.

17. Platt, *City Tavern*, 42–44.

18. Francisco de Miranda, who visited the City Tavern in 1784, found that "those who do not like to dance play cards on tables prepared for that purpose in nearby rooms" (ibid., 44 n. 80).

19. *Packet*, Oct. 25, 1773.

20. Lyman H. Butterfield, ed., *Diary and Autobiography of John Adams*, 2 vols. (Cambridge, Mass.: Belknap Press, 1961), Aug. 29, 1774, 2:114.

21. Platt, *City Tavern*, 93, 96.

22. Ibid., 113. Washington dined at the City Tavern on May 9, 12, 13, 16, 18, 20, and 29 and June 3, 7, and 12, 1776 (113 n. 202).

23. Ibid., 95 n. 167.

24. Ibid., 115, 148–149.

25. Marquis de Chastellux, *Travels in North America in the Years 1780, 1781 and 1782*, 2 vols., trans. Howard C. Rice (New York: Augustus M. Kelley, 1970), 1:141–142. Chastellux also noted that so as not to crowd the tables the congressmen divided into dinner groups and that the groups reflected geographical divisions.

26. See Platt, *City Tavern*, 118.

27. Ibid., 171.

28. Ibid., 172 n. 323.

29. Nash, *The Urban Crucible*, esp. 312–338; Billy G. Smith, *The "Lower Sort."* See also Stuart Blumin, *The Emergence of the Middle Class: Social Experience in the American City, 1760–1900* (New York: Cambridge University Press, 1989).

30. Nash, *The Urban Crucible*, 395.

31. For a discussion of the origins and themes of the economic policies that

Pennsylvania's small-producers hoped the newly independent state would pursue, see Schultz, *The Republic of Labor*, 37–102.

32. For a powerful discussion of the significance Americans attached to equality and its place within the Revolution, see J. R. Pole, *The Pursuit of Equality in American History* (Berkeley: University of California Press, 1993).

33. Cited in Schultz, *Republic of Labor*, 28.

34. Guardians of the Poor, Alms House Daily Occurrences Docket, 1787–1790, MSS, CPA. Millenar: Nov.1, 1787; Paulin, Aitkens, and Boy: Dec. 1787. See also Billy G. Smith, ed., *Life in Early Philadelphia: Documents from the Revolutionary and Early National Periods* (University Park: Pennsylvania State University Press, 1995), 29–130.

35. Guardians of the Poor, Alms House Daily Occurences Docket, 1787–1790, CPA. McDonald: Oct. 11, 1789; McClure and Fritz: Nov. 1, 1787.

36. Ibid., Nov. 21, 1789, Dec. 13, 1789.

37. Graydon, *Memoirs*, 119.

38. Boggs and Boggs, "Inns and Taverns," 88.

39. Cited in Frederick D. Stone, "Philadelphia Society One Hundred Years Ago: or, the Reign of Continental Money," *PMHB*, 3 (1879), 377–378. See also Ethel E. Rasmussen, "Democratic Environment—Aristocratic Aspiration," *PMHB*, 90 (1966), 155–182.

40. Platt, *City Tavern*, 150.

41. Ibid., 108, n.192.

42. Nelson, Diary, May 5, 12, 1781.

43. For a discussion of hardening temperance attitudes among the city's Quakers, see Jack D. Marietta, *The Reformation of American Quakerism, 1748–1783* (Philadelphia: University of Pennsylvania Press, 1984), esp. 105–108.

44. Nelson, Diary, Oct. 26, 1780.

45. W. J. Rorabaugh, *The Alcoholic Republic: An American Tradition* (New York: Oxford University Press, 1979).

46. Foner, *Tom Paine and Revolutionary America*, 63, 115; "Extracts from the Diary of Dr. James Clitherall," *PMHB*, 22 (1898), 471.

47. Guardians of the Poor, Alms House Daily Occurrences Docket, 1787–1790, CPA, Nov. 1788.

48. Cited in Schultz, *Republic of Labor*, 34.

49. *Pennsylvania Evening Post*, July 30, 1776.

50. Graydon, *Memoirs*, 115.

51. Gordon Wood has made one of the few attempts since Richard Hofstadter to examine the origins and influence of a "conspiratorial" mode of thinking in the revolutionary era. However Wood's study is mainly concerned with political thought and largely ignores social behavior. See "Conspiracy and the Paranoid Style: Casuality and Deceit in the Eighteenth Century," *WMQ*, 3d ser., 39 (1982), 401–441; Hofstadter, "The Paranoid Style in American Politics," in *The Paranoid Style in American Politics and Other Essays* (New York: Columbia University Press, 1965).

52. *Franklin Papers*, July 7, 1765, 12:202.

53. Hutson, "An Investigation of the Inarticulate," 5 n. 6.

54. Ryerson, *The Revolution is Now Begun*, 27; Graydon cited in Platt, *City Tavern*, 64 n. 112.

55. Cited in Platt, *City Tavern*, 187.

56. See "Examination of Isaac Atwood, July 11, 1776," in Linn and Egle, eds., *Pennsylvania Archives*, 2d ser., 1:611–615. See also "Minutes of a Meeting at the Indian Queen, Nov. 25, 1776," in Hazard, ed., *Pennsylvania Archives*, 1st ser., 5:74–75.

57. Linn and Egle, eds., *Pennsylvania Archives*, 2d ser., 1:562–563.

58. Passing testimony to the role of Bradford's coffeehouse as an unofficial headquarters of the independence movement can be seen in the fact that, following the first public reading of the Declaration of Independence a crowd tore down the royal coat of arms from the Pennsylvania statehouse and carried this symbol of tyranny to the coffeehouse. See Ryerson, *The Revolution Is Now Begun*, 239; Boggs and Boggs, "Inns and Taverns," 192–193.

59. "Diary of James Allen Esq. of Philadelphia, Counsellor-at-Law, 1770–1778," *PMHB*, 9 (1885), May 15, 1776, 187.

60. Boggs and Boggs, "Inns and Taverns," 195.

61. Barbara Clark Smith, "Social Visions of the American Resistance Movement," in *The Transforming Hand of Revolution: Reconsidering the American Revolution as Social Movement*, ed. Ronald Hoffman and Peter J. Albert (Charlottesville: University Press of Virginia, 1995), 30, 27–57. The association is reproduced in J. R. Pole, ed., *The Revolution in America, 1754–1788: Documents and Commentaries* (London: Macmillan, 1970), 24–28. See also Ann Fairfax Withington, *Toward a More Perfect Union: Virtue and the Formation of American Republics* (New York: Oxford University Press, 1991).

62. See, for example, the case of John Ireland, imprisoned by Philadelphia's committee of safety for drinking a toast damning Congress in a widow's tavern; Linn and Egle, eds., *Pennsylvania Archives*, 2d. ser., 1:741–742.

63. Mackraby to Sir Phillip Francis, Apr. 24, 1770, in "Philadelphia Society Before the Revolution," 493.

64. The following account is based on *Autobiography of Charles Biddle*, 72–73; Platt, *City Tavern*, 106; Ryerson, *The Revolution Is Now Begun*, 131–132; Withington, *Toward a More Perfect Union*, 239–240.

65. On May 2, 1775, a cobbler named Thomas Loosely was seized by a mob because he had vilified the measures of Congress in support of the people of Boston. He was placed outside the coffeehouse and "exhibited" to "a great number of respectable citizens" inside. Loosely gave sincere promises that his future conduct would be equitable and was eventually released; Christopher Marshall, *Passages from the Remembrances of Christopher Marshall, Member of the Committee of Observation and Inspection, of the Provincial Conference, And of the Council of Safety*, ed. William Duane (Philadelphia: J. Crissy, 1837), 22. See also Marshall's account of Jabez F[isher]'s recantation (21).

66. "Diary of James Allen," Mar. 6, 1776, 186. In the aftermath of crowd action taken against Dr. Kearsley, Philadelphia's Committee of One Hundred took steps to ensure that Philadelphians laid before it all charges of sedition or treason. In time

Congress removed cases of alleged treason from the jurisdiction of local committees. See Ryerson, *The Revolution Is Now Begun*, 132.

67. Linn and Egle, eds., *Pennsylvania Archives*, 2d. ser., 1:640.

68. "Diary of James Allen," Oct. 14, 1775, 186.

69. Thomson's views on debate were formed during his involvement in the Young Junto, a society for promoting useful knowledge founded in imitation of Franklin's Junto. At each meeting of Thomson's Junto a member, chosen by alphabetical rotation, proposed two improving questions for future discussion. Debate was strictly controlled, no visitors were allowed, and new members were admitted only by unanimous vote. Thomson was later instrumental in the founding of the American Philosophical Society. See Hendricks, *Charles Thomson and the Making of a New Nation*, 31–38; DuPonceau, *An Historical Account of the Origin and Formation of the American Philosophical Society*.

70. Cited in "Early Days of the Revolution in Philadelphia: Charles Thomson's Account of the Opposition to the Boston Port Bill," *PMHB*, 2 (1878), 421. In a letter to John Dickinson written in August 1776, Thomson charged that Dickinson's opposition to independence had had the effect of throwing Pennsylvania's affairs into the hands of "men totally unequal to them," men liable to commit "errors" in government through their "ignorance." Thomson to Dickinson, Aug. 16, 1776, cited in Ryerson, *The Revolution Is Now Begun*, 245.

71. *A Letter to the Freeholders and other Inhabitants of this Province . . .* (Philadelphia, 1742) [Evans 4988], 8.

72. Joseph Reed to Charles Pettit, Mar. 30, 1776, cited in Ryerson, *The Revolution Is Now Begun*, 166.

73. Platt, *City Tavern*, 77–78.

74. "Early Days of the Revolution in Philadelphia," 414 emphasis added, also 411.

75. Graydon cited in Platt, *City Tavern*, 127 n. 188.

76. Cited in Douglass, *Rebels and Democrats*, 265.

77. Pennsylvania's first constitution is reprinted in Pole, ed., *The Revolution in America*. See esp. 534.

78. Cited in Schultz, *Republic of Labor*, 53.

79. Cited in Douglass, *Rebels and Democrats*, 274.

80. Cited in Zuckerman, "The Irrelevant Revolution," 231.

81. Schultz, *Republic of Labor*, 52, 53.

82. Ibid., 56.

83. Ibid., 63.

84. John K. Alexander, "The Fort Wilson Incident of 1779: A Case Study of the Revolutionary Crowd," *WMQ*, 3d ser., 31 (1974): 599–604; Rosswurm, *Arms, Country, and Class*, 205–227; Nicholas B. Wainwright, ed., "Captain Samuel Shaw's Revolutionary War Letters to Captain Winthrop Sargent," *PMHB*, 70 (1946), 300; Schultz, *Republic of Labor*, 58–62.

85. On small-producer ideology, see Schultz, *Republic of Labor*, 3–35.

86. During the British occupation of Philadelphia, Daniel Smith, the City Tavern's first keeper, had not only continued trading but also assisted in the organi-

zation of dinners and dances in the tavern's long gallery. He had organized vendues of furniture and other property dubiously acquired. He fled Philadelphia with the retreating British and was eventually awarded an annual pension of £30 by Parliament. See Platt, *City Tavern*, 106, 130–133; Examination of Daniel Smith, Loyalist Transcripts, A.O.12 102, fol. 182 [Public Record Office, London] microfilm, the David Library, Washington's Crossing, Pa. In the aftermath of the Battle of Brandywine, Joseph Galloway hired a waiter at the City Tavern, James Jeremiah Rice, to acquire military intelligence. Rice made at least one trip behind American lines. See Loyalist Transcripts, A.O. 12 100, fol. 356, microfilm, David Library. The Indian King, renamed the British Tavern, also continued trading during the occupation; *Pennsylvania Ledger*, Apr. 15, 1778.

87. Foner, *Tom Paine and Revolutionary America*, 56.

88. Schultz, *Republic of Labor*, 61.

89. *By His Excellency Joseph Reed Esq.; . . . A Proclamation . . . October 6, 1779* [Library Company of Philadelphia].

90. For the background and outcome of the mutiny, see Kenneth R. Bowling, "New Light on the Philadelphia Mutiny of 1783: Federal-State Confrontation at the Close of the War for Independence," *PMHB*, 101 (1977), 419–450. The text of the demands the mutineers presented to Dickinson can be found in *PCC*, Item 38, Reel 45, fol. 27. See also John Byers to William Irvine, July 1, 1783, Irvine Papers, HSP.

91. Testimony of Benjamin Spykes, *PCC*, Item 38, Reel 45, fol. 59–61.

92. Elias Boudinot had called congress into special session but the meeting fell just short of a quorum; Bowling, "New Light on the Philadelphia Mutiny," 431–433. See also James Madison, "Notes on the Debates of Congress, June 21, 1783," in *The Papers of James Madison*, ed. William T. Hutchinson, William E. Raihal, Robert A. Rutland et al., (Chicago: University of Chicago Press and Charlottesville: University Press of Virginia, 1962-), 7:176–178; "Letter to the Editor," in *Freeman's Journal*, July 2, 1783.

93. *Madison Papers*, 7:176; Affidavit of Solomon Townshend, *PCC*, Item 38, Reel 45, fols. 49–52; Robert Shaw cited in Rosswurm, *Arms, Country, and Class*, 247. On the dispersal of the soldiers and the aftermath of the day's events, see *Freeman's Journal*, July 2, 1783; Bowling, "New Light on the Philadelphia Mutiny," esp. 435–439.

94. "Address of Colonel Butler to the Non-Commissioned Officers and Men of the Third Pennsylvania Regiment," *PCC*, Item 38, Reel 45, fol. 45.

95. "Notes on the Debates," June 21, 1783, in *Madison Papers*, 7:177.

96. Benjamin Rush to John Montgomery, July 4, 1783, in *Letters of Benjamin Rush*, ed. Lyman H. Butterfield, 2 vols. (Princeton, N.J.: Princeton University Press, 1951), 1:305. The idea of incendiaries surfaced in an address the mutineers presented to Congress June 25, 1783, *PCC*, Item 38, Reel 45, fols. 33–37.

97. Benjamin Spykes testified that Carberry and Sullivan had treated Sergeant Bennet at the Doctor Franklin tavern; *PCC*, Item 38, Reel 45, fols. 59–61, 65–69. Howe believed in draconian measures to suppress mutiny. See his description of the manner in which he suppressed a mutiny of the Pennsylvania line in 1781; Howe to George Washington, Jan. 27, 1781, cited in *The Writings of George Washington*, ed. Jared Sparks, 12 vols. (Boston, 1837–1858), 7:560–566.

98. *Freeman's Journal*, July 2, 1783.

99. Edmund S. Morgan, *Inventing the People: The Rise of Popular Sovereignty in England and America* (New York: W. W. Norton, 1988), 13. In marked contrast, Richard D. Brown's recent study presumes that it is possible to study the idea of an informed citizenry without reference to the origins and nature of the ideas that citizenry possessed and expressed in sites like taverns. See *The Strength of a People: The Idea of an Informed Citizenry in America, 1650–1870* (Chapel Hill: University of North Carolina Press, 1996).

100. Simon P. Newman, *Parades and the Politics of the Street: Festive Culture in the Early American Republic* (Philadelphia: University of Pennsylvania Press, 1997), 43.

101. Ibid., 186.

Epilogue

1. Benjamin Rush's account is in a letter of July 16, 1782, reprinted in "The French Fête in Philadelphia in Honor of the Dauphin's Birthday, 1782," *PMHB*, 21 (1897): 257–262. Citations are on 257, 259. See also Shields, *Civil Tongues and Polite Letters*, 1–5.

2. "The French Fête," 260.

3. Ibid.

4. Ibid., 261. Two weeks before the fete the French ambassador was among three hundred guests invited to a grand Fourth of July dinner held at the City Tavern. Enos Reeves noted that "the greatest variety of wines of the best brands" were "plied close." The company grew "noisy" but Reeves and a number of other guests left before the toasting could degenerate into excess. See John B. Reeves, ed., "Extracts from the Letter Books of Lieutenant Enos Reeves," *PMHB*, 21 (1897), Letter 153, 82.

5. "The French Fête," 262. Another guest, John Beatty, came to similar conclusions. He was put off by the ostentation of the event, describing it as a "great raree-show." He assured his brother, "suffice it to say it partook more of elegance than of pleasure and satisfaction. The largeness of the company, together with the heat of the season, conspired not a little to this purpose." John Beatty to Erkuries Beatty, July 16, 1782, in Beatty, "Letters of the Four Beatty Brothers," 228–229.

6. "The French Fête," 258. The chevalier's purse was instead distributed among indigent prisoners and patients in the city hospital.

7. Ibid., 262.

8. *Packet*, July 3, 10, 16, 1789.

9. Parsons, ed., *Diary of Jacob Hiltzheimer*, May 2, 1785, 73.

10. William Parker Cutler and Julia Perkins Cutler, eds., *Life, Journals and Correspondence of Rev. Manasseh Cutler, LL.D.*, 2 vols. (Cincinnati: Robert Clarke, 1888), 1:278–279. Cutler's account of the origins of the project credits a single, unnamed licensee. Eberlein and Hubbard attribute ownership of the gardens to the Gray brothers. See Harold Donaldson Eberlein and Cortlandt Van Dyke Hubbard, "The American 'Vauxhall' of the Federal Era," *PMHB*, 68 (1944), 150–175. The brothers owned the gardens during their period of greatest fame.

11. Cutler and Cutler, eds., *Life of Manasseh Cutler*, 1:275–276.

12. Ibid., 1:278. Henry Wansey compared the Grays' gardens with London haunts such as the Vauxhall or Bagnigge Wells. "The ground," he wrote "has every advantage of hill and dale, for being laid out in great variety; and it is neatly decorated with alcoves, arbors, shady walks etc." See Jeremy, ed., *Henry Wansey and His American Journal*, 112; Eberlein and Hubbard, "American 'Vauxhall,'" 150–152.

13. Cutler and Cutler, eds., *Life of Manasseh Cutler*, 1:275.

14. *Packet*, Sept. 29, 1789.

15. See Jared Browne, *The Theatre in America During the Revolution* (New York: Cambridge University Press, 1995); William S. Dye, Jr., "Pennsylvania *versus* the Theatre," *PMHB*, 55 (1931), 333–372.

16. See Carl Bridenbaugh, "Baths and Watering Places of Colonial America," in *Early Americans* (New York: Oxford University Press, 1981), esp. 230–231; F. H. Shelton, "Springs and Spas in Old-Time Philadelphia," *PMHB*, 47 (1923), 196–227. See also advertisements for John Coyle's Wigwam tavern and bathhouse; *Packet*, July 14, 1789, Sept. 6, 1790.

17. Cutler and Cutler, eds., *Life of Manasseh Cutler*, 1:279.

18. *Packet*, July 5, 1790.

19. Ibid., Oct. 15, 1789.

20. Boggs and Boggs, "Inns and Taverns," 196.

21. *Packet*, July 7, 1789.

22. *Gazette*, Feb. 4, 1789.

23. Jeremy, ed., *Henry Wansey and His American Journal*, 103–104.

24. The Dancing Assembly transferred their regular events from the City Tavern to Oeller's at the end of 1790; *Packet*, Sept. 7, 1790.

25. Boggs and Boggs, "Inns and Taverns," 160–163; Jeremy, ed., *Henry Wansey and His American Journal*, 103–104; *Moreau de St. Méry's American Journey: 1793–1798*, ed. Kenneth Roberts and Anna B. Roberts (Garden City, N.Y.: Doubleday, 1947), 309. In 1799 Oeller's Hotel was destroyed by a fire that started at Ricketts's circus; Boggs and Boggs, "Inns and Taverns," 163.

26. Gardner, *The St. Andrew's Society of Philadelphia*, 166.

27. On gentlemanly opposition to excessive drinking, see Mathew Carey, "Reminiscences on the Subject of Intemperance," in *Miscellaneous Essays* (Philadelphia: Carey and Hart, 1830), 318; Chastellux, *Travels in North America*, 1:92–93. For a further discussion, see Peter Thompson, "'The Friendly Glass,'" 560–569. The clerk George Nelson was among those Philadelphians who questioned the propriety of expensive state celebrations at a time when the poor could not afford the necessities of life; see Nelson Diary, May 12, 1781.

28. *An Historical Catalogue of the St. Andrew's Society, 1749–1907* (Philadelphia: St. Andrew's Society, 1907), 44.

29. Chastellux, *Travels in North America*, 1:92–93.

30. Carey described a gradual softening of convention. First a man was allowed to fill his glass as he pleased, though he still had to drink a toast as soon as his glass was full. Later a man could both drink and fill as he pleased. "Reminiscences on the Subject of Intemperance," 318.

31. *Moreau de St. Méry*, 269.

32. Ibid., 265–266.

33. The keeper of the City Tavern, Edward Moyston, announced the departure of the assembly in the *Packet*, Nov. 29, 1790.

34. Jeremy, ed., *Henry Wansey and His American Journal*, 104.

35. "The French Fête," 261.

36. *Moreau de St. Méry*, 333.

37. *Packet*, July 1, 1790. See also Newman, *Parades and the Politics of the Street*, 83–119.

38. Platt, *The City Tavern*, 120 n. 213, 121 n. 215.

39. *Autobiography of Charles Biddle*, 252–253; William Cobbett, "History of the American Jacobins" (1796), in *Peter Porcupine in America: Pamphlets on Republicanism and Revolution*, ed. David A. Wilson (Ithaca, N.Y.: Cornell University Press, 1994), 191–192. See also Newman, *Parades and the Politics of the Street*, 120–151.

40. See, for example, William Cobbett, "A Bone to Gnaw, for the Democrats," reprinted in Wilson ed., *Peter Porcupine in America*, 87–118.

41. Civis to Mr. Fenno, *Gazette of the United States*, Oct. 9, 1797; Boggs and Boggs, "Inns and Taverns," 209.

42. "Amusements and Politics in Philadelphia, 1794," *PMHB*, 10 (1886), 185.

43. Benjamin Rush, *The Drunkard's Emblem: Or an Inquiry into the Effects of Ardent Spirits Upon the Human Body* (1791; rpt., Newmarket, Va.: Ambrose Henkel and Co., 1812), 4–5.

44. See Bruce Laurie, *Working People of Philadelphia*, esp. 33–106; Blumin, *The Emergence of the Middle Class*, 66–107.

Selected Bibliography

Manuscripts

Boggs, Benjamin, and Mary Boggs. "Inns and Taverns of Old Philadelphia." Boggs Collection. Historical Society of Pennsylvania.

[Eight Partners'] Brewery Account Book, 1732–1737. Historical Society of Pennsylvania.

Guardians of the Poor. Alms House Daily Occurrences Docket, 1787–1790. City of Philadelphia Archives.

Haines, Reuben, and Godfrey Twells. Account Book, 1767–1771. American Philosophical Society.

Mayoral Court Docket, 1759–1764. City of Philadelphia Archives.

Mayor's Court Docket, 1767–1771. Historical Society of Pennsylvania.

Nelson, George. Diary. Historical Society of Pennsylvania.

Ogden, Joseph. Innkeeper's Account Book, 1769–1771. Historical Society of Pennsylvania.

Peters, Richard. Cash Book, 1755–1759. Moore Collection. Historical Society of Pennsylvania.

Philadelphia County. Miscellaneous Court Papers. Historical Society of Pennsylvania.

Philadelphia County Court of Quarter Sessions Docket, 1695. Historical Society of Pennsylvania.

Philadelphia County Tax List. Provincial, 1767. Rare Books Collection, Van Pelt Library, University of Pennsylvania.

Philadelphia County Tax List. Proprietary, 1769. Historical Society of Pennsylvania.

Philadelphia County Tax List. Provincial, 1772. City of Philadelphia Archives.

Philadelphia Court Records 1685–1686. Taken by Patrick Robinson. Historical Society of Pennsylvania.

Taylor, Joseph. Ledger. Historical Society of Pennsylvania.

Wallace Collection of Ancient Records of Pennsylvania. Historical Society of Pennsylvania.

West, James, and Gregory Marlow. Account Book. Historical Society of Pennsylvania.

Published Papers and Documents

——. "The First Tax List for Philadelphia County, A.D. 1693." Ed. William Brook Rawle. *Pennsylvania Magazine of History and Biography* 8 (1884), 82–105.

——. "Minutes of the Board of Property of the Province of Pennsylvania," Ed. John B. Linn and William H. Egle. 19 vols. *Pennsylvania Archives,* 2d ser. Harrisburg, Pa.: Lane S. Hart, 1890.

——. *Minutes of the Common Council of the City of Philadelphia, 1704 to 1776* Philadelphia: Crissy and Markley, 1847.

——. "Minutes of the Provincial Council of Pennsylvania: From the Organization to the Termination of Proprietary Government." Ed. Samuel Hazard. *Colonial Records of Pennsylvania.* 16 vols. Harrisburg, Pa.: Joseph Severns, 1852–1853.

——. "Presentments of the Grand Inquest of Philadelphia County, 1683." *Pennsylvania Magazine of History and Biography* 23 (1899):403–405.

——. "Some Indictments by the Grand Jury of Philadelphia." *Pennsylvania Magazine of History and Biography* 22 (1898): 496–498.

——. "Taxables in the City of Philadelphia, 1756." Compiler Hannah Benner Roach. *Pennsylvania Genealogical Magazine* 22 (1961), 3–41.

——. "Votes of the Pennsylvania House of Assembly." Ed. Gertrude McKinney et al. 8 vols. *Pennsylvania Archives.* 8th ser. Harrisburg, Pa.: State Printer, 1931–1939.

Adams, John. *Diary and Autobiography of John Adams.* Ed. Lyman H. Butterfield. 4 vols. Cambridge, Mass.: Belknap Press, 1961.

Allen, James. "Diary of James Allen Esq. of Philadelphia, Counsellor at Law, 1770–1778." *Pennsylvania Magazine of History and Biography* 9 (1885): 176–196, 278–296, 424–440.

Biddle, Charles. *Autobiography of Charles Biddle, Vice-President of the Supreme Executive Council of Pennsylvania, 1745–1821.* Ed. Charles Biddle. Philadelphia: E. Claxton, 1883.

Black, William. "The Journal of William Black." Ed. R. Alonzo Brock. *Pennsylvania Magazine of History and Biography* 1 (1878): 117–132, 232–249, 404–419; 2 (1879): 40–49.

Brown, Charlotte. "The Journal of Charlotte Brown, Matron of the General Hospital with the English forces in America, 1754–1756." In *Colonial Captivities, Marches and Journeys,* ed. Isabel M. Calder. New York: Macmillan, 1935.

Burd, Edward. *The Burd Papers: Selections from Letters Written by Edward Burd, 1763–1828.* Ed. Lewis Burd Walker. Pottsville, Pa.: 1899.

Carey, Matthew. *Miscellaneous Essays.* Philadelphia: 1830.

Chastellux, Marquis de. *Travels in North America in the Years 1780, 1781 and 1782.* 2 vols. Trans. Howard C. Rice. New York: Augustus M. Kelley, 1970.

Clitherall, James. "Extracts from the Diary of Dr. James Clitherall." *Pennsylvania Magazine of History and Biography* 22 (1898): 468–474.

Cutler, Manasseh. *Life, Journals and Correspondence of Rev. Manasseh Cutler, LL.D.* Ed. William Parker Cutler and Julia Perkins Cutler. 2 vols. Cincinnati: Robert Clarke, 1888.

Denny, William. "Memoir of Colonel William Denny." *Pennsylvania Magazine of History and Biography* 44 (1920): 112–115.

Fisher, Daniel. "Extracts from the Journal of Daniel Fisher, 1755." *Pennsylvania Magazine of History and Biography* 17 (1893): 263–278.

Franklin, Benjamin. *The Papers of Benjamin Franklin.* Ed. Leonard W. Labaree,

William B.Willcox, Claude-Anne Lopez, Barbara B. Oberg, et al. 32 vols. to
date. New Haven, Conn.: Yale University Press, 1959–1997.

——. *Benjamin Franklin: Writings*. Ed. J. A. Leo Lemay. New York: Library of
America, 1987.

Graydon, Alexander. *Memoirs of a Life, Chiefly Passed in Pennsylvania, Within the
Last Sixty Years.* 1811. Rpt., Edinburgh: George Ramsay, 1822.

Hamilton, Alexander. *"Gentleman's Progress": The Itinerarium of Dr. Alexander
Hamilton, 1744.* Ed. Carl Bridenbaugh. 1948; rpt., Pittsburgh: University of
Pittsburgh Press, 1992.

——. *The Tuesday Club: A Shorter Edition of* The History of the Ancient and
Honorable Tuesday Club *by Dr. Alexander Hamilton.* Ed. Robert Micklus.
Baltimore: Johns Hopkins University Press, 1995.

Hiltzheimer, Jacob. *Extracts from the Diary of Jacob Hiltzheimer of Philadelphia.
1765–1798.* Ed. Jacob Cox Parsons. Philadelphia: William F. Fell, 1893.

Mackraby, Alexander. "Philadelphia Society before the Revolution: Extracts of
Letters from Alexander Mackraby to Sir Philip Francis." *Pennsylvania Magazine of History and Biography* 11 (1887): 276–287, 491–494.

Marshall, Christopher. *Passages from the Remembrances of Christopher Marshall,
Member of the Committee of Observation and Inspection, of the Provincial Con-
ference, And of the Council of Safety.* Ed. William Duane. Philadelphia: J.
Crissy, 1839.

Mittelberger, Gottlieb. *Journey to Pennsylvania.* Ed. Oscar Handlin and John Clive.
Cambridge: Harvard University Press, 1960.

Moraley, William. *The Infortunate: The Life and Adventures of William Moraley, an
Indentured Servant.* Ed. Susan E. Klepp and Billy G. Smith. University Park:
Pennsylvania State University Press, 1992.

Moreau de Saint Méry, Médéric Louise Élie. *Moreau de St. Méry's American Journey:
1793–1798.* Ed. Kenneth Roberts and Anna B. Roberts. Garden City, N.Y.:
Doubleday, 1947.

Muhlenberg, Henry Melchior. *The Journals of the Rev. Henry Melchior Muhlenberg.*
Ed. Theodore G. Tappert and John Doberstein. 3 vols. Evansville, Ind.: Lutheran Historical Society, 1982.

Penn, Thomas. "Letters of Thomas Penn to Richard Hockley." *Pennsylvania Magazine of History and Biography* 40 (1916): 198–237.

Penn, William. *Correspondence Between William Penn and James Logan.* Ed. Edward
Armstrong. 2 vols. New York: AMS Press, 1970.

——. "A Further Account of Pennsylvania." *Pennsylvania Magazine of History and
Biography* 9 (1885): 64–81.

——. *The Papers of William Penn.* Ed. Richard S. Dunn and Mary M. Dunn. 5 vols.
Philadelphia: University of Pennsylvania Press, 1981–1987.

Porcupine, Peter [William Cobbett] *History of the American Jacobins, Commonly
Denominated Democrats.* Philadelphia: for William Cobbett, 1796.

Reeves, John B., ed. "Extracts from the Letter Books of Lieutenant Enos Reeves."
Pennsylvania Magazine of History and Biography 20 (1896), 302–323, 456–472;
21 (1897), 72–85, 235–256, 376–391, 466–476.

Rush, Benjamin. "The French Fête in Philadelphia in Honor of the Dauphin's

Birthday, 1782." *Pennsylvania Magazine of History and Biography* 21 (1897): 257–262.

———. *The Drunkard's Emblem: Or an Inquiry into the Effects of Ardent Spirits Upon the Human Body* 1791. Newmarket, Va.: Ambrose Henkel and Co., 1812.

———. *Letters of Benjamin Rush.* Ed. Lyman H. Butterfield. 2 vols. Princeton, N.J.: Princeton University Press, 1951.

Thomson, Charles. "Early Days of the Revolution in Philadelphia: Charles Thomson's Account of the Opposition to the Boston Port Bill." *Pennsylvania Magazine of History and Biography* 2 (1878): 411–423.

Wansey, Henry. *Henry Wansey and His American Journal: 1794.* Ed. David John Jeremy. Philadelphia: American Philosophical Society, 1970.

BOOKS AND ARTICLES

Alexander, John K. "The Fort Wilson Incident of 1779: A Case Study of the Revolutionary Crowd." *William and Mary Quarterly,* 3d. ser., 31 (1974): 589–612.

Bailey, F. G. *Gifts and Poison.* New York: Oxford University Press, 1971.

Blumin, Stuart M. *The Emergence of the Middle Class: Social Experience in the American City, 1760–1900.* New York: Cambridge University Press, 1989.

Borsay, Peter. "The English Urban Renaissance; the Development of a Provincial Urban Culture, c. 1680–c. 1760." *Social History* 5 (1977): 581–605.

Brennan, Thomas. *Public Drinking and Popular Culture in Eighteenth-Century Paris.* Princeton, N.J.: Princeton University Press, 1988.

Bridenbaugh, Carl. "Baths and Watering Places of Colonial America." In *Early Americans.* New York: Oxford University Press, 1981.

Brobeck, Stephen. "Revolutionary Change in Colonial Philadelphia: The Brief Life of the Proprietary Gentry." *William and Mary Quarterly,* 3d ser., 33 (1976): 410–434.

Brown, Richard D. *Knowledge Is Power: The Diffusion of Information in Early America, 1700–1865.* New York: Oxford University Press, 1989.

———. *The Strength of a People: The Idea of an Informed Citizenry in America, 1650–1870.* Chapel Hill: University of North Carolina Press, 1996.

Calhoun, Craig, ed. *Habermas and the Public Sphere.* Cambridge: MIT Press, 1992.

Chartier, Roger. *The Cultural Origins of the French Revolution.* Ed. Lydia G. Cochrane. Durham, N.C.: Duke University Press, 1991.

———. *On the Edge of the Cliff: History, Languages and Practices.* Ed. Lydia G. Cochrane. Baltimore: Johns Hopkins University Press, 1997.

Clark, Peter. *The English Alehouse: A Social History, 1200–1830.* New York: Longmans, 1983.

Cleary, Patricia. "'She Will Be in the Shop': Women's Sphere of Trade in Eighteenth-Century New York and Philadelphia." *Pennsylvania Magazine of History and Biography* 119 (1995): 181–205.

Cohen, Norman S. "The Philadelphia Election Riot of 1742." *Pennsylvania Magazine of History and Biography* 92 (1968): 306–319.

Conroy, David Weir. "The Culture and Politics of Drink in Colonial and Revolutionary Massachusetts, 1681–1790." Ph.D. diss., University of Connecticut, 1987.

——. *In Public Houses: Drink and the Revolution of Authority in Colonial Massachusetts.* Chapel Hill: University of North Carolina Press, 1995.

——. "Puritans in Taverns: Law and Popular Culture in Colonial Massachusetts, 1630–1720." In *Drinking: Behavior and Belief in Modern History,* ed. Susanna Barrows and Robin Room. Berkeley: University of California Press, 1991.

Cummings, Hubertis. *Richard Peters: Provincial Secretary and Cleric, 1704–1776.* Philadelphia, 1944.

Daniels, Bruce C. *Puritans at Play: Leisure and Recreation in Colonial New England.* London: Macmillan, 1995.

Davis, Susan G. *Parades and Power: Street Theatre in Nineteenth-Century Philadelphia.* Berkeley: University of California Press, 1988.

Diamondstone, Judith. "The Philadelphia Corporation, 1701–1776." Ph.D. diss., University of Pennsylvania, 1969.

Doerflinger, Thomas M. *A Vigorous Spirit of Enterprise: Merchants and Economic Development in Revolutionary Philadelphia.* Chapel Hill: University of North Carolina Press, 1986.

Douglass, Elisha P. *Rebels and Democrats: The Struggle for Equal Political Rights and Majority Rule During the American Revolution.* New York: Quadrangle/The New York Times, 1965.

Downard, William L. *Dictionary of the History of the American Brewing and Distilling Industries.* Westport, Conn.: Greenwood Press, 1980.

Duby, Georges, ed. *A History of Private Life: Revelations of the Modern World.* Cambridge: Harvard University Press, 1988.

Duis, Perry. *The Saloon: Public Drinking in Chicago and Boston, 1880–1920.* Urbana and Chicago: University of Illinois Press, 1983.

Dunn, Richard S., and Mary M. Dunn, eds. *The World of William Penn.* Philadelphia: University of Pennsylvania Press, 1986.

Epstein, James. "Radical Dining, Toasting and Symbolic Expression in Early Nineteenth-Century Lancashire: Rituals of Solidarity." *Albion* 20 (1988): 271–291.

Foner, Eric. *Tom Paine and Revolutionary America.* New York: Oxford University Press, 1976.

Gilbert, Daniel R. "Patterns of Organization and Membership in Colonial Philadelphia ClubLife, 1725–1755." Ph.D. diss., University of Pennsylvania, 1952.

Gildrie, Richard P. *The Profane, the Civil and the Godly: The Reformation of manners in Orthodox New England, 1679–1749.* University Park: Pennsylvania State University Press, 1994.

Gilje, Paul A. *The Road to Mobocracy: Popular Disorder in New York City, 1763–1834.* Chapel Hill: University of North Carolina Press, 1987.

Gough, Robert. "Towards a Theory of Class and Social Conflict: A Social History of Wealthy Philadelphians, 1775–1800." Ph.D. diss., University of Pennsylvania, 1977.

Habermas, Jürgen. *The Structural Transformation of the Public Sphere: An Inquiry into a Category of Bourgeois Society.* Trans. Thomas Burger. Cambridge: MIT Press, 1989.

Harris, Tim, ed. *Popular Culture in England c. 1500–1800*. London: Macmillan, 1995.

Hindle, Brook. "The March of the Paxton Boys." *William and Mary Quarterly*, 3d. ser., 3 (1946): 75–92.

Horle, Craig, and Marianne Wokeck, eds. *Lawmaking and Legislators in Pennsylvania A Biographical Dictionary*. 2 vols. Philadelphia: University of Pennsylvania Press, 1991–1997.

Hutson, James. *Pennsylvania Politics, 1746–1770: The Movement for Royal Government and Its Consequences*. Princeton, N.J.: Princeton University Press, 1972.

Isaac, Rhys. *The Transformation of Virginia, 1740–1790*. Chapel Hill: University of North Carolina Press, 1982.

Jenkins, Howard. *The Family of William Penn*. Philadelphia, 1899.

Jennings, Francis. *Benjamin Franklin, Politician: The Man and the Mask*. New York: W. W. Norton, 1996.

Kelley, Joseph J., Jr. *Life and Times in Colonial Philadelphia*. Harrisburg, Pa.: Stackpole Press, 1973.

Lapsanksy, Emma Johns. "South Street Philadelphia, 1762–1854: A Haven for Those Low in the World." Ph.D. diss., University of Pennsylvania, 1975.

Laurie, Bruce. *Working People of Philadelphia, 1800–1850*. Philadelphia: Temple University Press, 1980.

Lender, Mark Edward, and James Kirby Martin. *Drinking in America: A History*. Rev ed. New York: The Free Press, 1987.

Manges, Frances May. "Women Shopkeepers, Tavernkeepers and Artisans in Colonial Philadelphia." Ph.D. diss., University of Pennsylvania, 1958.

Marietta, Jack D. *The Reformation of American Quakerism, 1748–1783*. Philadelphia: University of Pennsylvania Press, 1984.

Middlekauff, Robert. *Benjamin Franklin and His Enemies*. Berkeley: University of California Press, 1996.

Morgan, Edmund S. *Inventing the People: The Rise of Popular Sovereignty in England and America*. New York : W. W. Norton, 1988.

Nash, Gary B. *Quakers and Politics: Pennsylvania, 1681–1726*. Rev. ed. Boston: Northeastern University Press, 1993.

——. "The Free Society of Traders and the Early Politics of Pennsylvania." *Pennsylvania Magazine of History and Biography* 89 (1965): 147–173.

——. *The Urban Crucible: Social Change, Political Consciousness, and the Origins of the American Revolution*. Cambridge: Harvard University Press, 1979.

Newcomb, Benjamin H. *Franklin and Galloway: A Political Partnership*. New Haven, Conn.: Yale University Press, 1972.

Newman, Simon P. *Parades and the Politics of the Street: Festive Culture in the Early American Republic*. Philadelphia: University of Pennsylvania Press, 1997.

Parker, Peter J. "Rich and Poor in Philadelphia, 1709." *Pennsylvania Magazine of History and Biography* 99 (1975): 3–19.

Platt, John D. R. *The City Tavern*. Denver, Colo.: National Parks Service, 1973.

Rediker, Marcus. *Between the Devil and the Deep Blue Sea: Merchants Seamen, Pirates and the Anglo-American Maritime World, 1700–1750*. New York: Cambridge University Press, 1987.

Roach, Hannah Benner. "A Philadelphia Business Directory for 1690." *Pennsylvania Genealogical Magazine* 23 (1963–1964): 95–129.

———. "The Planting of Philadelphia: A Seventeenth-Century Real Estate Development." *Pennsylvania Magazine of History and Biography* 92 (1968): 3–47, 143–194.

Rorabaugh, W. J. *The Alcoholic Republic: An American Tradition.* New York: Oxford University Press, 1979.

Rosenzweig, Roy. *Eight Hours for What We Will: Workers and Leisure in an Industrial City, 1870–1920.* Cambridge: Cambridge University Press, 1987.

Rosswurm, Steven. *Arms, Country, and Class: The Philadelphia Militia and the "Lower Sort" during the American Revolution, 1775–1783.* New Brunswick, N.J.: Rutgers University Press, 1987.

Ryerson, Richard Alan. *The Revolution Is Now Begun: The Radical Committees of Philadelphia, 1765–1776.* Philadelphia: University of Pennsylvania Press, 1978.

Schultz, Ronald. *The Republic of Labor: Philadelphia Artisans and the Politics of Class, 1720–1830.* New York: Oxford University Press, 1993.

Schwartz, Sally. *"A Mixed Multitude": The Struggle for Religious Toleration in Colonial Pennsylvania.* New York and London: New York University Press 1987.

Sennett, Richard. *The Fall of Public Man: On the Social Psychology of Capitalism.* New York: Vintage Books, 1978.

Shammas, Carole. "The Female Social Structure of Philadelphia in 1775." *Pennsylvania Magazine of History and Biography* 107 (1983): 69–84.

Shi, David E. *The Simple Life: Plain Living and High Thinking in American Culture.* New York: Oxford University Press, 1985.

Shields, David S. *Civil Tongues and Polite Letters in British America.* Chapel Hill: University of North Carolina Press, 1997.

Smith, Billy G. *The "Lower Sort": Philadelphia's Laboring People, 1750–1800.* Ithaca, N.Y.: Cornell University Press, 1990.

Soderlund, Jean R., ed. *William Penn and the Founding of Pennsylvania, 1680–1684. A Documentary History.* Philadelphia: University of Pennsylvania Press, 1983.

Spera, Elizabeth Grey Kogan. "Building for Business: The Impact of Commerce on the City Plan and Architecture of the City of Philadelphia, 1750–1780." Ph.D. diss., University of Pennsylvania, 1980.

Stone, Frederick D., "Philadelphia Society One Hundred Years Ago: or, the Reign of Continental Money." *Pennsylvania Magazine of History and Biography* 3 (1879): 360–381.

Tolles, Frederick B. *James Logan and the Culture of Provincial America.* Boston: Little, Brown, 1957.

———. *Meeting House and Counting House: The Quaker Merchants of Colonial Philadelphia, 1682–1763.* New York: W. W. Norton, 1963.

Trexler, Richard C. *Public Life in Renaissance Florence.* Ithaca, N.Y.: Cornell University Press, 1991.

Tully, Alan. *Forming American Politics: Ideals, Interests, and Institutions in Colonial New York and Pennsylvania.* Baltimore: Johns Hopkins University Press, 1994.

Turner, Victor S. *Drama, Fields and Metaphors: Symbolic Action in Human Society.* Ithaca, N.Y.: Cornell University Press, 1974.

Warner, Michael. *Letters of the Republic: Publication and the Public Sphere in Eigh-teenth-Century America.* Cambridge: Harvard University Press, 1990.

Warner, Sam Bass, Jr. *The Private City: Philadelphia in Three Periods of Its Growth.* 2d ed. Philadelphia: University of Pennsylvania Press, 1987.

Watson, John F. *Annals of Philadelphia, and Pennsylvania, in the Olden Time.* 1st ed. Philadelphia: E. L. Carey, 1830.

Webb, Sidney, and Beatrice Webb. *The History of Liquor Licensing: Principally from 1700 to 1830,* Rpt., Hamden, Conn.: Archon Books, 1963.

Wendel, Thomas. "The Keith-Lloyd Alliance: Factional and Constitutional Poli-tics in Colonial Pennsylvania." *Pennsylvania Magazine of History and Biogra-phy* 92 (1968): 289–305.

Wiebe, Robert H. *The Segmented Society: An Introduction to the Meaning of America.* New York: Oxford University Press, 1975.

Wilson, David A., ed. *Peter Porcupine in America: Pamphlets on Republicanism and Revolution.* Ithaca, N.Y.: Cornell University Press, 1994.

Withington, Ann Fairfax. *Toward a More Perfect Union: Virtue and the Formation of American Republics.* New York: Oxford University Press, 1991.

Wolf, Stephanie Grauman. *Urban Village: Population, Community, and Family Structure in Germantown, Pennsylvania, 1683–1800.* Princeton, N.J.: Princeton University Press, 1976.

Wood, Gordon S., "Conspiracy and the Paranoid Style: Casuality and Deceit in the Eighteenth Century." *William and Mary Quarterly,* 3d ser., 39 (1982): 401–441.

Zimmerman, John S. "Governor Denny and the Quartering Act of 1756." *Pennsyl-vania Magazine of History and Biography* 91 (1967): 266–281.

Zuckerman, Michael. "The Fabrication of Identity in Early America." *William and Mary Quarterly,* 3d ser., 34 (1977): 183–214.

——. "Identity in British America: Unease in Eden." In *Colonial Identity in the Atlantic World,* ed. Nicholas Canny and Anthony Pagden. Princeton, N.J.: Princeton University Press, 1987. 115–159.

——. "The Irrelevant Revolution: 1776 and Since." *American Quarterly* 30 (1978): 224–242.

Acknowledgments

This project's journey to published manuscript could not have been accomplished without the help of numerous individuals and two institutions. While a graduate student at the University of Pennsylvania, and thereafter, I have luxuriated in the friendly rigor of the research environment at the McNeil (formerly the Philadelphia) Center for Early American Studies. My reading of an aspect of Philadelphia's past in this book owes a great deal to the knowledge and generosity of all those scholars who have passed through the center over the past decade and to successive directors of the center—Richard Beeman, Stephanie Grauman Wolf, and Richard Dunn. I could not have finished this book without timely intervention, in the form of a term's leave from teaching, from the University of Oxford's Faculty of Modern History. Many thanks are due those overburdened colleagues, especially Clive Holmes of Lady Margaret Hall, who lightened my teaching load. I am particularly indebted to Nick Mayhew of St. Cross College, Oxford, who deputized for me as Tutor for Admissions in order that I might complete this project. I would also like to record my gratitude to Sydney L. Mayer, whose benefaction to Oxford allowed me to travel to Philadelphia to search for illustrations and elusive references.

Much of the primary research for this book was conducted in the manuscripts room of the Historical Society of Pennsylvania. I found Linda Stanley, until recently the society's Curator of Manuscripts, to be unfailingly helpful and informative. Her example was followed by the rest of the society's library staff. Jim Green, Erika Piola, and Jennifer Ambrose of the Library Company of Philadelphia also provided invaluable assistance. Librarians and archivists at the American Philosophical Society and the Rare Books Department of the University of Pennsylvania's Van Pelt Library treated me with great courtesy and efficiency. The staff of the City of Philadelphia's Archive Unit gave me a large welcome in their cramped quarters in City Hall Annex. Thanks are also due to Jack Lindsay at the Philadelphia Museum of Art and to Joseph Benford at the Free Library of Philadelphia.

Craig Horle shared with me both his general expertise and his transcriptions of seventeenth-century Philadelphia's two surviving court dockets. Patricia Cleary helped me think about the importance of tavernkeeping as a trade for women. Professor Sharon Salinger shared with me her work on Philadelphia's insurance records and expertise on much else besides.

Many friends listened to me on the subject of taverns with greater patience, and more generosity, than any author has a right to expect. I thank Kathy Brown, Martin Conway, Saul Cornell, Marcus Daniel, Joel Kaye, Robert Middlekauff, Simon Newman, Nancy Rosenberg, and Mike Wheeldon for all their counsel. Susan Klepp and Michael Meranze gave me extremely helpful readers' reports. Jerry Singerman and the staff at the University of Pennsylvania Press have made publishing a pleasurable process. Richard Dunn and Michael Zuckerman have challenged, advised, and supported me throughout. My debt to Mike Zuckerman—dazzling intellectual and inspiring mentor—is simply enormous. This book is dedicated with much love to my wife, Alex.

Index

Tavernkeepers, Petitioners for Tavern Licenses, and Public Houses

General Index